THE JOY OF BREEDING
YOUR OWN SHOW DOG

*Until one has
loved an animal
a part of one's soul
remains unawakened.*

ANATOLE FRANCE

Ch. Mayfair Barban Loup-de-Mer was the first Mayfair Barban Yorkshire Terrier born with that special quality that set him apart and made him a natural in the show ring. He was the first breakthrough in bringing to the surface correct body coat color genes for his breeders. "Loupy" was top Yorkie in 1974 and 1975. In 1976 he was top Yorkie and No. 5 in the Top Ten Toys. He sired three litters, a total of six get, four of which became champions. Then the hand of fate struck the author's breeding program a cruel blow. The little dog contracted viral enteritis at a show, resulting in an extremely high temperature which rendered him sterile. Nonetheless, "Loupy" is the great, great, greatgrandsire of the majority of Mayfair Barban show Yorkies today.

The JOY of Breeding Your Own Show Dog

by Ann Seranne

with foreword by Julia Gasow

Illustrations by Donna L. Morden

First Edition

HOWELL BOOK HOUSE
New York

Howell Book House
Macmillan Publishing Company
866 Third Avenue, New York, NY 10022
Collier Macmillan Canada, Inc.

Library of Congress Cataloging-in-Publication Data

Seranne, Ann, 1914–
    The joy of breeding your own show dog.
    Bibliography: p. 267
    Includes index.
    1. Dogs—Breeding.   I. Title.   II. Title:
Show dog.
SF427.2.S45   636.7′0888   80-16081
ISBN 0-87605-413-0

Macmillan books are available at special discounts for bulk purchases
for sales promotions, premiums, fund-raising, or educational use.
For details, contact:

            Special Sales Director
            Macmillan Publishing Company
            866 Third Avenue
            New York, NY 10022

20   19   18   17   16   15   14   13

Printed in the United States of America

Affectionately dedicated to
my friend and partner,
BARBARA WOLFERMAN
without whom Mayfair Barban Yorkies
would not be winning
Groups and Bests in Show.

For Peter

Contents

About the Author

ANN SERANNE has devoted most of her life to good food and good dogs. She is one of the foremost Yorkshire Terrier authorities in the United States and co-breeder, with Barbara Wolferman, of Mayfair Barban Yorkshire Terriers. She is the author of *All About Small Dogs in the Big City,* and is currently writing a monthly department in *Pure-Bred Dogs—American Kennel Gazette,* "Serving the Fancy," dedicated to the proposition that the dog exhibitor has an alternative to the frankfurter as standard dog show fare.

One-time Food Editor of the *New York Post* and food consultant to NBC, *Reader's Digest,* Waring Products and others, she is also the author of some twenty cookbooks, and has edited forty others, the most recent a series of regional Junior League cookbooks. She is a frequent contributor to *Family Circle* and other service magazines.

Ann told us that her father was a great nature lover. "Each summer we travelled north to an isolated island in Georgian Bay, where he taught me, as a child of four years, how to tell the age of trees, to recognize poisonous mushrooms from the edible varieties, how to watch for, but not to fear, the rattlesnakes that inhabited the island and to catch a bumble bee in flight in my bare hands without harming it.

"Chipmunks, wild rabbits and squirrels were my playmates rather than dolls. They all ate from my hand and the chipmunks would allow me to dress them in tiny vests cut from colorful material.

One summer, when I was seven, a wild rabbit adopted me, followed me into the cottage and remained there throughout the summer months. He was housebroken, slept on my bed and begged for crusts of bread from the table. It was such a heartache to have to bid farewell to him at the end of the summer and send him back to his forest home that, upon returning to the city, my father bought me my first dog—a Pekingese. That was the first time I knew that one could buy a dog of a particular breed. I just thought you picked them up off the street!''

From that time on, through her college years at Queen's University, in Kingston, Ontario, where she was expelled from first-year pre-med for letting all the laboratory experimental cats out the window, and later as food chemist at a food packaging plant in a tiny village in upper New York State during the war years, she always had a pair of Pekingese by her side. One day someone gave her a brown Standard Poodle, "Susie," who followed the newspaper boy on his bicycle each morning as he made his rounds and carried the newspapers in her mouth from sidewalk to door mat.

When the war ended and Ann relocated in New York City, she reluctantly took the Pekingese to Canada to live with her sister, and gave Susie to the newspaper boy. She did not feel it was practical at that time for her to have a dog in the city.

Back in New York, Ann joined the staff of *Gourmet Magazine* where she was catapulted in a couple of short years from receptionist to Executive Editor. After six years she resigned from *Gourmet* to start her own food publicity firm of Seranne and Gaden, which operated most successfully for thirteen years. It was during this time that Ann felt sufficiently established in a career that she bought her first Yorkshire Terrier. That was in 1958. A couple of years later she decided to begin breeding on a limited scale.

Since then she has been the co-breeder and/or owner of 62 Yorkie champions (six of them multiple Best in Show winners), half a dozen Standard Poodles (two of them multiple Best in Show winners) and a couple of Shih Tzus. In 1978 she was approved by the American Kennel Club to judge all varieties of Poodles, and Shih Tzu. Ann Seranne feels she has reached an exciting new plateau in the world of purebred dogs, and looks forward to many more years of enjoying dogs and writing books and articles in her top-of-the-hill test kitchen in Blairstown, New Jersey.

Foreword

IF ONLY *The Joy of Breeding Your Own Show Dog* had been written forty years sooner! It is by far the best book of its kind I have ever read—fascinating reading and an invaluable aid for all breeders, no matter what breed they own.

For beginners, it's a real bonanza. If you contemplate breeding dogs, PLEASE first read this book. And then keep it at hand where you can turn to it frequently for help and suggestions. You'll be grateful for every page.

In thorough and orderly presentation, Miss Seranne takes you through every step—progressing over setbacks, cautioning you of pitfalls, and encouraging you on to the great satisfaction that lies ahead. The fruits of her years of intense study and scientific research are here given to all who love dogs and are anxious to breed good ones.

Miss Seranne lightly observes at one point, "75% of successful dog breeding depends on luck and 25% on skill." My words, too—until reading her book. *The Joy of Breeding Your Own Show Dog* refutes us both—it leaves no areas to luck.

It is a delightfully written book, easy to understand and with a charm and lightness that keeps it from ever becoming dull, even in the "heavier" portions dealing with genetics. The Mendelian theories and the scientific developments that have followed, difficult for laymen to comprehend when presented in the technical language of most textbooks, are here made very clear for us. And when followed, as they are here, by interesting explanations of the four methods of breeding, everything falls naturally into place. It's intriguing reading—and once started, you will find it difficult to put the book down.

When the beginner has read *The Joy of Breeding Your Own Show Dog,* I urge him—before taking his first step—to go back and re-read the section, "Getting a Foot in the Door." Nothing scientific or involved here—just good advice that will save him more trouble than you might imagine.

I am touched by Ann Seranne's deep love of dogs, her knowledge, her sincerity. But most of all, I am touched by her total unselfishness. I quote:

> The challenge before us is to capture all the qualities in one gorgeous, animated package and lock those genes into our genetic lines so that our dogs will eventually breed true. We may not be able to accomplish this in the remaining span of our lives, but we hope that we will be able to leave the foundation for such a dream to an equally interested person who will be able to accomplish in his lifetime what we will attempt to strive for in ours.

What better creed could any devoted dog breeder aspire to?

—JULIA GASOW

Preface

It was ch. alekai marlaine that caught a strand of my heartstrings and hooked it immediately and forever into the colorful and complex tapestry of the dog show world.

Standing poised in the ring, looking inquiringly into the face of her handler—no one with an appreciation of beauty and balance could fail to sense something special about her. In motion she was a poem, seeming to float down the ring, her feet barely touching the ground.

Marlaine was a white Standard Poodle bred and owned by Mrs. Henry J. Kaiser. Her handler was a young professional named Wendell Sammet. I was in the lowest echelons of know-it-all-breeder-exhibitors participating in a five-day dog show circuit with my first homebred "show quality" Yorkshire Terrier. Each day, after breed judging, I found myself, Yorkie in arm, racing to the Poodle ring to watch Marlaine. When she lost, I cried; when she won, I cried. It was then I knew that someday I was going to breed, own and show a dog with that special star quality.

That was many years ago, and between that time and now, many strands of sweat, tears, heartbreak, anguish, joy and pride have been added to that tapestry. Some are bright, artistic, creative additions; others are disturbing, their colors soiled and stained by the ugly facets that inevitably infiltrate any sport depending on human judgment and weakness.

For the next few years, circumstances made me mark time with my breeding dreams. I finished a few homebred champions but, living and working as I did in the heart of New York City, I had neither the time, space nor money to breed and show on an extensive scale.

It was not until I met Barbara Wolferman, also a New Yorker, who had owned and loved Yorkies for 25 years, that my dreams became a reality. We met at a cocktail party, and it didn't take us long to find out that we had much in common: a love of the theatre (we both had produced a show on Broadway), a fondness of fine foods, and a passionate devotion to the Yorkshire Terrier breed.

Barbara had never been to a dog show and believed that putting a Yorkie through the rigors of the show ring was tantamount to cruelty. I persuaded her to go with me to the Bronx County Kennel Club show the following weekend. It was, perhaps, the worst choice I could have made. The armory was as cold as a tomb, dirty, smelly, its thick stone walls reverberating with the barking of a thousand dogs. But Barbara, blue to the bones, sat stoically through not only the Yorkie breed judging (we lost) but the Groups and Best in Show. She loved every bone-chilling moment of it. She took to dog shows like the proverbial duck, and immediately wanted to buy a show dog. It was not long before we joined forces and moved to an 11-acre hilltop ranch in northern New Jersey.

Although differing in temperament, personality, and capabilities, we were remarkably complementary to each other, and by pooling our resources, our combined talents, and varied interests in breeding and showing, we were able to launch a full-scale breeding-showing program.

I was an ardent student of genetics; Barbara was gung-ho for the shows, so together we made a good team. We both had reached an age when we had the education, intelligence, financial security and ambition to dare to attempt to develop a strain of Yorkshire Terriers within our interpretation of the breed standard that would someday breed true.

I knew it was not going to be easy, but little did I realize the heartbreaks along the way. And although, through the years and now into our seventh generation of homebreds, we have managed to produce a constant stream of show-quality Yorkies, many of them Group winners, and several multiple Best in Show dogs, there have been countless times when I have been ready to call it a day. If not for Barbara, I would have retired to the living room with my needlepoint long ago. She gave me the stamina to ride through the rough periods and, if we eventually make a valuable contribution to purebred dogs, it will be entirely due to her confidence and encouragement.

Breeding dogs is not only a science but an art, with a good portion of luck thrown in. *The Joy of Breeding Your Own Show Dog* takes a puppy from the moment of its conception to its first show. It was written for the novice breeder with the hope that it may be a lifeline when he is in trouble and will inspire him to delve more deeply into all aspects of dog breeding. This is only the tip of the iceberg.

ANN SERANNE

Acknowledgments

MY SINCERE THANKS and appreciation to Terri Shumski and Kenneth J. Davis, D.V.M., for their permission to use all or any part of the photographs and text from the manuscript *Puppy Arrival and Survival,* and to those dedicated breeders who took time out from busy schedules to supply me with details of their breeding systems and samples of their pedigrees, which have become an important part of this book.

My thanks also to Merrit B. Wooding, D.V.M., for patiently answering all my questions.

Mel McIntire

15

To the dedicated breeder, every litter, every puppy represents an investment in time, study, planning and hope. Breeding fine dogs and doing it right can never be called a casual exercise, but to the serious breeder the satisfaction of consistently producing fine dogs always justifies the effort involved. These six-month-old Cairn Terrier puppies, bred by Mr. and Mrs. Taylor Coleman, personify the sincere breeder's best effort.

1

Before You Breed

BREEDING DOGS is a serious business and should not be undertaken without a great deal of thought and purpose in mind. It is a combination of art and science, of common sense and intelligence, to which must be added a modicum of luck and a tremendous amount of intestinal fortitude.

Breeders have a grave responsibility to the lives they create—living, loving creatures of bone, blood and muscle, that might never have been born had not a breeder taken it into his hands to mate a certain dog to a certain bitch. Granted, if all goes well, it can be a stimulating, rewarding experience, but the many failures along the way can be devastating and heart-breaking.

How many times have I heard myself say, "I'll *never* breed another dog!" But, somehow, with the irrepressible optimism of a dedicated breeder, I begin to think how lovely a litter might be from that new champion bitch if bred to that beautiful young male. I manage to pick up the broken pieces and begin again. Each breeding is more exciting than the last, and the projected pedigree of the antipicated litter promises exceptional quality.

Breeding dogs is a privilege and not a means of making money. That is not to say that if you can breed quality animals and still make a profit, there is any law against it, but to enter the field of breeding dogs primarily as a money-making project is not what serious breeding or this book are all about.

Hopefully *The Joy of Breeding Your Own Show Dog* will discourage many who "just want to have a litter," will make an equal number stop long enough to consider if they are ready, equipped physically, mentally and emotionally to begin a breeding program, and will help the intelligent enthusiast begin the right way.

What You Should Know Before Breeding Dogs

There is much you should know before breeding your first litter—*must* know if you are going to be successful in raising a litter of healthy, well-adjusted pups.

First, you should have some practical knowledge of mating, care of the bitch in whelp and in whelping and conditioning the litter. I hope to be able to guide you through these aspects of breeding, by passing along to you the successes and failures of almost twenty years experience which, while extensive, is by no means complete. New techniques are being discovered every day, and what might be the right way to do something today may be improved upon or replaced with an entirely different method tomorrow.

The Breed Standard

In addition to these obvious requirements, a breeder must be able to understand and interpret the American Kennel Club's *Standard of Perfection* for his breed, and have a clear mental picture of what he considers the perfect specimen or the ideal. This can be done only by an intensive study of his breed's background, and by careful scrutiny of numerous specimens of the breed, both in and out of the show ring, accompanied by an unprejudiced evaluation of these dogs against the standard.

Then there is type. How will you be able to select good foundation stock without an understanding of type? You may have the soundest dog in the world, perfect in color, coat and temperament, but without that undefinable feature—type—any dog will fall short of his standard and will seldom bring home the ribbons from a dog show.

Genetics

Once you have selected your foundation bitch, how are you going to select the stud dog that could best produce quality, typey puppies, unless you have a working knowledge of genetics and breeding principles?

In order to breed intelligently, the dog breeder must know how a characteristic is transmitted from one generation to another. Why do some characteristics appear generation after generation while others disappear, only to crop up in the great- or great-great-grandchildren? Why do puppies from one bitch differ so drastically from puppies out of a full sister to that bitch?

The answers to these questions lie in the science of genetics which is, unfortunately, no sure road to perfection. Somehow Nature has a way, now and then, of throwing in a joker, and it is only by understanding the laws of heredity that you will know where that joker may have come from and the best way to eliminate it from your line.

I do not profess to be an expert in the field of genetics, but I hope to be able to pass along to you, in the simplest terms possible, what it has taken me years to absorb from the many technical books written by qualified geneticists, and to show you how to apply this knowledge to your breed.

After all is learned, planned, charted and projected, genetics, at best an applied science and experience, combined with an analytical mind, can be your best teacher. A breeder must constantly test the mechanics of heredity within the genetic structure of his particular strain of dogs. If a recognized theory works for him, it can be used time and time again. If not an alternate must be found.

Structure and Locomotion

Like love and marriage, structure and locomotion "go together" and cannot be divorced from each other. A study of both is essential for every dog breeder and for every judge.

Just as the artist or sculptor needs knowledge of anatomy in order to sketch or sculpt the human body, so must the breeder or judge know what lies beneath the skin and coat to be able to evaluate the true quality of a dog.

To move properly a dog must be built correctly, and the functional principles of a dog's structure remain the same whether the breed is the diminutive Yorkshire Terrier or the giant Irish Wolfhound. Each has the same number of bones and muscles, and the way these parts fit together remains the same for all breeds. When a dog is correctly built, its movement will be smooth, graceful and efficient.

The skeletal system of a dog is divided into two general parts: One is the *axial* skeleton consisting of the skull, spine, sternum, ribs and pelvis. These are the bones that protect the vital organs. Two is the *appendicular* skeleton composed of the shoulder blades, forelegs and hindlegs.

It's not necessary to memorize all the medical terms of the bones in a dog's body. Leave that to your veterinarian. But it is important to be familiar with common terms such as patella, croup, pastern, stifle, hock and to understand such "doggie" expressions as cow-hocked, splay-footed, reach of neck, out at the elbow, roach backed and so on.

In the front assembly, the shoulder blade or scapula is a focal point and no dog can be better than the set of this bone. Since it is not possible to measure the angles and lengths of bones and joints in a live dog with scientific accuracy, the term generally used to describe optimum slant of the shoulder is "good layback." A good shoulder, together with an upper arm correctly positioned against the chest wall, should function like a smooth, shock absorbing mechanism as it accepts thrust from the rear quarters and lifts and carries the body forward. What many of us fail to realize is that the shoulder blade is quite a mobile bone, attached to the rib cage only by muscle. In motion it glides up, forward and slightly inward as its upper tip pivots in elliptical fashion against the withers. Shoulder assemblies vary in different types of dogs, with consequent varying styles of gait. In any dog, however, a correctly positioned scapula contributes to topline and good head carriage, giving the neckline a pleasing transition into the withers, and breadth and strength to the forequarters.

When watching any dog move, whether a Working dog or a Toy, keep your eye on the withers. They tell a lot. You will never, or should never, see a top-winning dog with withers that rise and fall abruptly as it moves. If they do, that dog is poorly structured.

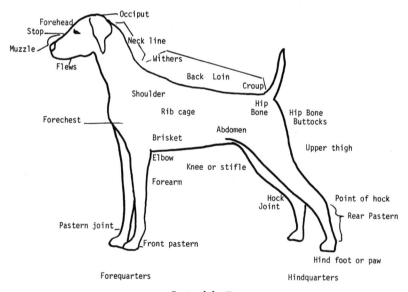

Parts of the Dog

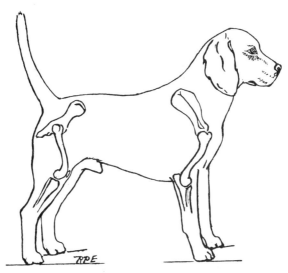

Front and rear angulation in the dog.

Rachel Page Elliott

The rear assembly of a dog supports its body and supplies the drive in motion. A pelvis that slopes at a 30-degree angle to the spine permits greater efficiency of stride than any other angulation of this assembly.

Many good books have been written on the subject of structure or anatomy, movement or locomotion. One that should be required reading for all dog people is *The Dog in Action,* by McDowell Lyon. It explains by word and illustration, often humorously, always interestingly, what I have tried briefly to outline here, and much more. The subjects are far too comprehensive to be more than touched on in this book.

Don't expect to digest Lyon's book the first time you read it. Use it for reference and reread it as frequently as you find yourself able to apply its principles to the evaluation of your dogs.

Another most important book to own for quick reference is the charmingly and effectively illustrated *Dogsteps, Illustrated Gait at a Glance,* by Rachel Page Elliott.

A Good Eye and a Gentle Hand

No matter how many books you read and how much technical information you amass, your study must go hand-in-hand with practical experience or it will be of little use to you. Your hands must be

21

able to tell you how a dog is built. Your eye must be trained to confirm the findings of your hands as you watch the dog standing stationary before you and in motion, and to quickly evaluate its general condition, characteristics and type.

Hands need not be rough. You can outline the slope of a shoulder blade or pelvis, determine the angulation of a stifle, the straightness of a leg more accurately with a gentle finger than with the entire hand. Try pressing your hand hard against your jaw bone, then run the tip of your finger gently around its perimeter. Which touch tells you more about the formation of your jaw? In the same way, a light touch will tell you more about your dog than a rough, sometimes hurtful one.

The eyes and hands of a judge in the show ring should do their best to seek out the virtues of a dog, but it is up to the eyes and hands of the breeder to find the faults of the dogs in his kennel and then set about eliminating them from his breeding program.

What You Should Have Before Breeding Dogs

Interest, knowledge, time and stamina are only a few requirements for breeding dogs. You must also have proper facilities and enough money to invest in quality stock. If you start with nothing you get nothing. The novice, who thinks he can breed a pet quality bitch to a pet quality dog and come up with a treasure, will pay out over the years, in his attempt to improve, a great deal more than if he had begun with one good bitch. This is especially true if he purchased that bitch from a breeder who had already spent many years weeding out, discarding and selecting only the best to carry on his bloodlines. It won't come cheap but, no matter what the initial cost, you will be far ahead of the game, and your starting investment is relatively unimportant.

Should you be lucky enough to find one or more such bitches, and they will not be easy to come by because breeders are reluctant to let quality bitches go into inexperienced hands, by all means listen to any advice the breeder is willing to pass along to you. No one will know better than he the correct mate for the bitch. He will be able to explain to you why he feels a particular dog is likely to give you best results. He knows the background of his stock and the quality of the progeny they have produced in the past. You have nothing to lose and everything to gain by putting your faith and trust in the breeder of your foundation. It won't be long before you will be able to try your own wings.

Proper Facilities

In the beginning, depending on the breed you have selected, you may allow your foundation stock to be a part of your family—living, eating and sleeping with you. But the time will come when you will have to designate a room in your house, which is quiet and away from the main stream of house traffic, in which to whelp and raise your first litter. Often a family room, an extra bedroom or an outmoded dining room can serve as a starting kennel. It should have plenty of cross ventilation, adequate heat, sunshine and, if possible, egress to a fenced-in patch of lawn or graveled driveway.

Prior to entering into any breeding program you will have, of course, checked the dog laws of your community and, hopefully, live in an unrestricted county or township. If not, you had better start thinking about when and where you are going to move when your dog family exceeds the legal limit.

If you have no limitations and enjoy a permanent life-style, you should begin to plan on enlarging your present facilities, before your home becomes sheer bedlam. You might just as well face the fact that, any time you have a litter, your "family" is likely to grow. So now is not too soon to anticipate your future needs.

Seek expert advice on modern kennel construction. Design a kennel which is best suited and practical for your breed. If a kennel doesn't work for you, and by that I mean make your life easier, then it isn't worth building. At the same time the well-being of the dogs must be considered if you are going to continue to raise happy puppies. It's not as easy in a kennel as in the home, where the pups are in constant touch with people, and the hustle and bustle of a variety of activities. As your breeding stock multiplies it becomes increasingly difficult to give each and every puppy, whether show quality or pet, the necessary time to assure its essential conditioning during the critical periods of its young life.

Psychologically a kennel should be a safe, happy place for dogs and, while it must be practical, thought should be given to various ways to keep the dogs amused. Boredom can manifest itself in constant barking, circling, licking, chewing, fence fighting, loss of weight and other undesirable habits. "Constant suppression of activity and unending confinement in the same drab concrete and chain-link enclosure, day after day, is a form of torture . . . . for man or beast!" This is a quote from an excellent article published in *Western Animal News,* and I have permission to reprint from it some constructive suggestions.

Building a kennel as an extension of the home, provides greater security for both dogs and people. This kennel tailored for Toys, is an integral unit. It has its own furnace, water pump, electrical panel and kitchen. The main building, with guest entrance centered on its length on the driveway side is 64 feet long by 24 feet wide. On each side of the main entrance are four, eight by six foot stalls, with sliding glass doors leading to individual screened outdoor runs. A door at one end of the kennel leads to a quiet whelping room, a puppy room and an isolation area, which can double as an additional bedroom for kennel assistants.

For starters, when building a kennel avoid at any cost building square runs. The square is the best way to encourage a dog to just sit and do nothing. A rectangle, or any other shape, at least encourages the dog to walk up and down. Try to provide a view of some sort.

Plant a tree or put in a planter. Who wants to look at a solid wall all the time? If you are using concrete blocks, you can offset them enough to provide peepholes, or buy blocks with openings.

And even if you already have an existing kennel you can, with a little imagination, change it physically from time to time.

Puppy runs are fun runs! Instead of sitting and waiting for the time to pass, they should be running and playing most of the day . . . and developing strong bodies and minds. Several large rough stones, just big enough for a puppy to sit on and play "king of the mountain," liven up the area.

One of the best boredom-breakers is large cement drainage tiles. They are large enough to make a snug tunnel or to climb on and off. They come in a variety of sizes and shapes and can be moved from one area to another fairly easily.

Whenever you do any pruning of trees or bushes, save a few good pieces to toss into the runs. Many dogs delight tearing them up, playing wild games of tug-o-war, or just carrying them around. Any empty card-board boxes (except those joined with staples) should make a stop in a dog run before being destroyed. They end up in pieces, but not before providing a lot of energy release to the dogs.

Balls of all sizes (except those small enough to be swallowed) brighten the days, cost little, and help develop canine personalities. Periodically, throw some kind of fresh fruit or vegetables in with them as a different kind of toy.

The bitterness of a lemon or grapefruit fascinates many dogs . . . and an apple or an orange is just a sweet-tasting ball! Potatoes, celery stalks and carrots are crunchy toys that provide vitamins!

Any change is a help. The runs may seem all alike to you, but they aren't to the dogs. Move them around from one kennel to another periodically. Move their sleeping platforms (or pillows) and water dishes around. Do anything for change.

Sure there are some drawbacks to this kind of thinking. Bits of cardboard, branches and vegetables are a bother to pick up at cleaning time. But compare this small nuisance to the results of enforced monotony on the dog. Many forms of undesirable behavior are rooted in boredom. And the worst of all is the slow stagnation of character caused by the prison-camp form of confinement.

There are endless little ways of breaking the chain of monotony if you will just give it a little thought. The only limit is your imagination.

I would like to add—and your common sense.

Inside the Toy kennel is plenty of sunshine and color. Banks of fiberglass cages are used for individual feeding and sleeping quarters. The doors are removable and the rounded corners prevent food and germs from accumulating in them.

Dogs appreciate looking out at something beside chain-link fences and cement. Bushes, trees and pots of blossoming flowers, help relieve kennel boredom.

26

Seaward Kennels (Newfoundlands)

Elinor Ayers, a celebrated breeder of Landseer and black New-foundlands, tired of coping with remodelled kennel buildings, designed and built her ideal kennel for large dogs on a seventy-acre property in North Rupert, Vermont. Miss Ayers was kind enough to send photographs of the kennel, taken for the Winter, 1977 issue of *Gaines Progress,* and an architect's floor plan for use in this book.

A tremendous amount of advance planning went into perfecting every detail of Seaward Kennels, to make both work and living conditions for her employees as attractive as possible. Miss Ayers, also was careful to take into consideration the community and her immediate neighbors.

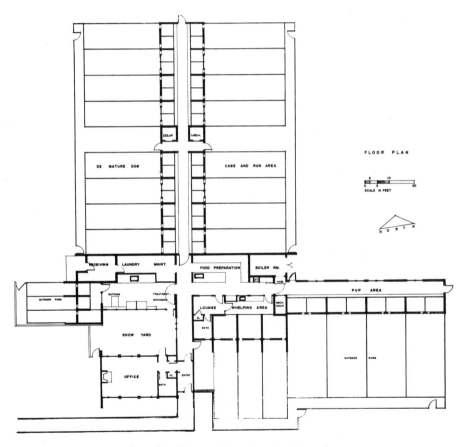

FLOOR PLAN

SCALE IN FEET

NORTH

Floor plan of Seaward Newfoundland Kennels.

Artistically set into a woodland grove, Seaward Kennels is the ultimate in careful planning and design. Fencing is so arranged that the dogs cannot see approaching cars and visitors. Rows of evergreens contribute to the "protective coloration" of the kennel. *William Forsyth*

Back of the boarding section of Seaward Kennels. Note the three-foot wide, wire-enclosed path which runs the entire length of the outside runs and doubles as a deterent for Vermont's wildlife, which causes wild excitement if any approach the runs. *William Forsyth*

There is little, if any, barking. Walls and fencing of the kennel are so arranged that dogs cannot see cars or visitors approaching. Music within the kennel masks the sound of approaching cars. All interior floors slope toward a trough punctuated by drains which carry off water and solid waste. Outside runs also slope downward, making the kennel easy to clean by a simple hosing. Excess moisture is mopped dry.

The interior whelping pens are 10 by 10 feet. The area referred to on the floor plan as pup area, really the boarding section, has interior pens that are 8 feet long and 6 feet wide, and open out onto 30 feet long runs that are 20 feet wide. All the runs with the exception of three small runs to the left of the building, referred to as isolation runs, are 30 feet long and 10 feet wide. In this isolation area the runs are about 7 feet wide and 25 feet long. Usually they are used for visiting bitches, escape artists, or small dogs in board.

Miss Ayers is happy with her ideal kennel, with one exception. She writes:

> The only problem we have, was due to the architect not believing me when I told him how dogs can destroy things, has been with our kennel guillotine doors. They have never been satisfactory. The dogs, when bored, tear out the weatherstripping liners and, because they were placed on the outside of the building, they often freeze after we have washed the interior cages, and it requires the personnel having to kick them loose so they can open the door.

The kennel is heated by oil with the exception of the whelping area. This is fully electric and, in the event of power failure, an electric generator takes over. Panel heating is supplemented by infrared lighting and heat.

There is a separate kitchen and an adjoining area called the "lounge" which really is a one-room apartment for the convenience of whoever might be keeping the nighttime vigil with a bitch about to whelp.

Most breeders hope to produce a Best in Show dog at least once in a breeding lifetime, and winning the top spot at Westminster is, to many, the ultimate success story. The 1979 Westminster BIS winner, Irish Water Spaniel, Ch. Oak Tree's Irishtocrat, affectionately known as "Dugan," is shown here winning BIS at the Maryland KC in November, 1978 under English judge Reginald Gadsden just prior to his Westminster triumph. "Dugan" was bred by Mrs. Anne E. Snelling, Ottawa, Ontario, and was expertly handled by W.J. Trainor, who now co-owns him with his breeder.   *Gilbert*

2

The Mechanics
of Heredity

MANY FINE DOGS have been produced by breeders who never heard of Mendel and his laws, but the great ones, if any, will be few and far between. More likely such breeders will ride along forever on the wave of mediocrity while breeders who understand Mendel's laws of inherited traits and use them wisely, as a short cut to improvement, will succeed.

But because of the complexities of genetics and the many variables in the transference of inherited characteristics, such a breeder must be willing to gamble with nature, taking the worst along with the best. With the courage of his convictions, if he is able to ride through those times when nothing seems to be going according to rules, he will eventually emerge triumphant and a great dog will be born.

A Monk Counts His Peas

An Austrian monk named Gregor Mendel is recognized as "the Father of Genetics," the science of heredity. His discoveries as to how a characteristic is passed from one generation to another are not theory but proved laws accepted by every biologist and used by every successful breeder.

Mendel began his experiments by planting two different kinds of pea plants, one tall and one short. When the seeds of a tall plant were crossed with the seeds of another tall plant, all resulting plants were tall, and when he crossed the seeds of a dwarf or short plant with another dwarf plant all resulting plants were short. He called these plants PURE for their size—that is, tall or short.

But Mendel discovered that when he crossed the seeds of one *pure tall* plant with those of a *pure short* plant, instead of getting medium-size plants, which one might expect, all were tall. There were no short plants at all.

Continuing into another generation, Mendel crossed the seeds of these plants with each other and found that 75% of the resulting plants were tall and 25% were short. He further discovered that when the dwarf seeds resulting from this cross were mated to each other, all plants were dwarf and again became *pure* for the short characteristic. However, only one out of three of the tall seeds resulting from that cross, when mated to each other, bred true or was *pure* for the tall characteristic. The other two carried in their simple cell structure the ability to produce tall and dwarf plants in the proportion of 50-50. He called these plants HYBRIDS.

After thousands of cross-breedings and after counting millions of peas, Mendel eventually arrived at a method of inheritance by which he was able to predict results with mathematical certainty.

Dominant and Recessive "Particles"

Mendel found that certain "particles," later to become known as GENES, were inherited in related pairs, one from each parent and that, when one particle was inherited from each of two parents which showed different or contrasting characteristics, the particle inherited from one parent suppressed the particle inherited from the other. He called the particle which expressed itself in the offspring DOMINANT and the one which was hidden or suppressed RECESSIVE.

Mendel's Law of Segregation

Mendel proved that two pure dominant parents would produce all pure dominant progeny and that two pure recessive parents would produce all pure recessive progeny. But, when one parent was pure dominant for a given characteristic or trait and the other was pure recessive for the contrasting characteristic or trait, all the immediate progeny were hybrid or impure and when bred together produced offspring in the ratio of 25% pure dominant, 25% pure recessive and

50% hybrid dominant. This meant that the offspring would exhibit the dominant characteristic even though it carried a particle for each contrasting characteristic in its seed or germ cell.

By symbolizing the DOMINANT particle with a capital letter and the recessive particle with the same letter only in lower case, we can equate Mendel's discoveries when he crossed PURE tall and PURE dwarf plants as follows.

Let a pure dominant plant for the tall trait be symbolized by TT.

Let a pure recessive plant for the short trait be symbolized by tt.

Any offspring inheriting one particle from each of the parent plants would be Tt or hybrid for these traits.

The first parental generation is called P_1 or what we dog breeders would call the sire and the dam; the second P_2, or what we know as grandparents, P_3 would be great grandparents and so on.

The offspring of the first pair of parents would be the first filial generation or F_1, the offspring of F_1 would be F_2 and so on through each generation of descendants.

With these abbreviations it is easy to formulate Mendel's Laws of Segregation, which is the breeder's key to a working knowledge of genetics.

P_1 TT × tt =Tt Tt Tt Tt F_1: 100% tall in appearance
                                      100% hybrid in cell structure
P_2 Tt × Tt =TT Tt Tt tt F_2: 75% tall and 25% short in appearance
                                      25% pure dominant, 25% pure recessive and 50% hybrid in cell structure.

These formulas illustrate that the particles in the cell structure, not the physical appearance, pass along the physical characteristics to future generations.

Mendel found there were six possible ways in which a pair of particles could combine with another pair, and that the combinations were mathematically predictable if the parent plants produced a minimum of sixteen offspring.

Red and White Equals Pink

The garden peas with which Mendel experimented provided contrasting characteristics in their physical appearance. The plants were either tall or short: their seeds were smooth or wrinkled. But when he applied his principles to four o'clock plants and crossed a pure white four o'clock with a pure red four o'clock, instead of getting all white or all red flowers in the first generation, as he

33

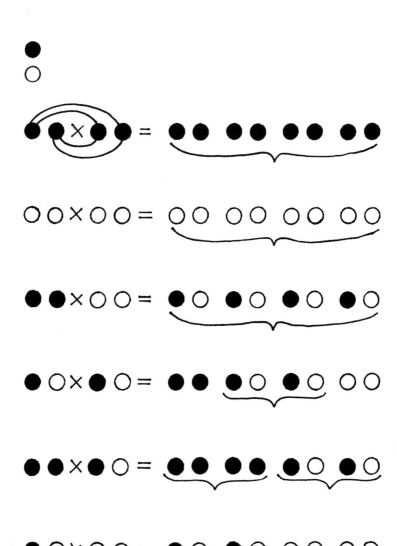

The six possible ways in which one pair of "particles" can combine with another pair.

anticipated, he got all pink flowers. The crossing of the white and red flowering plants produced a blend of the parental colors in the blossoms of the progeny.

However in the second generation when he cross-fertilized the seeds of the first generation he found that the blended color effect was only in the blossoms and not in the germ cell. The red and white particles inherited from their parents were carried as separate units and reproduced in the same ratio as his hybrid peas.

We must keep in mind that Mendel was dealing with simple plant life and not the complicated structure of a dog.

Before delving more deeply into genetics and attempting to apply its laws to the breeding of dogs, we must understand a little about biochemistry and how an animal develops from the union of two cells.

The Cells—Sperm and Ovum

Nature works in mysterious ways its wonders to perform, and the greatest of these is the creation of life itself.

The beginning of life is a cell which results from the union of two germ cells, one from the male, called the sperm cell, the other from the female, called the egg cell or ovum.

The egg cells or ova are produced in the ovaries of the female and the sperm cells are generated in the testicles of the male. In a normal mating, the male ejects millions of sperm cells from its penis into the vagina of the female.

Nature provided these sperm cells with propelling tails which enable them to wiggle or "swim" their way up the vagina, through the cervix of the female, up the horns of the uterus into the Fallopian tubes where the ripened eggs are waiting to be fertilized. The head of the first of those millions of sperm to reach one of the eggs pierces the outer membrane surrounding the ovum, penetrates it, and the two cells unite to become one. A fertilized cell or ZYGOTE is formed. In this split second of penetration, all traits, good ones and bad ones, contained in that fertilized cell are locked in forever. Nothing can change them; no external influence such as weather, food or training can affect them. Color, quality and quantity of coat, structure, ear set, temperament—every characteristic is predetermined in the fertilized egg.

As soon as the head of a sperm buries itself in the ovum, the ovum walls harden to prevent the penetration of any other sperm, and as soon as all the eggs have been fertilized, the remaining sperm die. With them die all the genetic inheritance they contained. The little

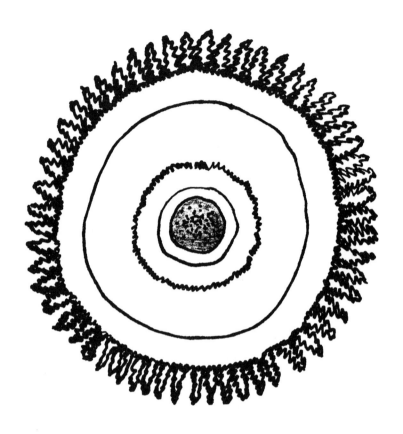

The female germ cell or ovum, showing chromosomes in the center.

one-celled zygotes descend from the Fallopian tubes into the uterus and attach themselves to its walls. The uterus provides heat, food and protection. Contrary to beliefs prior to Mendelism, the blood of the female does not flow through the zygotes. The only part the mother plays is to serve as an incubator for the growth of the fertilized cells.

Here in the incubator or uterus of the female the united cell or zygote begins the process of dividing, first into two cells, then the two become four, the four eight and so on. Eventually millions of cells result in a living breathing animal. All the cells are descended by continuous division from the original zygote, some of them specializing in bone, others in blood, some in muscle, some in brain and still others in the different organs of the body.

Early in the zygote's growth, one particular pair of cells begins a special process and divides into the reproductive organs, the ovaries in the female and the testicles in the male. It is in these organs of the fully developed embryo that the inherited characteristics of both the original germ cells will be carried to future generations.

Understanding how those characteristics are passed along provides the breeder with a short cut to improvement. At the same time, if we stop to consider the enormity of why one sperm is chosen, from the millions discharged into the vagina of the female, to fertilize a particular egg, we will have a better understanding of the odds we breeders take when we gamble with nature.

Chromosomes and Genes

Within the head of the sperm and the nucleus of the ovum are networks of rod-like structures known as CHROMOSOMES, or color bodies so called because their size and shape can be determined by the use of various stains. These chromosomes come in pairs and, strung out along their length, like beads on a string, are thousands of GENES, which also come in pairs. Each pair occupies the same position on each of the pair of chromosomes. The genes are the carriers of genetic information.

The dog has 39 pairs of chromosomes or a total of 78; man has 23 pairs or a total of 46; the cat has 19 pairs or a total of 38, and the fruit fly has but 4 pairs or a total of 8.

If both the sperm and the ovum contributed all their chromosomes in the process of fertilization, the resulting zygotes in a dog would have increased to 156. Then these would continue to increase with each successive generation.

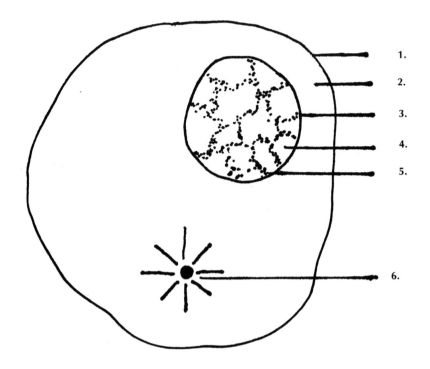

A Typical Cell.

1. Cell Wall
2. Cytoplasm
3. Nuclear membrane
4. Nucleus
5. Chromatic Network
6. Centrosome

Nature solves this problem by ridding the sex cells of half their chromosomes before they meet and unite. The sperm cell divides in half, making two sperms, each containing only one half of each of the 39 pairs of chromosomes. The ovum, however, performs its reduction act at the precise moment of fertilization by discarding half its pairs of chromosomes in a tiny cell called the polar cell. By these different methods of division, one gene from each pair of genes in the sire is contributed to the offspring and one gene from each pair of genes in the dam is contributed by the dam. In other words, both sire and dam give one half their genes to each puppy. The genes are not the same each time, and so it is possible for a zygote to receive from either the sire or the dam all their combined bad genes or all their good genes, or a mixture of good and bad.

And because both the sire and dam received half their genes from their sire and half from their dam, it is quite possible for one of them or both to pass along a concentration of the genes of its parents. In such a case a puppy would be more closely related to its grandparents than to its sire or dam.

Of the 39 pairs of chromosomes in the dog, the two members of each pair look alike except for one pair—the sex chromosomes. The sex chromosome of the female is made up of two X chromosomes, while the male has one X and one Y. When the ovum discards half its chromosomes it must of necessity discard an X, but when the sperm divides into two sperms, one of them will carry the X chromosome and one will carry the Y. If the Y-bearing sperm penetrates the ovum the resulting sex cell will be XY and the puppy will be a male. If the X-bearing sperm penetrates the ovum the resulting sex cell will be XX and the puppy will be a female. And so it is the male, not the female, which determines the sex of the puppies.

Four Important Words

Mendel knew nothing of genes and chromosomes. To analyze his discoveries he had to take for granted the presence of "particles" responsible for the transmission of inherited characteristics. It was long after his death that the study of cell structure or *cytology* lead to the discovery of chromosomes and their genes.

With this discovery came a whole new scientific language of tongue-twisting, unfamiliar terms. Because of them, it is little wonder that breeders think the science of heredity is beyond their intelligence. Nothing could be further from the truth. By understanding the meaning of only FOUR words, any breeder can master a working knowledge of Mendel's laws.

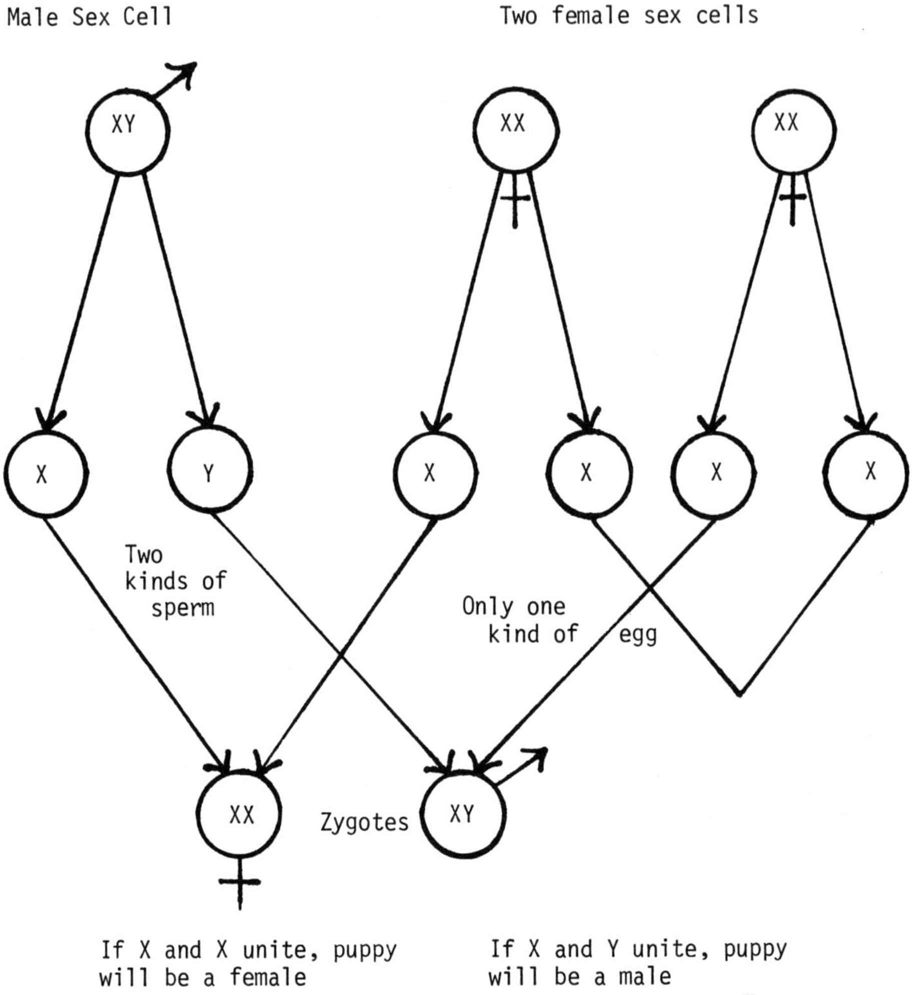

Male Sex Cell

Two female sex cells

XY

XX

XX

X

Y

X

X

X

X

Two
kinds of
sperm

Only one
kind of egg

XX   Zygotes XY

If X and X unite, puppy
will be a female

If X and Y unite, puppy
will be a male

The male sex cell or sperm divides into two sperm and each will carry a different chromosome. The egg also divides but discards one of its chromosomes into what is known as the polar cell. Only one kind of egg survives, and it has an X chromosome. It is pure chance whether an X or a Y sperm penetrates the X ovum.

Homozygous and Heterozygous

A breeder must know the meaning of these two unfamiliar words that are part of the genetic vocabulary. Everyone today understands the meaning of the words homosexual and heterosexual. Let's define them. A homosexual prefers a member of the same sex, while a heterosexual prefers one of the opposite sex.

You know that a zygote is a fertilized cell or the union of two sex cells, the sperm and the ovum, and you know that in this cell lie the 39 pairs of chromosomes and the thousands of genes that contribute to the development and manifestation of specific traits in the living animal, the dog.

Now you should understand the meaning of homozygous and heterozygous. HOMOZYGOUS means two of the same genes or an identical pair. It is what Mendel called PURE and his pure plants bred true for the characteristics that the pair influenced.

HETEROZYGOUS means two differing genes in a pair or mixed genes, one of each kind, and is what Mendel called a hybrid. His hybrid plants were impure and did not breed true.

The pairs of homozygous genes may be either dominant or recessive, but the heterozygous genes must be one of each, or one dominant and one recessive.

Genotype and Phenotype

These are the other two most important words in a breeder's vocabulary and, unless a breeder recognizes that every animal is in reality two different beings, he cannot breed with any degree of skill.

What an animal looks like on the outside, its physical appearance, is its PHENOTYPE. It is the phenomenon of how certain genes came together to create its appearance. What a dog looks like on the inside is its GENOTYPE, or the make-up of the genes responsible for all the good and bad qualities that can be seen in its PHENOTYPE and many others that remain hidden within. The GENOTYPE is the blueprint of every trait it inherited from its ancestors and can pass along to future generations.

We must constantly remind ourselves that how a dog looks or acts or moves may be no guide whatsoever to the qualities it can pass on to its offspring.

Applying Mendel's Laws to the Breeding of Dogs

If science is ever successful in duplicating the cell structure of the dog in the laboratory, and perfect dogs begin to roll off the scientific assembly line, there will be no need for breeders. Until that time comes, breeding dogs, to many, will continue to be a stimulating adventure with genetics the clues to the "treasure."

If you like jigsaw puzzles and card games you will enjoy putting your knowledge of genetics to work. It is very much like any other game, where 75% is luck and 25% is skill. Still, many faults can be eliminated from a bloodline and superior qualities introduced by a combination of selectivity and. an understanding of the laws of heredity.

We know that everything is inherited, even a dog's show spirit or its ability to perform tricks. We also know that a dog's true qualities are not necessarily evidenced in its phenotype (physical appearance) but are often concealed in its genotype (genetic framework).

We know there are three genotypes for every trait.

DOUBLE DOMINANT or pure for a character =DOMINANT HOMOZYGOUS

DOUBLE RECESSIVE or pure for a character =RECESSIVE HOMOZYGOUS

MIXED GENES OR HYBRIDS =HETEROZYGOUS

Homozygosity Is the Breeder's Key to Genetic Purity

A great many breeders labor under the mistaken idea that all good traits are dominant and all bad qualities are recessive. This is probably because most of the serious faults in dogs—cleft palate, club foot, canine hip dysplasia, hare lip, under or overshot jaw, night blindness—are caused by recessive genes. So, too are many desirable qualities such as good lay-back of shoulder, nicely angulated stifle, dark pigment on white dogs, a smooth gait covering the maximum of ground with the minimum of effort and other traits which may be virtues in one breed but faults in others.

This is why genetics is an applied science and its principles must be applied to a particular breed and even to a particular strain or type within the breed. For example, in my breed, which you must know by now is the Yorkshire Terrier, more than 50% of its desirable qualities are governed by recessive genes. And once a breeder lucks into these recessives it is easy to lock them into his genetic framework forever.

Any dog or bitch which displays a characteristic known to be due to a recessive gene must have inherited this gene from both parents and therefore possesses it in a double dose. It is pure for this characteristic. It cannot do anything but pass on the recessive gene to each of its offspring because it does not possess the contrasting dominant gene. It is homozygous for this trait and, if bred to another dog which also displays the trait, will always breed true.

A recessive is a gene that is suppressed and not one that is inferior to a dominant gene. And so it is the extent to which a dog is homozygous or pure for a particular quality, and able to pass this quality along to all its offspring, that is more important than whether this purity was the result of dominant or recessive genes.

Achieving genetic purity, however, with recessive genes is much easier than with dominant ones. Because dominant genes in a single dose cause the dog to exhibit the trait, it is only by test breeding that the breeder is able to ascertain whether the other gene of the pair is dominant or recessive.

If all the qualities we wished to perpetuate in our dogs were controlled by a single pair of genes, producing perfect dogs would be fairly simple. Unfortunately most traits are controlled by two or more pairs and the breeder's work is infinitely more challenging.

A Single Pair of Genes

Most geneticists agree that ear carriage is controlled by a single pair of genes. Erect ears are dominant over recessive drop ears. We have proved this fairly conclusively with our Yorkies which, originally were a drop-eared breed, but now must have ears which are carried fully erect. There is little doubt that many other genes influence the ears such as their size and shape and the way they are set on the head. But let us assume that the simple mechanism of whether they are carried up or down is governed by a single pair of genes.

Let the gene for erect ear be the symbol E and the gene for the contrasting characteristic or drop ear be e. The genes from the sperm are represented by a single letter and the genes from the ovum are represented by a single letter, but the genes resulting from the fertilized cell are represented by double letters.

When we breed a dog and a bitch, both homozygous or pure for erect ears, the possible combinations of the genes would be:

E E × E E

DAM

		E	E
S	E	EE	EE
I			
R	E	EE	EE
E			

All offspring will have erect ears, will be homozygous or pure and will produce only erect ears in the offspring.

When we breed two dogs which are both heterozygous for erect ears we get the following combination:

E e × E e

DAM

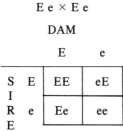

		E	e
S	E	EE	eE
I			
R	e	Ee	ee
E			

In a litter of four or more, three of the offspring may have erect ears and one may have drop ears. The drop-ear will breed true if bred to another drop-eared dog (if this is what you're looking for you're "in business!"), but only one of the 25% of the erect eared offspring will breed true. The others will be heterogzygous.

THE PRESENCE OF EVEN ONE DROP-EARED PUPPY IN A LITTER OF FOUR SHOWS US THAT BOTH THE SIRE AND DAM ARE CARRYING THE RECESSIVE DROP-EARED GENE.

If drop ears is a fault in your breed, you should sell the drop-eared puppy as a pet and eliminate it from your breeding program. Also you should be careful to breed any other of the offspring in the litter to a dog with a dominant gene for an erect ear.

If there were three erect-eared puppies in this litter, you might not want to keep them all. Most likely you would keep the one showing the most potential in other qualities and sell the other two. If you are a completely ethical breeder you will advise the people to whom you sell these puppies that the puppies *might* be carrying a drop-ear recessive, and might produce one in a litter of four if mated to a dog which is also carrying the recessive gene for drop ears. You should also explain that in small litters, the chance of a drop ear popping up is three to one. The same sire and dam might be bred several times without a drop-ear appearing in the litters. This does not mean that the drop-ear gene has disappeared, it has only been hidden by the dominant gene and 50% of the offspring will continue to pass the fault on to future generations.

The Back-Cross

Now, what about the best puppy in the litter that you kept for future breeding? You might very much like to know if this superior puppy is homozygous or heterozygous for an erect ear, so you make a test mating, known as a *back-cross*. You breed the puppy to a drop-eared mate. If all the puppies in a litter of four or more have erect ears, the dog being tested is homozygous for this characteristic. If it is heterozygous, half the puppies will be drop-eared and half will be erect-eared.

a)   e e × E e

DAM

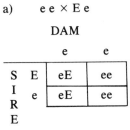

		e	e
S	E	eE	ee
I	e	eE	ee
R			
E			

When we test breed an erect-eared dog to a drop-eared bitch, our gene combination will be one of the following two:

a) Half the puppies will have erect ears and half will have drop ears. Therefore our sire is heterozygous for the drop-eared trait.

b)   e e × E E

DAM

		e	e
S	E	eE	eE
I	E	eE	eE
R			
E			

b) All the puppies have erect ears but will carry the drop-ear gene. They will all be heterozygous for this trait. Our sire, however, is homozygous DOMINANT, and if bred to another with the same pure pair of dominant genes will produce all pure or HOMOZYGOUS DOMINANT PUPPIES.

Two Pairs of Genes and the Law of Independent Assortment

When two pairs of contrasting genes are involved, each parent will have in its genotype two different kinds of unit characters in the germ plasm. Each pair will separate independently of the other pair. This is Mendel's second law known as the Law of Independent Assortment.

Using the genetic symbol A for one dominant characteristic and B for the others, and a and b for the contrasting recessives, we formulate the germ cells of both the sire and dam as ABab.

The genes can come together in 16 different combinations. In a litter of 16 puppies there would, theoretically, be nine offspring containing either a single or double gene for both dominant characters; there will be three carrying one or two genes for A and none for B; there will be three carrying one of the two genes for B and none for A, and there will be one offspring which will express both the recessive genes.

So, if we breed a heterozygous short-haired black dog to a heterozygous long-haired blue bitch we could, again theoretically, expect to see expressed in the offspring nine short-haired black dogs, three long-haired black dogs, three short-haired blue dogs and one long-haired blue dog.

The division of the two gene pairs and their recombination is illustrated in the following diagrams.

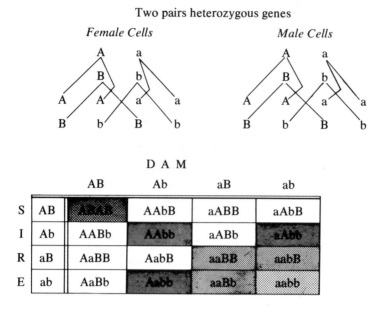

Two pairs heterozygous genes

When we are dealing with two pairs of heterozygous genes, or a double hybrid, known as a *dihybrid cross,* four possible phenotypes are produced in the approximate ratio of 9: 3: 3: 1.

9 will exhibit both dominant traits but only one of these will be PURE for both traits for HOMOZYGOUS DOMINANT ■

3 will be hybrid dominant for A and homozygous recessive for B ■

3 will be hybrid dominant for B and homozygous recessive for A ▨

1 will be HOMOZYGOUS RECESSIVE for both traits. ▨

Three Pairs of Heterozygous Genes or a Trihybrid

When we work out the gene combination possible from parents with three contrasting characteristics we reach a point of diminishing returns. The puppies in the first generation would all be *trihybrids,* and all would show the three dominant traits in their phenotype. However, each would carry recessive genes and these genes would produce in the next generation eight different phenotypes which may occur in 64 different ways in a ratio of 27: 9: 9: 9: 3: 3: 3: 1. Only one would exhibit all three recessive traits.

Facing Reality

While it is theoretically possible to determine the ratio of any number of contrasting traits, such calculations are of no practical use to the dog breeder.

Even with a single pair of genes involved, it might be necessary to breed several litters before a desired recessive would occur. With three pairs, a breeder might wait all his life for that one to appear, because any and all combinations of genes occur in the offspring by pure chance.

It is far better for a breeder to move slowly toward his eventual goal by tackling one problem at a time, locking the virtues into his genotype and discarding the obvious faults through strict selectivity. At all times the overall dog must be kept in mind.

It can be done, and we have proved it in our own breeding program.

When we first began to breed, our handful of Yorkies were not faultless but, basically, they had strong legs and straight toplines. They were sound little dogs with good terrier movement and spirit. Both my partner and I felt these were qualities we wanted to keep in our future Yorkies. But there were other desirable traits which were lacking in our foundation dogs. One of these was the controversial color and texture of a Yorkie's coat. The Yorkies we saw in the show ring in those early days possessing paler, silkier coats were rather miserable specimens of the breed in most other respects. Their backs were roached, their bodies were too long for their legs, the gold on head and legs was pale, lacking depth and brilliance, their movement was faulty.

Rather than attempting to deal with this obvious assortment of heterozygous genes, we decided for the time being to let the color chips fall where they wanted to. We began to build our genetic mosaic gene by gene and desirable trait by desirable trait. We knew we had a long way to go, but we weren't in any hurry.

We introduced three lovely shades of old gold head color from one dog—elegance, leg, neck and head refinement from still another. Then we reached out for tissue and muscle, which we felt were being lost in our puppies and, finally, that elusive recessive "blue" silky coat appeared in one of our litters, which was neither too light nor too dark. It was sheer luck. We knew, from research, that the recessive genes were back there in our pedigrees and all it took was time to have them appear. Along the way we had managed to retain the qualities we started with, but had refined and improved them and introduced new desirable qualities. At all times we kept the picture of

47

our ideal Yorkie in mind, and this is the secret of success. If a breeder concentrates on one single characteristic of a dog to the exclusion of basic soundness, movement, spirit and type, he is taking a shortcut to disaster.

This all sounds so easy, but it has taken twenty years and a vast sum of money. We are still far from producing a "great" in every litter. Often it seems as if we take one step forward and two back but, we know we have, here in our dogs, all the potential necessary to breed our "ideal" Yorkie. The challenge before us is to capture all the qualities in one gorgeous, animated package and lock those genes into our genetic lines so that our dogs will eventually breed true.

We may not be able to accomplish this in the remaining span of our lives, but we hope that we will be able to leave the foundation for such a dream to an equally interested person who will be able to accomplish in his lifetime what we will continue to strive for in ours.

Returning to Mendel

Back we go to Mendel's second Law of Independent Assortment which provides an opportunity for genes, which have developed separately, to come together. Like all laws it has its exceptions and, today, it is known that this law is not categorically valid. There are many variables which must be taken into consideration when it is applied to the complex structure of the dog.

I'll touch on these only briefly. If you find yourself engrossed in the fascinating subject of genetics, there are many excellent books written by qualified geneticists for you to read. But for the average breeder, these variables are only the odds we take when we start playing God.

Linked Inheritance

When two or more pairs of genes on a chromosome remain together they are inherited together, instead of separately as expected. They stay in their original formations and are known as linked genes. But even this variation has its invariable due to a phenomenon known as *crossing-over*. Some of the chromosomes which are paired closely together become intertwined and part of one changes place with part of its corresponding member. This crossing-over prevents any possibility of all the genes on one chromosome being inherited in their entirety, assuring the individuality of every offspring.

Incomplete Dominant Genes

These are quantitative characters that have no sharply opposed opposites. They are nature's way of gravitating toward the norm. Many inherited characteristics, such as temperament, intelligence, body height, weight and length of leg fall into this category.

Modifying Genes

These control certain aspects of conformation such as upright shoulders, straight stifles, shallow brisket and other inherited characteristics expressed by multiple genes. The traits produced by these genes are referred to as *polygenetic*.

Lethal Genes

When a lethal gene is inherited in a double dose, one from each parent, it is usually self-eliminating. When homozygous it causes the death of the embryo in the uterus or, if born alive, will destroy the puppy early in its neonatal period. These genes usually surface as a result of close breeding practices, which serve the purpose of getting rid of them in future generations. If inherited singly, a lethal gene, like all recessives, may be carried along in the genotype for years without a breeder knowing it is in the genotype of his breeding stock.

Sex-Linked Genes

These are located only in the X and Y chromosomes and can alter expected ratios.

Of interest to many breeders, who have trouble controlling the size of their puppies, is the theory that a bitch is genetically larger for her size than a dog. When two dogs of the same size are bred, the male offspring are often larger than their dam and the female offspring are likely to be smaller than their sire.

On the other hand, because of quantitative genes it is possible to breed a large bitch to a small male and have a litter of average-size puppies. This applies only to the first generation. When these puppies are bred, there will be a substantial variation in the size of their offspring.

Atavism or Reversion

When close breeding produces something which resembles a remote ancestor more closely than either the sire or dam, it is probably due to the reappearance of an old characteristic or the reunion of two heterozygous recessives, which finally come together against great odds. The chance of these two ancestral genes, needed for its manifestation, getting together is about as likely as two remaining members of the class of 1920, jogging from New York to California for a reunion.

Mutations

Mutations produce a change in the original theme. They are unexpected differences, generally unpredictable, in the individual organism.

For a long time it has been known that mutations can be caused by radiation, X-rays and certain chemicals and gases, such as mustard gas. Some mutations, considered to be an asset to a breed, such as the screw tail of the Boston Terrier or the short legs of the Dachshund, were deliberately retained by breeders through selection and inbreeding. But the majority of mutations are considered undesirable and usually die out. Possibly many more mutations occur than we hear of because breeders dispose of offspring at birth which exhibit an irregularity, and are reluctant to talk about it. This is foolish, of course, because a mutation is not a genetic fault. Something happened to prevent the exact duplication of a cell and a variation of the original gene is produced.

Modern Advances in Genetics

In the past two decades great strides have been made in the knowledge of heredity. Two chemicals have been identified as the substance of the materials of heredity, and these have literally opened the door to an understanding of the process of life itself.

Genes are now known to be molecules of a protein substance called deoxyribonucleic acid or DNA. Furthermore the gene has a built-in mechanism for the repetition of its own structural pattern, so that it duplicates itself from cell to cell and from generation to generation. The duplicating mechanism is another protein substance identified as RNA. When scientists combine DNA and RNA, the same self-copying job performed by nature in the division of the cells can be performed in the laboratory.

DNA and RNA are known as the "Language of Heredity." Certain codes, already identified, are believed to be the basis for the differences in various species. It is believed that further "cracking of the codes" of the language of heredity, will eventually lead to the control, if not the elimination of mutations and inherited diseases. If, however, the laboratory is ever allowed to become breeders of mice and men, it will indeed be a strange new world, stranger than even Aldous Huxley ever dreamed.

Until that time, we dog breeders will continue to gamble with the odds, combining the basic laws of heredity with the discoveries of geneticists who have been able, through years of breeding, to identify some of the dominant genes and their recessive counterparts.

Genetically Dominant and Recessive Traits

Following is a list of genetically dominant and recessive traits as agreed upon by the majority of geneticists and breeders. It must be kept in mind that some are incompletely dominant, some are linked and others, such as a cleft palate, are lethal.

Dominant	Recessive
Long head	Short head
Large or long ears	Small or short ears
Low set ears	High set ears
Wide ear leather	Narrow ear leather
Coarse skull	Fine skull
Short foreface	Long foreface
Erect ears	Drop or tipped ears
Dark eye	Light eye
Normal eye	Large bulging eyes in some breeds
Brown eyes	Blue eyes
Wire coat	Smooth coat
Short coat	Long coat
Curly coat	Straight coat
Poor layback of shoulder	Good layback of shoulder
Poorly angulated stifle	Well angulated stifle
High set tail	Low set tail
Heavy bone	Light bone
Deep chest	Shallow chest
Straight topline	Sway back
Good spring of rib	Poor spring of rib
Short stifle	Long stifle
Light pigment	Dark pigment on skin of white dogs
Normal hearing	Deafness
Good eyesight	Night blindness
Good eye pigment	Wall eyes
Self-color	Parti-color
Black nose	Dudley nose
Good mouth	Overshot or undershot
Normal palate	Cleft palate
Normal lip	Hare lip
Straight tail	Kinked or bent tail

Black is dominant to red, but red is dominant to liver, brown, orange or lemon. Black is dominant to white.

A long, reaching gait covering a maximum of ground with a minimum of effort is recessive and dependent on good angulation both fore and aft and on the balance of angulation between the front and rear assemblies.

Dark pigment on nose, lips, eyelids and toenails is recessive to light pigment, but not tied in with the dark eye.

These Dachshund puppies were permanently stamped with their complete genetic heritage at the moment of conception.

3

Pedigrees and Breeding Systems

A PEDIGREE is a blueprint of a dog's genetic past. The value of information contained in it is in direct proportion to a person's ability to interpret it—to the amount of time he is willing to spend researching the good and bad qualities of the dogs named in it.

What a dog transmits to its descendants depends on its genotype and may be completely uninfluenced by the number of champions sometimes emphasized in red ink in its pedigree. The idea that an inferior breed type will produce something greater than itself because it has an impressive pedigree is fallacy. A sire or dam can put into its puppies only the qualities it inherited from the genetic structure of its parents and their parents before them. Unless it carries in its genotype the gene combinations for a desired quality, it cannot pass it along to its progeny.

Breeding dogs is similar to making a good soup or stew. The finished dish can be no better than the ingredients that went into its making. And if we want to know the kind of "ingredients" in our breeding stock, we must turn to their pedigrees.

What Pedigrees Tell the Breeder

At first a pedigree may look just like the names of many dogs who were mated together over the years. Actually it tells us what breeding systems, if any, were used to produce a particular dog, and what qualities that particular dog is apt to pass along to its progeny. Its real significance can only be appreciated by a person who has a clear picture of his breed type in mind, who understands the breeding systems used by experienced breeders and has a sound knowledge of the basic principles of genetics. Once the simple mechanics of heredity have been grasped, a pedigree becomes a very revealing document. It enables a breeder to plan his matings, and through systematic methods of inbreeding and linebreeding, accompanied by rigorous selection, he can accumulate and concentrate the desirable genes in his breeding stock.

The average pedigree consists of four or five generations of ancestors and a total of either 30 or 62 dogs: the immediate sire and dam (2), four grandparents, eight great grandparents, 16 great-great grandparents and in five-generation pedigrees 32 great-great-great grandparents.

If you can think of each of these ancestors, not as names of dogs but as thousands of genes neatly arranged on 39 pairs of chromosomes, any one of them capable of expressing a particular quality in a dog, you will be taking a giant step forward in your ability to analyze a pedigree.

Although not genetically precise, we can assume for the purpose of analyzing pedigrees, that a dog inherits half its genes and chromosomes from its sire and half from its dam; one-quarter of which could be from each of its four grandparents, one-eighth from each of its eight great-grandparents, and so on. Theoretically, a dog's immediate ancestors have the greatest influence on the progeny and, while it is reasonable to assume that the ancestral influence on the inherited traits of a particular dog diminishes with each successive generation of ancestors, it is still possible for a dog to inherit one or more good or bad qualities from ancestors as far back as six or seven generations—even further. A dog receives its heritage in a purely chance fashion. Some of its ancestors may give it much, some little, some nothing at all. Should a sire happen to pass along a batch of genes that is received from its sire, then that particular puppy could be more related to its grandsire than to its immediate sire.

An Open Pedigree

In an open pedigree the name of a dog appears only once. The usual pedigree consists of four or five generations but, for the sake of brevity, we will confine our diagrams to only three.

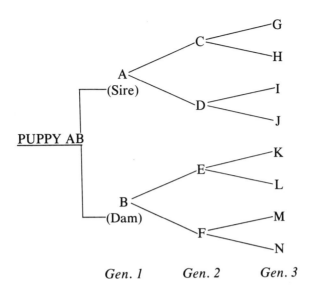

| | Gen. 1 | Gen. 2 | Gen. 3 |

PUPPY AB

A (Sire)
B (Dam)
C
D
E
F
G
H
I
J
K
L
M
N

The above chart illustrates a three-generation open pedigree. No dog appears more than once and PUPPY AB could have inherited one or more qualities or a combination of qualities from 14 different ancestors.

In a five-generation open pedigree, a dog could have inherited both its physical and genetic qualities from 62 different purebred ancestors. The billions of genes involved are mind-boggling. And, unless every dog in such a pedigree is phenotypically high in quality and genetically pure or homozygous for good qualities, the results are likely to be a mishmash of heterozygous puppies bearing little resemblance to any one ancestor in particular. To begin a breeding program with an open-pedigree foundation is doing it the hard way, to put it mildly. It would take the rest of a person's life, and perhaps another lifetime to reach a point from which he could have begun had he started with a carefully bred dog from select stock.

For useful foundation stock you must turn to the experienced breeder who, by means of proved breeding systems, has considerably reduced the number of ancestors in a five-generation pedigree. Such a breeder knows he cannot create any qualities not already present in the genetic structure of his dogs. His objective is to consistently upgrade his dogs by accumulating the desirable genes and concentrating them in the hereditary make-up of his breeding stock. He deliberately sets forth to double the genes of one or more particularly high-quality ancestor to build a valuable gene bank.

note

Building a gene bank can be compared to stacking a deck of cards. If, over the generations, a breeder persists in discarding the deuces, threes, fours, and so on (the poor qualities), replacing them with face cards (good qualities) the chances of dealing a "full house" or a high percentage of quality puppies are greatly increased.

Nevertheless it takes a lot of knowledge, determination, perseverance and plain good luck to be either a good poker player or a fine breeder. Just when you feel you have discarded all the spot cards and replaced them with Aces, Kings and Queens, Mother Nature has a way of turning up a joker.

It must be clearly understood that success in breeding depends to a large extent on the ability of the breeder to make a correct assessment of the genetic potentialities of a dog's ancestors and to be completely objective in evaluating his own breeding stock.

A Genetic Card Game

There are four options or breeding systems open to breeders and these are known as inbreeding, linebreeding, outbreeding and outcrossing. Every breeder, whether he intends to use any of these systems in particular or a combination of them all, should have a clear understanding of what they mean and where one leaves off and another begins.

Inbreeding

This system implies the breeding of closely related individuals, no further separated in the pedigree than one generation: brother to sister, son to dam, sire to daughter or half-brother to half-sister. It concentrates the genes of one or more particular individuals and reduces the overall number of different hereditary combinations that can enter the zygote (germ cell).

If the genotype of the dogs which appear more than once in a pedigree consists of Aces, Kings, Queens and Jacks, the deck or gene bank is being stacked with quality cards or genes. On the other hand, if the genotype consists of low cards or a combination of both good and bad, a breeder is putting those cards into his gene bank to be expressed in future generations.

Inbreeding is likely to concentrate good qualities in some puppies and poor qualities in others in the same litter. The individuals inheriting a double dose of these genes, whether faults or virtues, are apt to be prepotent for these qualities and in turn will pass them along to their progeny.

Inbreeding fixes type more quickly than any other method but, unfortunately, it fixes faults as firmly as it does good qualities. It can be the ruination of a breeder rather than the salvation, unless he has extensive knowledge of both the physical qualities of the dogs in a pedigree and their genetic prepotency as expressed in their progeny.

Suffice it to say that inbreeding should never be used by the novice or by any breeder who lacks the ability to be entirely objective in evaluating his dogs. Some people have no "eye" for a dog and are totally incapable of seeing either their faults or virtues. Nor should the decision to inbreed be based on the number of ribbons the dog has won in the show ring.

If inbreeding were restricted to outstanding dogs, the system would not be so controversial. Geneticists know that it is not the system that is at fault but its application by breeders using unsuitable stock.

Inbreeding has been called a "double-edged sword." For the knowledgeable breeder it can be a powerful tool; for the novice a dangerous one. Inbreeding never creates any qualities, good or bad. It only expresses those qualities already existent in the dog's genetic structure. Inbreeding will in no way upgrade the quality of the original population unless those qualities are already present in the genotype of the sire and dam.

Inbreeding is sometimes employed by a breeder who wants to expose faulty gene combinations that he suspects lurk in the genotype of his dogs. He is then able to dispose of them and eliminate them from his breeding stock.

If inbreeding is used, it must be accompanied by drastic culling of inferior puppies, otherwise it is all to no avail. It is not a breeding system for either the soft in heart nor those with dollar signs in their eyes.

In the following charts we have used 100%, 50%, 25% and 12½% for the first, second, third, and fourth generations in order to arrive at a percentage of prepotency that could theoretically be accumulated in the genes of a puppy. Other percentages can be used as long as the principles behind the breeding system are understood. Actually, any numerical analysis of pedigrees must be viewed in the light of actual breeding experiences within the confines of a particular breed. And as Mr. Onstott so wisely said in *The New Art of Breeding Better Dogs,* "we must never let the pedigree wag the dog."

Brother-Sister Inbreeding

Brother to sister mating is the closest inbreeding that can be made. It reduces the number of dogs in a three generation pedigree by almost 50%.

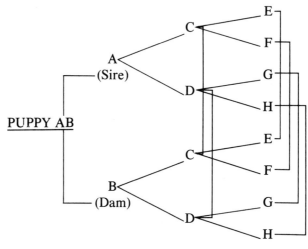

G. Parents   G.G. Parents

Only eight different ancestors are in the above chart of PUPPY AB as contrasted to the 14 in an open pedigree. The diagram (pedigree) shows us that ancestor C is not only the sire of the sire but the sire of the dam and that ancestor D is not only the dam of the sire but the dam of the dam. We know that ancestor C and D each contributed half of their genes to both the sire and dam of the puppy and 25% to the puppy itself. By adding the genetic contribution of ancestors C and D it becomes evident that ancestors C and D could have contributed as much to PUPPY AB as either the sire or the dam.

Father-Daughter or Dam-Son Inbreeding

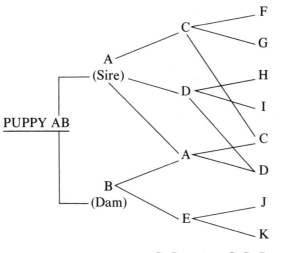

G. Parents   G.G. Parents

Father to daughter mating as diagrammed above shows that the ancestors are reduced less quickly than in full brother to full sister breedings or from 14 to 11 or 25% in a three-generation pedigree. Because Sire A and Grandsire A are the same dog, PUPPY AB will have inherited more genes from it than from its dam.

Theoretically both A and B could contribute 50% of their genes to PUPPY AB. Grandparent C, D or E could contribute 25% of its genes, through the genes of the sire, to puppy AB. But A, which is both sire and grandsire, is likely to contribute more of its qualities (both good and bad) to the puppy than the dam, actually in a ratio of 3 to 2 or 75% to 50% of the puppy's total inheritance.

If any one of the great grandparents could contribute 12½% of its genes, then grandparents C and D are likely to contribute a greater percentage of their qualities to PUPPY AB through ancestor A, than the other grandparent E. in the ratio of 5 to 4 or 37½% to 25%.

Half-Brother—Half-Sister Inbreeding

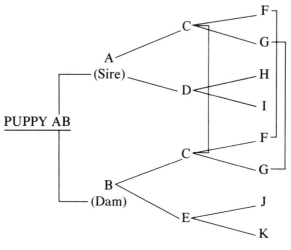

G. Parents   G.G. Parents

Half-brother to half-sister matings reduce the number of ancestors in a three-generation pedigree by the same percentage as sire to daughter matings or 25% but, instead of collecting the genes of the grandsire, it gives equal opportunity to sire and dam and grandsire C to influence PUPPY AB genetically.

The Pros and Cons of Inbreeding

Some geneticists recommend inbreeding for several generations in order to establish a genetic purity or homozygosity in breeding stock.

Dr. S.A. Asdell, author of a highly technical book on reproduction and genetics, *Dog Breeding,* believes that close breeding tends to weaken the vitality of a strain and, therefore outcrosses to other strains may be advisable to preserve the necessary vitality. Contrary to this, Leon Shiver, in a speech published in *Dog Lover's Digest,* May, 1973, advises breeders not to be misled by well-meaning friends who tell us that breeding too close for any length of time will result in loss of size and stamina. "Very true," he says, "If you breed small dogs to small bitches and continue to breed this way in the same family, you will most certainly produce small dogs."

Mr. Shiver bred half-brothers and half-sisters together for generation after generation with outstanding results but, it is worthy of

60

note, and should be kept in mind before such close breedings are attempted by the novice, that Mr. Shiver never uses a stud that is not closely bred and the product of at least three generations of champion sires. He breeds it to a bitch, which is also the product of very close breeding for at least three generations of top show dogs on both sire's and dam's side. Obviously Mr. Shiver had done a great deal of "weeding out" before he set forth on this experiment.

Dr. Leon Whitney developed a beautiful strain of tropical fish by breeding brothers to sisters for ten consecutive generations. For the first four generations the fish became noticeably smaller and less vigorous than each previous generation but, suddenly there was an improvement. In the fifth generation and in each generation thereafter the fish gained in both vigor and color.

Another experiment was made with a strain of fighting cocks in which brother-sister matings were continued for more than one hundred generations, and the end products were finer and larger than the original pair.

But breeding fish and fighting cocks, mice and fruit flies is a very different kettle of flesh and bones than breeding dogs and, even with large breeds which produce large litters, the amount of time and money necessary to attempt such a program make it impractical for most breeders. With small breeds and small litters it would be virtually impossible. Defects and hidden recessives in the genotype of ancestors from many generations back would surface, and the chances are that lethal genes would terminate such a program before it could be completed.

Inbreeding is common among wild animals without any apparent degenerative effects, but this is probably due to the fact that Nature is ruthless in destroying the weak and defective. We, as dog breeders, should respect the "survival of the fittest," and not force weak puppies to live by tube feeding or other supplementary methods, and we must cull mercilessly in any kind of a breeding program. This does not mean necessarily that we must destroy all but perfect specimens. It does mean that we must eliminate them from our breeding program or from anyone's breeding program by finding them good homes and supplying registration papers only on proof of spaying or castration.

I would like to stress again that the system of inbreeding is not at fault, but rather the quality of stock used by breeders who are unable to evaluate their dogs objectively.

However, if we all had nothing but perfect dogs, it would be much too easy to breed perfection, and most of the challenge of breeding would be lost.

61

Our last diagram illustrates brother-sister matings for three-generations. An open pedigree would, by this method, be reduced from fourteen ancestors to six. If such matings were continued for five generations, the resulting puppies would carry the accumulative genes of only ten ancestors in their genotype instead of 62.

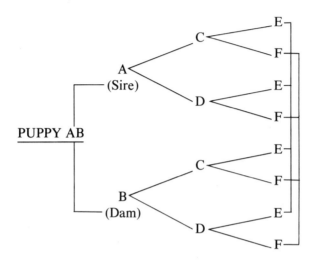

All six dogs in this pedigree could contribute equally to PUPPY AB. Sire and dam could each contribute 50%; grandsire and grand-dam C and D could each contribute 25% plus 25% or 50% of their accumulative genes, and great-grandsires and great granddams could each contribute 12½% times four, or 50% of their accumulative genes. PUPPY AB is just as likely to resemble great grandsire E as it might resemble sire A. The actual percentage of genes that a puppy inherits from each ancestor is very much a matter of luck, or how the cards are dealt.

Linebreeding

This system of breeding brings together individuals further removed than one generation and is favored by the majority of serious breeders because it is less drastic than inbreeding. When linebreeding it will take a breeder longer to obtain uniformity of type or increase homozygosity in his dogs than if he resorted to inbreeding or a combination of inbreeding and linebreeding.

Linebreeding means the mating of individuals which are closely related to a common ancestor, but are little, if at all, related to each other. So, when someone tells you proudly that his dog is linebred, he should name the ancestor in the pedigree that is common to both the sire and the dam.

The object of linebreeding is to accumulate the genetic contributions of one outstanding ancestor, and this ancestor becomes of paramount importance. If a breeder continues to breed to this particular dog, in several generations the accumulation of its genes and its ability to express itself in its progeny can be in excess of the influence of either the sire or the dam. On the other hand, unless linebreeding is continued, it will be only a matter of three or four generations before the genetic contribution of the outstanding ancestor is reduced to an unimportant level.

It should not be necessary to point out that, unless the dog to which one linebreeds is truly an outstanding example of its breed, both physically and genetically, the breeder may be downgrading his stock rather than upgrading it. Linebreeding to a poor specimen can do nothing but produce poor quality puppies, and the more often the breeder returns to that poor specimen, the worse his puppies will become.

It is heartbreaking to stand by and watch a novice breeder seriously attempt to improve his stock by linebreeding to a dog which has been touted by its owners as "perfect." In reality it can make little genetic contributions, if any, to future generations, regardless of how many ribbons it accumulated in the show ring. So, beware the breeder who tries to "sell" you on the virtues of his stud dog or speaks derogatorily about a competitor's stud dog. Use your own head and get a firm picture in mind of the type of dog you wish to eventually breed. Many novice breeders, with a knowledge of movement and structure, have that priceless "eye for a dog," and are more realistic in their appraisal of adults and puppies than some who have been in the act for a long time.

Before you finally decide on the dog to whom you are going to linebreed, make sure it is or was both physically and genetically a good one. Then, if linebreeding works for you, continue it for several generations. If one or more particular faults occur too often for comfort, you will have to turn to another system of breeding or take drastic action to correct those faults. Remember you are linebreeding, not inbreeding, so you will not be breeding to the dog itself but rather to a grandson or uncle, which is also a quality dog.

Keeping in mind that a puppy receives approximately 50% of its inheritance from each parent, 25% from each grandparent, 12½% from each great grandparent, and so on, we can readily calculate the percentage of genes that a puppy shares with the ancestor to which its dam or sire was linebred.

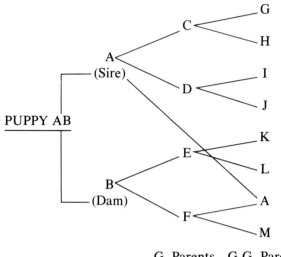

G. Parents G.G. Parents

The above chart illustrates linebreeding sire to granddaughter. In an open pedigree it reduces the number of ancestors in three generations by only one, or from 14 to 13. It also serves to illustrate the veteran breeder's favorite quote, "Let the sire of the puppy (a future sire or dam) be the grandsire of the dam on the dam's side."

By counting the number of times a name is repeated in a pedigree we get a glimpse of which ancestor made the greatest contribution to a puppy. It is not difficult, however, to calculate the percentage of genes that PUPPY AB is apt to share with ancestor A, which is 62½%.

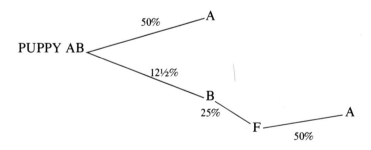

Linebreeding the progeny of brothers and sisters (cousin to cousin) reduces the number of ancestors in a four-generation pedigree from 30 to 24, and PUPPY AB would likely carry 25% of the same genes as both of its cousins I and J. If I and J received some of the identical genes (hopefully desirable ones) from their sires and dams (QR and ST), the actual breeding coefficient of PUPPY AB would be even greater. In order to illustrate cousin to cousin breeding, a four-generation pedigree is needed.

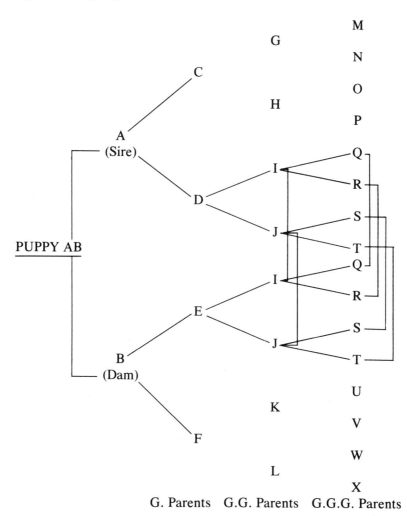

G. Parents   G.G. Parents   G.G.G. Parents

Uncle to niece breeding is diagrammed below. By reversing the sire's and dam's role, it would then be the mating of nephew to aunt. Such matings reduce the number of ancestors in a four-generation pedigree to 24 from 30, the same reduction as mating cousin to cousin, but PUPPY AB is apt to have 37½% of the same genes as both its Uncle C and Niece D.

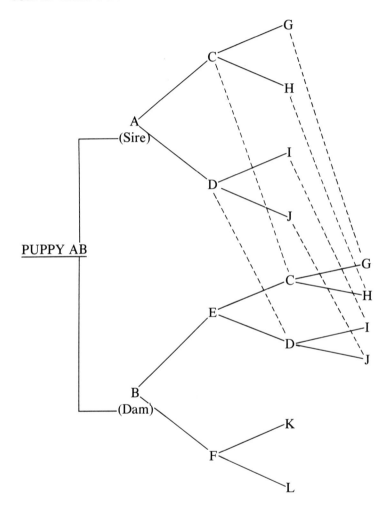

Uncle C and Aunt D could each pass 50% of their genes to Sire A, who could pass 25% of each of their genes to PUPPY AB. Nephew C and Niece D could give 50% of their genes to E, which could pass 25% to Dam B and Dam B could give 12½% of the genes to both

Nephew and Niece to PUPPY AB. The accumulative genes of both these ancestors in PUPPY AB would be 37½%.

Linebreeding great grandson to great grandaughter (a popular breeding technique) or vice versa, reduces the number of ancestors in four generations by six. PUPPY AB is likely to have inherited 25% of the same genes as those of his great grandsire. Let's call him ADAM. If ADAM was outstanding in quality, a breeder might consider taking the best puppy in the litter and breeding back to this ancestor, increasing not only the number of genes that the resulting progeny and ADAM would have in common, but the breeding coefficient or homozygosity as well.

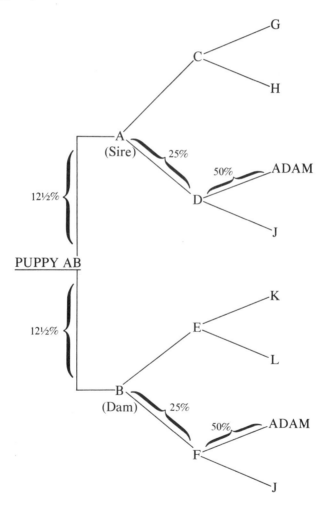

By breeding PUPPY AB back to ADAM the accumulation of ADAM'S genes in a resulting puppy would be 62½%. The puppy would have a genetic prepotency similar to ADAM in excess of either ADAM (the sire) or the dam. Let's hope ADAM is a superior specimen of the breed!

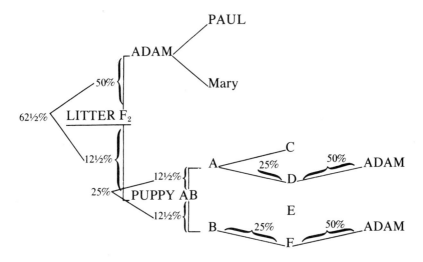

Reduction of number of dogs in a pedigree through various systems of breeding.

Type of Pedigree	No. Dogs		
	3-gen.	4-gen.	5-gen.
Open	14	30	62
Inbreedings			
Brother to Sister	8	16	32
Father to Daughter Mother to Son Half-Brother to Half-Sister	11	23	47
Linebreedings			
Cousins Nephew to Aunt Niece to Uncle G. Grandaughter to G. Grandson Grandson to Granddaughter		24	48
Grandfather to Granddaughter Grandmother to Grandson		27	55

Outbreeding

Outbreeding is not so much a system as a lack of system. The mating of close relatives is deliberately avoided, and only distantly related animals are mated for generation after generation in a haphazard manner. It is generally used by "breeders" with little or no knowledge of genetics who are able to maintain a fairly profitable breeding operation within a kennel. By outbreeding they avoid the costs and problems which face the serious breeder, working constantly to upgrade his breeding stock.

Occasionally such a devil-may-care attitude may produce a fairly good dog, because of a tendency of nature to gravitate toward the norm. Also because of the high degree of heterozygosity and disassortment in the offspring, the average level of quality is inferior to that obtained by means of an intelligent breeding program.

Outbreeding is generally the method employed by the pet owner who finds an adorable little dog down the street, which happens to be of the same breed as his bitch. This, then becomes the most convenient and cheapest way to impregnate his pet bitch and have a litter of "cute little pups." Pet shops are filled with such cute pups and millions are destroyed each year for lack of homes in which to place them.

Outcrossing

Outcrossing is generally considered to be the mating of animals with no common ancestors within five generations. It increases genetic heterozygosity and diminishes prepotency. It should not be confused with crossbreeding, which is the mating of different breeds and, unless conducted with a purpose in mind of developing a new breed, results in mongrels.

There are two reasons why a breeder will deliberately outcross. The first is an attempt to introduce genetically into his own line one or more desirable qualities lacking in his breeding stock. He sets out to find an animal which displays these qualities. Ideally it will be a carefully linebred or even an inbred dog, prepotent or homozygous for the desired qualities and therefore genetically able to pass them to its offspring in a double dose. The best would be not only an outstanding example of the breed, but a top-producer as well.

If the sire and dam are carefully selected, the phenotype of the puppies in the first generation (F_1) will generally be good or a combination of good and bad. Unfortunately the breeder has introduced a lot of unknown qualities and possibly unwanted genes into the genotype of the puppies along with the desirable ones. The intelligent breeder will return immediately to his own stock and, by means of Mendelian segregation in the F_2 (second generation), he will be able to see the results of his cross. He can then select the best with the hope that the qualities he was seeking will express themselves in future generations. The remaining pups should be sold as pets without papers.

Dr. Roy C. Fanguay, in a fascinating article on *Pedigree Utilization in Breeding*, states that the wise breeder will consider carefully before outcrossing.

> All too often breeders resort to outcrossing to correct a particular weakness in their dogs (like soft backs) instead of correcting it through selection within their own breeding stock. What they fail to realize is that you cannot just "order" one part. You may improve the backs as a result of this outcross, but in the process you may have picked up weak legs.

He advises the breeder to use extreme caution in making outcrosses and only to resort to them when selection within his own line fails.

The second reason for outcrossing is to increase vigor within a particular strain of a breed. This can only be achieved if both lines are closely inbred. The result is puppies which grow more rapidly to a

70

larger size, have increased productivity and are less susceptible to stress.

Geneticists call this *hybrid vigor*. It is based on the theory that the most desirable genes in a breed, whether recessive or dominant are homozygous, and will express themselves in the first generation.

It is a system often employed by breeders who measure their success by how many show dogs they produce, not on how successful they are in developing a strain which will breed true to type. It's a short term policy at best, because of the increased genetic heterozygosity in the first generation of puppies. While they will be phenotypically superior in every way to their sire and dam, they should not be introduced into a breeder's main line. If they are, it will be just like starting all over again.

Many successful breeding operations, not only in animals but in plants, are based on the crossing of two strongly inbred lines. The biggest, meatiest cattle, the largest ears of corn, the reddest and juiciest tomatoes in your garden are usually hybrids. If you are a gardener as well as a breeder you will notice that many of the packets of seeds you buy state that the seeds are hybrid and carry the following warning:

"The seeds from the resulting produce should not be used for future plantings." In other words, they will be "bad" seeds.

Non-Genetic Breeding Systems

It is most surprising that many intelligent breeders believe the only way to breed quality is phenotypically, and to such Mendelism and pedigrees are of little consequence.

Like-to-Like

Breeders who employ this method of breeding believe that mating quality to quality can not produce anything but quality. They depend on their eye to select individual specimens of similar body type, coat and temperament. It is a hit-or-miss method of breeding, and has not proved successful in many instances.

When it is successful, it is generally because those little chromosomes and genes are in there doing their work whether the breeder knows it or not. When a particular type of dog appeals to him and he selects another with similar appeal, it is not unusual to find an outstanding, inbred ancestor common to both dogs, which was responsible for producing the similarity in the two dogs in the first place.

Divergent Breeding

This type of breeding is based on correcting faults by breeding to a dog which displays the contrasting virtue, such as long legs to short, long necks to short, sway backs to level backs. If the breeder happens to be dealing with a modifying gene (long legs to short legs) he might occasionally get what he is looking for in the first generation but, where does he go from there? No place but down.

Many new breeders think that if they mate an oversize bitch to an undersize male, they will produce the correct size puppies. Nothing could be further from the truth. Chances are there will be half small and half large puppies in the litter.

Two wrongs do not make a right either in a court of law or in the breeding of dogs.

The Nick

Sometimes, regardless of what breeding system is employed, Nature has a way of throwing in a handful of Aces, and a breeder finds a certain dog mated to a particular bitch results in offspring that are superior to either of the parents. This is known as a "nick" or a happy combination of the genes of the sire and the dam. Should such a mating be repeated? Sure. Why not? Wouldn't you?

Conclusion

Nothing is ever as clear cut and simple as the illustrations in this chapter. Many are the permutations and combinations of breeding methods and systems, some of which may work for you and others which may not. It is my hope that the diagrams will serve to stress that a breeder is working in the dark unless he knows a great deal about the dog to whom he breeds, and that he must learn as much as possible about the qualities, both good and bad, in the genotype of his own breeding stock.

This is why breeding is an applied science. No matter how much you know about Mendel's Laws of Heredity, of genes and chromosomes, of breeding systems, without an immense accumulation of data on your particular breed, an "eye" for a good dog, and generations of breeding experience, genetics can be fascinating but of little practical value.

Probably one rule stands out above any other and that is—either inbreeding, linebreeding or outcrossing, breed only the best to the best and don't be satisfied with anything less.

4

Pedigrees and Progeny

THE TRUE BREEDER is not interested in occasionally producing a good dog, but in improving the average level of all the dogs in his kennel. His eventual aim is to develop a line of dogs that produces superior animals that will, in turn, produce offspring of better than average quality.

Which Breeding System is Best?

The system that works best for you and your breed is the best one.

And regardless of what system or combination of systems a breeder uses, his objective should be to consistently upgrade his breeding stock.

Breeding is an art as well as a science. To this blending of art and science, a large measure of courage must be added. Without the courage to ride through the inevitable difficult periods along the way, when everything seems to be going against you, your breeding program is doomed to failure right from the beginning. Breed books illustrate only too vividly how new breeders come on fast and strong, become overnight experts but, in a few years, one hears no more about them, and their contribution to the breed becomes insignificant. The genes of the dogs they bred become diffused and rapidly fade into the genetic structure of the breed as a whole.

No breeding system can be successful without a background knowledge of what genes individual dogs are likely to possess in their genotype and may pass along to their offspring.

No breeding system can be successful without rigid selectivity. This means that the breeder must have a clear picture in mind of the type of dog he wishes to breed. Without this how can he be selective?

No breeding system can be successful unless the breeder is completely objective in evaluating his breeding stock and the puppies they produce. "Kennel blindness" is the worst fault that can crop up in any kennel and unless quickly "cured" can become lethal.

Far too many breeders are totally incapable of recognizing the faults in the dogs they show or breed. The objective breeder is seldom satisfied with his dogs. He is always able to fault them and usually will fault them more strictly than others would. He knows that "the only perfect dogs are bred by novices."

When a breeder can be thrilled at the sight of a good dog regardless of who owns it or bred it, he can consider himself truly objective.

No breeding system can be successful without an "eye" for a good dog. Some breeders, exhibitors and judges are unable to recognize either faults or virtues. They are responsible for allowing faults to creep into a breed. By either ignoring them or rewarding them with a placement ribbon, the faults soon become accepted qualities of the breed, even though they may be in direct opposition to the official standard. A good eye, an honest eye, is essential in breeding dogs, and the final responsibility rests firmly on the shoulders of the judges who should withhold ribbons from any dog that is not sound, typey and conforms to the official standard—"the only standard of excellence by which a breed shall be judged."

A Few Breeding Tips Based Solely on Experience

Since I am not a geneticist, I do not intend to tell you how to breed but, after twenty years of breeding and exhibiting dogs and feeling close to the heartbeat of the dog fancy, I might be able to help you avoid some of the mistakes that are all too easy to make.

1. Be prepared to make a fresh start. Take a good hard look at your breeding stock. Watch them standing free, and moving, and evaluate their best qualities and their faults. Are they worth breeding? If not, be courageous and transfer them to good pet homes.

2. It is better to breed an overall high quality bitch with one major fault than to attempt to correct a lot of small faults in an otherwise mediocre specimen. It would take more than your lifetime to breed them out, and chances are the bitch is not worth breeding

anyhow. A major fault that you can see is caused by a homozygous gene and is very easy to eliminate from future breeding stock.

3. Until you have bred a great many litters and have considerable experience with your breed, don't attempt close breedings. Linebreed cousin to cousin, uncle to niece, granddaughter to grandsire.

4. Never mate two dogs exhibiting the same fault or that you know are carrying the same faulty genes.

5. Don't try to correct an exaggeration by mating to an opposite one. Mate to a well-balanced, correctly proportioned and structured dog.

6. Avoid excessive inbreeding and outcross only when absolutely necessary. When outcrossing use a distantly related stud dog or a closely linebred or inbred stud. A closely linebred or inbred sire, itself a quality dog, is likely to introduce fewer faults than one that is widely linebred.

7. After outcrossing, select the best puppies and mate them back to their parents or grandparents. You won't really know what faults or virtues have been introduced into your breeding stock by the outcross until the second generation. Half the progeny should show the quality you wanted to introduce into the genetic structure of your dogs.

8. Breed to correct one fault or to improve one quality at a time. And, if possible, do this by selection within your own family rather than resorting to an outcross. Remember that each time you outcross you open a "new can of worms."

9. If possible develop two complementary strains that can be bred together. A third related line to use for outcrossing is Utopia but impractical for most of us.

10. Keep track of the dogs you sell with the thought of returning to them if necessary.

11. Don't rush to breed to the top-winning dog. First investigate the qualities of its sire. Often it is far better to breed to the dog that sired the top winner than to the top winner itself. *note!*

12. Set your sights high and don't falter. When the going gets rough, remember that Mendelian selection is sorting out the good genes from the bad ones. The next generation will be better. Don't give up too quickly.

Interpreting Pedigrees

Now let's look at the careers of some of the most successful, veteran breeders in America. From them we can learn what kinds of

A full brother to Dream Walking and Debutante, Ch. Jay Mac's Cavalier was top-winning Miniature Pinscher in 1976. He is shown with John McNamara, his owner breeder.

breeding systems were used to produce some of our top-winning dogs, both past and present.

Jay-Mac Miniature Pinschers

Mr. & Mrs. John McNamara were the breeders of some very high quality Miniature Pinschers, including Ch. Jay-Mac's Dream Walking, Ch. Jay-Mac's Impossible Dream and Ch. Jay-Mac's Miss Debutante.

Mr. McNamara wrote me from his home at Mexico, Missouri, where he is retired and almost out of dog breeding, but his comments will be of inspiration to every novice breeder.

After a few false starts in Miniature Pinschers, I finally got the idea of what I wanted to produce in the type of Min Pin from a pen-and-ink drawing on an early-day breeder's letterhead. I had never seen a Miniature Pinscher to compare to this drawing and I have never been able to produce one that compares completely with the drawing. I am still trying, as this was the ideal image of the Min Pin I wanted. I have found that the Min Pin is not an easy breed to breed to the standard or to the standard we have set for ourselves at Jay-Mac.

Twenty years ago, many of the Min Pins were short, cobby little dogs with quite heavy heads and thick necks set on four rather short, heavy-boned legs. The ears were short-cropped as was the tail and in many cases, they lacked the elegance or style that I wanted. There are still some breeders today who like and still breed that type of German Miniature Pinscher, but we wanted one with more racy lines and more refinement.

It was about 1962 that we finally decided on the type of Min Pin we wanted to breed. We evaluated the stock we had on hand and decided they were not adequate for what we had in mind. They were all sold as pets. Then we bought two of the best Miniature Pinscher bitches we could find from Dr. Boshell. They were definitely show puppies and the very tops in breeding. One bitch was a double Von Kurt breeding and the other one Von Kurt and Alema cross. Both finished their championships quickly and were ready for breeding on their second season.

In looking for suitable studs to mate them with, we decided to go to Tipton's Casanova with one of them and to Booher's Ch. Dobe with the other. Both of these studs were tops in breeding and conformation and both had the style and elegance we were looking for.

From these two breedings we got some outstanding puppies and were on our way at last to establish our line. We never bred the two bitches to the same stud as we wanted to develop two lines that we could crisscross.

Ch. Jay-Mac's Dream Walking accumulated during her
show career, 33 Bests in Show and 129 Group Firsts. She
was the result of close breeding from a sire and dam, both
linebred to Ch. Rebel Roc's Casanova V. Kurt.

Martin Booth

Full sister to Dream Walking is
Ch. Jay-Mac's Miss Debutante.

Lee Lane

As our puppies developed, we decided we would have to use a longer ear-crop and a longer tail-crop to balance the longer necks and head set, and for a time we were the butt of many jokes from other breeders for our long ears and longer tails that they thought we should tie flags on. I told them I thought the long tails were good to tie first place ribbons on. However, we also had some objections from the good judges who thought we were getting away from the Min Pin standard calling for a sturdy little dog.

We have always kept some of our best champion bitches for breeding stock, and if we can point to any one reason we have had some success, good bitches would be our first answer. I know some breeders who hold that some of the less desirable bitches in a litter should produce the same quality as the real good bitches, as they all carry the same genes, but we have never found this to be true. We firmly believe that if you breed second best, you will come up with second best puppies. Most of our breeding is planned on paper but, if the results are not satisfactory, we go back to where the deviation became apparent and try to correct it.

In looking for stud dogs, we first look for one with eye-appeal and showmanship. If he has those qualities, we then are interested in his pedigree, but will insist that the pedigree goes back to some of the great foundation lines in this country without skips into the pet line. We do not like complete outcrosses, and try to locate a relationship at least within the third or fourth generation. If the outside stud does not bring us some of the things we are looking for, he is soon discarded. We must constantly move forward.

I believe the Miniature Pinscher has to be a real outstanding specimen to compete successfully in the Toy Groups today. The long coats give us real competition. He must be alert, with head and tail held high and move with assurance that he's got it and in the right places. He has no long coat to catch the judge's eye or to cover possible faults. The Min Pin is out there in his underwear, and if a foot turns in or out, it is obvious to the judge as well as ringside. The Min Pin has to have elegance and soundness bred into him to be able to compete.

We at Jay-Mac have not revolutionized or changed the breed in any great way nor have we wanted to. We do believe we have improved our line and for our own satisfaction are getting quite a few of the type we had in mind. If given time, we hope to complete a few more of our plans. In our own minds, at least, we have been able to compete successfully and as an added reward we have met and made many friends in the wonderful world of dogs. Impossible Dream, Dream Walking and several others have made some of our dreams come true.

The McNamaras bred more than 100 champions. Among them were seven Best in Show winners.

The litter which included Ch. Jay-Mac's Ramblin Rose was the beginning of the answer for the McNamaras. She was born in February, 1967, and lived until June, 1978. During her productive years she was the dam of 22 champions of record, three of which were Best in Show winners. She herself, won 49 Bests in Show and 211 Group Firsts. She was ten years old at the time this free-standing picture was taken. *Martin Booth*

Probably the greatest Miniature Pinscher of all time was Ch. Rebel Roc's Casanova Von Kurt or "Little Daddy." He was owned and bred by Mrs. E. W. Tipton, Jr, and handled by E. W. Tipton, Jr. Born in September, 1959, he lived until March 1974.

If we study the pedigree of Dream Walking we can see the great contribution that E.W. Tipton's Ch. Rebel Roc's Casanova V. Kurt played in his genetic contribution to the Jay-Macs. The McNamaras returned to "Little Daddy" several times and, in this way, were successful in bringing forward not only Casanova's genes but those of two great Min Pins in his background, Ch. Eldomar Sentry and his illustrious sire, Ch. King Allah V. Siegenburg.

		Ch. Sgt. Fritz Von Enztal
	Bel Roc's Sniklefritz	Bel Roc's Redwing Von Enztal
	Ch. Bo-Mar's Drummer Boy	Ch. Little Buzzard of Alema
	Ch. Bo-Mar's Ebony Belle	Ch. Rebel Roc's Cora V. Kurt
	Ch. Bo-Mar's Brandy of Jay-Mac	Ch. Baron Anthony V. Meyer
	Ch. Rebel Roc's Jupiter V. Kurt	Rolling Green's Sparkle
	Ch. Bo-Mar's Blythe Spirit	Ch. Tip Topper of Alema
	Ch. Rebel Roc's Cora V. Kurt	Rolling Green's Sparkle
Ch. Bo-Mar's Roadrunner		Ch. Eldomar Sentry
	Ch. Baron Anthony V. Meyer	Bel Roc's Dina Von Enztal
	Ch. Rebel Roc's Casanova V. Kurt	Ch. Mudhen Acres Red Snapper
	Rolling Green's Sparkle	Ch. Bel Roc's Sugar V. Enztal
Bo-Mar's Dancing Doll		Ch. Baron Anthony V. Meyer
	Ch. Rebel Roc's Jupiter V. Kurt	Rolling Green's Sparkle
	Ch. Bo-Mar's Drum Song	Ch. Little Buzzard of Alema
	Ch. Bo-Mar's Ebony Belle	Ch. Rebel Roc's Cora Von Kurt

CH. JAY-MAC'S DREAM WALKING, MISS DEBUTANTE, CAVALIER and PIPPIN

	Ch. Baron Anthony Von Meyer	Ch. Eldomar Sentry
	Ch. Rebel Roc's Casanova V. Kurt	Bel Roc's Dina Von Enztal
	Rolling Green's Sparkle	Ch. Mudhen Acres Red Snapper
	Ch. Rebel Roc's Jackpot	Ch. Bel Roc's Sugar V. Enztal
	Ch. Rebel Roc's Casanova V. Kurt	Ch. Baron Anthony V. Meyer
	Ch. Rebel Roc's Yo-Yo	Rolling Green's Sparkle
	Ch. Rebel Roc's Sugar V. Enztal	Ch. Bel Roc's Dobe V. Enztal
Ch. Jay-Mac's Miss Michigan		Bel Roc's Mischief V. Enztal
	Ch. Bo-Mar's Drummer Boy	Bel Roc's Sniklefritz Von Enztal
	Ch. Bo-Mar's Drum Song of Jay-Mac	Ch. Bo-Mar's Ebony Belle
	Bo-Mar's Penny Von Enztal	Ch. Sgt. Fritz Von Enztal
	Ch. Jay-Mac's Ramblin' Rose	Bo-Mar's Sassy Von Enztal
	Ch. Rebel Roc's Jupiter V. Kurt	Ch. Baron Anthony V. Meyer
	Ch. Bo-Mar's Drum Song	Rolling Green's Sparkle
	Ch. Bo-Mar's Ebony Belle	Ch. Little Buzzard of Alema
		Ch. Rebel Roc's Cora Von Kurt

Dream Walking's grandsire was the result of sire to daughter inbreeding, while her sire and dam were progeny of half-brother, half-sister matings.

Ch. Cede Higgens

To Mrs. John Clark, Seattle, Washington, goes the credit for setting the genetic stage that produced Ch. Cede Higgens, the enchanting Yorkshire Terrier that was Top Toy for 1978 and BIS at Westminster that same year.

By studying the pedigree one can see how expertly Mrs. Clark juggled and brought forward two related but separate lines. She bred her original foundation bitch, Clarkwyn Miss Debutante, imported from Clonmel Kennels in 1958, to Ch. Wildweir Pomp 'N' Circumstance, a double grandson of Ch. Star Twilight of Clu-Mor. Two years later, a Yorkie, named Toy Clown of Rusklyn won the CC at Crufts, and Mrs. Clark imported him for her foundation stud. Toy Clown became a top winner in America with ten Toy Groups and many other Group placements to his credit. He was also a top producer, sire of five champions and grandsire of many more.

Mrs. Clark bred Toy Clown to Miss Debutante, to Miss Debutante's daughters, granddaughter and great granddaughter, gradually building a prepotency of Toy Clown's genes in both the sire and dam of Higgens. It should be further noted that 50% of Toy Clown's genes are the same as those in the genotype of Anston Blue Emperor, Toy Clown's double grandsire.

The pedigree shows that when Mrs. Clark felt she needed to introduce some new genes into her breeding stock, she bought Dansel Mollie Brown, an inbred daughter and granddaughter of Ch. Buranthea's Doutelle, thereby introducing into her linebred Toy Clown stock, the genes of another outstanding ancestor, International Ch. Mr. Pim of Johnstounburn, one of England's top producers. Mr. Pim appears in the background of most of the quality Yorkies in America today.

If another generation were added to Higgens' pedigree, we would see that Mr. Pim was also the sire of Ch. Burghwallis Vikki.

It is interesting that both these outstanding ancestors, Mr. Pim and Blue Emperor, are prominent in the pedigree of Ch. Blairsville Royal Seal, the number one dog (all-breeds) and "Dog of the Year," in England in both 1976 and 1977. It is also interesting to note how two dogs, differing so drastically in structure and type, could fall within the confines of the standard of perfection for the Yorkshire Terrier breed. The one point they seem to have in common is quality of coat.

One English critic who had judged both dogs reported that Higgens, with his baby face and large eye, would have done little, if any, winning in England, while Royal Seal, with his extreme terrier stamp, might have had trouble getting out of the breed in America.

Ch. Cede Higgens, all-time top-winning Yorkshire Terrier, was bred by C.D. Lawrence and owned by Charles W. and Barbara A. Switzer. He was Top Toy in 1978 and the winner of the coveted Westminster BIS that same year. He was expertly handled by the Switzers' daughter Marlene Lutovsky. *MikRon*

PEDIGREE OF CH. CEDE HIGGENS

Ch. Toy Clown of Rusklyn
Ch. Clarkwyn Johnny Co-Co
Ch. Clarkwyn Dreamy Doll
Ch. Clarkwyn Nipsey Doodle
    Ch. Wildweir Pomp 'N' Circumstance
Ch. Clarkwyn Dreamy Doll
    Clarkwyn Miss Debutante
Ch. Clarkwyn Jubilee Eagle
    Sorreldene Master Cutler
Ch. Toy Clown of Rusklyn
    Rusklyn Dinkie Duffles
Ch. Clarkwyn Fanciful Sue
    Clarkwyn Lancelot
Ch. Clarkwyn Saucy Sue
    Clarkwyn CoCo's Co-Kette

    Ch. Wildweir Pomp 'N' Circumstance
Ch. Wildweir Sugar Daddy
    Ch. Sorreldene Sugar Plum
Clarkwyn Billie Boy
    Ch. Buranthea's Doutelle
Dansel Mollie Brown
    Wildweir Time Marches On
Cede Bonnie

    Ch. Wildweir Poppycock
Clarkwyn Lancelot
    Ch. Clarkwyn Dreamy Doll
Ch. Clarkwyn Saucy Sue
    Ch. Toy Clown of Rusklyn
Clarkwyn CoCo's Co-Kette
    Clarkwyn Flirtation

Sorreldene Master Cutler
Rusklyn Dinkie Duffles
Ch. Wildweir Pomp 'N' Circumstance
Clarkwyn Miss Debutante
Ch. Wildweir Cock of the Walk
Capri Venus
Cactus Model
Caroline of Clonmel
Anston Blue Emperor
Sorreldene Mignonette
Anston Blue Emperor
Theodore of Winpal
Ch. Wildweir Poppycock
Ch. Clarkwyn Dreamy Doll
Ch. Toy Clown of Rusklyn
Clarkwyn Flirtation
Ch. Wildweir Cock of the Walk
Capri Venus
Ch. Burghwallis Vikki
Sorreldene Mimosa
Ch. Mr. Pim of Johnstounburn
Buranthea York Sensation
Ch. Buranthea's Doutelle
Wildweir Time and Tide

Ch. Wildweir Pomp 'N' Circumstance
Ch. Wildweir Lucky Star
Ch. Wildweir Pomp 'N' Circumstance
Clarkwyn Miss Debutante
Sorreldene Master Cutler
Rusklyn Dinkie Duffles
Ch. Toy Clown of Rusklyn
Clarkwyn Miss Debutante

Ch. Blairsville Royal Seal

Ch. Blairsville Royal Seal, or "Tosha" as he is affectionately called by his breeders and owners, Brian and Rita Lister, is obviously the product of superior homozygous ancestors in what appears to be an open pedigree for four generations, but by extending the pedigree for another generation, we find that Ch. Pagnell Peter Pan and Ch. Burghwallis Vikki were full brothers and that Ch. Prism of Johnstouburn was the daughter of the famous International Ch. Mr. Pim of Johnstounburn.

Whether or not "Tosha" was the result of "lucky" genes or an expression of Mr. Pim will only be known through his progeny.

Ch. Burghwallis Little Nip
Ch. Pagnell Peter Pan
          Prism of Johnstounburn   Ch. Mr. Pimm of Johnstounburn
Ch. Beechrise Superb
      Beechrise Sensation
   Beechrise Pixie
      Beechrise Tina
Ch. Beechrise Surprise
      Anston Blue Emperor
   Sorreldene Shadow
      Tena of Neverbends
Jane Cutler
      Deans Tiny
   Amber Socks
      Barnsley Bess

PEDIGREE OF CH. BLAIRSVILLE ROYAL SEAL

      Dusty Jimmy of Aspenden
   Ravelin Little Jimmy
      Chingford Sweet Sue
Ch. Whisperdales Temujin
      Ch. Ravelin Gaiety Boy
   Ch. Whisperdales Phirno Carmen
      Blue Biddy
Ch. Blairsville Most Royale
      Leodian Smart Boy
   Ch. Blairsville Boy Wonder
      Blairsville Lady
Ch. Blairsville Shirene
      Ch. Burghwallis Vikki   **Ch. Burghwallis Little Nip**
   Blairsville Belinda   Prism of Johnstounburn
      Leodian Kandy Katy

Ch. Blairsville Royal Seal, Yorkshire Terrier, bred and owned by Brian and Rita Lister, was hailed in England as one of the greatest show dogs of all time. He was #1 Dog and "Dog of the Year," in 1976 and 1977; Reserve Best Toy at Crufts, 1978. He was also BIS at 12 all-breed championship shows, 16 times a runner up, and had a total of 33 groups and 50 CCs, all under different judges, by the time he was just past four years of age. *Diane Pearce*

A casual, free-standing photo of Ch. Mayfair Barban Verikoko, at 16 months of age. He is a seventh generation homebred owned by the author and her partner, Barbara Wolferman.

Falling mid-way between Royal Seal and Higgens in type, the author feels he is the best Yorkie they have bred to date and very close to her ideal of the breed. He may never attain his full potential in the show ring, because he is only six months younger than his half-brother, Ch. Mayfair Barban Quinnat, that at only 2½ years of age is one of the top Toys in the East at this writing.

The common denominator among all three Yorkies is the dark blue, silky coat.

Kennel Manager, Peter d'Auria, holds a carefully linebred litter of champions three, at three months of age, grandsons of 12 times BIS Ch. Mayfair Barban Loup-de-Mer. From left to right they are: Ch. Mayfair Barban Yummy, Ch. Mayfair Barban Yo-Hoo, and Ch. Mayfair Barban Yogurt. Yo-Hoo is the sire of both Verikoko and Quinnat.

Ch. Mayfair Barban Quinnat, half-brother to Verikoko, shown winning one of his many Bests in Show. This one under E. Irving Eldredge. Wendell Sammet is the beaming handler. *Ashbey*

Ch. Mayfair Barban Verikoko

If you compare the pedigrees of Higgens and Verikoko it can be seen that the same kind of linebreeding produced them both.

Higgens resulted from the mating of Ch. Clarkwyn's Saucy Sue's grandson to her daughter and both sire and dam were closely linebred to Ch. Toy Clown of Rusklyn.

Verikoko is the result of mating Ch. Mayfair Barban Loup de Mer's grandson to his daughter, and both sire and dam were closely linebred to Ch. Gaytonglen's Teddy of Mayfair. "Teddy" had four Bests in Show to his credit, while "Loupy" had an even dozen. An extended pedigree would show 13 crosses to International Ch. Mr. Pim of Johnstounburn and "Koko" bears a striking resemblance to this outstanding ancestor.

The number of ancestors in both Higgens' and Koko's five-generation pedigrees have been reduced from 60 to 34.

```
                                    Ch. Devanvale Jack-in-the-Box            Ch. Devanvale Sonny Jack
                        Ch. Mayfair Barban Loup-de-Mer                       Ch. Yorkfold Little Pixie of Theale
                                    Ch. Mayfair Barban Ladyfinger            Ch. Gaytonglen's Teddy of Mayfair
            Ch. Danby Belziehill Oscar                                       Mayfair's Poor Pitiful Pearl
                                    Ch. Mayfair Barban Mocha Mousse          Ch. Gaytonglen's Teddy of Mayfair
                        Ch. Danby Belziehill Matilda                         Ch. Mayfair's Upsa Daisy
                                    Danby's Belziehill Abigail               Kelpie's Belziehill Dondi
Ch. Mayfair Barban Yohoo                                                     Daisy of Libertyhill
                                    Ch. Progress of Progreso                 Ch. Don Carlos Of Progreso
                        Ch. Gaytonglen's Teddy of Mayfair                    Ch. Coulgorm Chloe
                                    Gaytonglen's Golden Tammie               Tenbliss Coat of Arms
            Mayfair Barban Ximinie                                           Tenbliss Craig's Golden Glow
                                    Ch. Mayfair Barban Mocha Mousse          Ch. Gaytonglen's Teddy of Mayfair
                        Ch. Danby Belziehill Raindrop                        Ch. Mayfair's Upsa Daisy
                                    Danby's Belziehill Abigail               Kelpie's Belziehill Dondi
PEDIGREE OF CH. MAYFAIR BARBAN VERIKOKO                                      Daisy of Libertyhill
                                    Ch. Devanvale Sonny Jack                 Ch. Devanvale Jack's Son
                        Ch. Devanvale Jack-in-the-Box                        Devanvale Marvel Queen
                                    Ch. Yorkfold Little Pixie of Theale      Yorkfold Grand Pim
            Ch. Mayfair Barban Loup-de-Mer                                   Burghwallis Buttons
                                    Ch. Gaytonglen's Teddy of Mayfair        Ch. Progress of Progreso
                        Ch. Mayfair Barban Ladyfinger                        Gaytonglen's Golden Tammie
                                    Mayfair's Poor Pitiful Pearl             Ch. Danby Diamond of Mayfair
Mayfair Barban X-Presso                                                      Ch. Devanvale Jenifer
                                    Ch. Progress of Progreso                 Ch. Don Carlos of Progreso
                        Ch. Gaytonglen's Teddy of Mayfair                    Ch. Coulgorm Chloe
                                    Gaytonglen's Golden Tammie               Tenbliss Coat of Arms
            Ch. Mayfair Barban Chili Petine                                  Tenbliss Craig's Golden Glow
                                    Ch. Devanvale Sonny Jack                 Ch. Devanvale Jack's Son
                        Ch. Mayfair's Upsa Daisy                             Devanvale Marvel Queen
                                    Danby's Belziehill Anya                  Ch. Yorkfold Jackanapes
                                                                             Danby's Belziehill Tanque
```

Both sire and dam were closely linebred to Ch. Gaytonglen's Teddy of Mayfair, but it should be kept in mind that Teddy was likely carrying three-quarters of the same genes as Ch. Progress of Progreso, his BIS sire and grandsire. In addition to three BIS winning dogs among the 34 champions in this pedigree, Mocha Mousse and Upsa Daisy were multiple Group winners.

Redway Silky Terriers

Another example of excellent line breeding to an outstanding ancestor is illustrated by the following pedigree of Ch. Redway Danny Boy O' Wexford, a Silky Terrier, bred and owned by Mrs. Merle E. Smith, in California.

An extended pedigree shows 32 crosses to Ch. Wexford Pogo, an Australian-born Silky imported by Mrs. Smith. Pogo completed his American championship in 1960 at seven and one-half years of age, after the breed was recognized by AKC. Prior to this he was undefeated in the Miscellaneous class for five years. He is the sire of 15 champions and grandsire of 81 champions with seven top-producing get.

Pogo was bred to his daughter to produce Ch. Redway Buster, one of the top-producing progeny. Buster inherited an accumulation of Pogo's genes, resulting in a prepotency which he, in turn, was able to pass on to future generations. Buster is Danny's great-grandsire, great-great-grandsire and great-great-great-grandsire. Pogo is also the grandsire of Danny's dam, Ch. Redway Wexford Peter's Poppy. As a result of all these lines going back to Pogo, Danny should carry in his genotype about 42% of the same genes as those of his illustrious ancestor.

Danny's full brother was bred to Danny's litter sister, Ch. Redway Silky Acres Samantha that Mrs. Smith co-owns with Patricia Walton. Both owners were pleased with the results.

Readers should keep in mind that Mrs. Smith linebred very cautiously for five generations, before she felt she had her genetic deck so well stacked with Aces and Kings that she dared the closest inbreeding possible.

Ch. Redway Danny Boy O' Wexford, bred and owned by Merle E. Smith, has demonstrated his value to the Silky Terrier breed in the show ring, and as a prepotent force at stud.   *Callea*

Ch. Wexford Pogo was over fourteen years old when this unusually large litter of Silkies, which he sired, was born. It was his last contribution to the breed. The six-week old puppies show more uniform type than is usually seen in a litter of Silkies. On the far right is Ch. Redway Black Eyed Susan, grandam of Ch. Redway Danny Boy O' Wexford.

Phillip J. Planert

Ch. Wexford Pogo was a remarkable dog that exerted a profound influence on the Silky Terrier. Whelped June 14, 1952 and died June 9, 1967, he finished his championship at seven and a half years, after the breed was officially recognized. He sired fifteen champions and his 81st grandget to finish did so in March 1980, almost 13 years after Pogo's death.

Ch. Wexford Pogo
Ch. Redway Buster
Redway Smith's Gamble
Ch. Rebel Dandy Andy
Aldoon Skipper
Rebel April Angel
Millburn Tiger
Ch. Silky Acres Dandy Dude
Ch. Nukara Dandy Dan Son of Pogo
Ch. Redway Tomales Ton
Redway Blue Chip
Silky Acres Sassy Susie
Ch. Redway Buster
Ch. Silky Acres Tiny Toby
Little Snooki
PEDIGREE OF CH. REDWAY DANNY BOY O'WEXFORD
Hayes' Junior de la Ek
Ch. Gem-G's Kool Hand Luke
Hayes' Lady Tina de la Kreaux
Ch. Redway For Pete's Sake
Ch. Midland's Fancy Frankie
Ch. Soblu My Fancy
Ch. Just a Smiden of Dixie
Ch. Redway Wexford Peter's Poppy
Baulkham Royal John
Ch. Wexford Pogo
Elouera Joy
Ch. Redway Black-Eyes Susan, C.D.
Ch. Smithfield Lover Boy
Canberra Cupie
Frosty Miss

Baulkham Royal John
Elouera Joy
Ch. Wexford Pogo
Brenhill Splinters
Aus. Ch. Aldoon Sivam
Aldoon Lassie
Ch. Redway Lord Michael
Millburn May Lady
Ch. Wexford Pogo
Artarmon's Nukara Tirrita
Prairie Roger
Ch. Redway Splinters
Ch. Wexford Pogo
Redway Smith's Gamble
Frisky
Koonoona Tiny
Hayes' Eaulde Kreaux
Hayes' Michelle de la Kreaux
Ch. Hayes' Gem Kreaux
Crusher
Aus/Am. Ch. Koonoona Bo Bo
Ch. Lylac Jan
Ch. Redway Buster
Ch. Aldoon Bonnie Lass
Aus. Ch. Ellwyn Gold Prince
Lady Patsy
Niobe Tim
Tecoona Tessie
Aus. Ch. Miami Gold Flash
Prairie Vicky
Ch. D'Imber Lilibet O'Teatime
Waratah Trade Winds

Alekai Standard Poodles

Mrs. Henry J. Kaiser is one of the few breeders I have talked to who does not believe in linebreeding. Like to like is the only way, she told me at a luncheon about a year ago.

Mrs. Kaiser fortunately had and still has a fantastic eye for a dog. When she bought her foundation stock she purchased the best bloodlines and individuals that money could buy. They all had similar characteristics and traits that Mrs. Kaiser admired in a Poodle but, as it turned out, some of the same ancestors produced these traits. Her like to like breeding theory turned out to be excellent linebreeding.

From Puttencove Kennels she bought Ch. Puttencove Kaui, by Ch. Puttencove Promise out of Ch. Puttencove Moonglow. From Ivardon Kennels she acquired Ch. Ivardon Winter, granddaughter of Ch. Blakeen Bali Ha'i, and Ch. Ivardon Kenilworth of Ensarr, a grandson of Ch. Puttencove Promise. Promise was also a grandson of

Ch. Alekai Pokoi, top-winning white Standard Poodle, bred by Mrs. Henry J. Kaiser and owned by the author and her partner, Barbara Wolferman. *Ben Burwell*

PEDIGREE OF CH. ALEKAI POKOI

Ch. Alekai Nohea

- Ch. Puttencove Promise
  - Ch. Loabelo Jonny
    - **Ch. Blakeen Bali Ha'i**
    - Ch. Vulcan Champagne Carmen of Blakeen
  - Astron Lily of Puttencove
    - **Ch. Pillicoc Barrister**
    - Ch. Astron Silver Star
- Ch. Davdon Suma Cum Laude
  - Ch. Valeway Temptation of Davdon
    - Ch. Hillandale C'Est Vrais
    - Ch. Betsal Lane Poupee Blanc
  - Pantaloon Altair of Cartlane
    - Ch. Cartlane Cockade
    - Cartlane Constellation

Ch. Ivardon Winter

- Ch. Puttencove Banner
  - **Ch. Blakeen Bali Ha'i**
    - **Ch. Pillicoc Barrister**
    - Blakeen Morning Star
  - Puttencove Snow Bunting
    - Ch. Vulcan Champagne Carmen of Blakeen
    - Blakeen Morning Star
- Ch. Cartlane Michele
  - Ch. Loabelo Coup of Cartlane
    - Cartlane Collinet
    - Ch. Vulcan Champagne Carmen of Blakeen
  - Cartlane Collectrice
    - Cartlane Alcindor
    - Donna Maria of Brush Hollow

Ch. Blakeen Bali Ha'i. From the de la Fontaine Kennels in Canada came Ch. Tambarine de la Fontaine whose sire was Ch. Puttencove Promise.

From Davdon Kennels she also bought the inbred Ch. Davdon Captivation, sired by Ch. Hillandale C'Est Vrai out of a C'Est Vrai daughter, and Ch. Davdon Summa Cum Laude, a C'Est Vrais granddaughter.

With such fabulous quality and prepotent genes, Mrs. Kaiser bred an impressive list of top winning and top producing white Standards.

Promise, himself, was bred to Ch. Davdon Summa Cum Laude and produced a litter of five champions, two of which were Best in Show winners, and a third was Best of Winners at the Poodle Club of America Specialty. Ch. Davdon Captivation was bred to Ch. Alekai Kila to produce the gorgeous Ch. Alekai Marlaine.

Ch. Alekai Pokoi was bred by Mrs. Henry Kaiser and owned by the author and her partner Barbara Wolferman. She was the top-winning Standard Poodle of all time until Frank Sabella came along with Lollipop and broke her record of 16 Bests in Show. Bred to Ch. Alekai Ahi, Pokoi was the dam of Ch. Alekai Luau of Mayfair and Ch. Alekai Bali of Mayfair, who won the Non-Sporting brace at Westminster in 1968. That just happened to be the year of Westminster's last show at the old Garden, and two noted figures in the dog fancy, Anne Rogers Clark and Percy Roberts were being honored. The "boys" remained subdued "in the wings" during the long speeches. By the time they entered the ring to compete for Best Brace in Show, they decided they had HAD it. They played and horsed around while Wendell Sammet tried unsuccessfully to control them. Needless to say, they did not win. I felt badly for Mrs. Kaiser with whom we were sitting and said, "Oh, I'm so sorry!" Mrs. Kaiser's reply endeared her to us forever. "Don't be silly," she said, "I'd much rather have them act like Poodles than win!"

Pokoi was born in June 16, 1961 and died at Mayfair on March 15, 1976.

Ch. Salilyn's Aristocrat, made all-breed history by winning Best in Show 45 times in one year (1967). He was owned and bred by Mrs. F.H. Gasow.

Williams

Salilyn English Springer Spaniels

Mrs. Julia Gasow, Troy, Michigan, is the breeder of an almost continuous succession of top-winning English Springer Spaniels. She is a strong supporter of judicious linebreeding from superior breeding stock. When her Ch. Salilyn's Citation II, a grandson of Ch. King Peter of Salilyn, was bred to a daughter of King Peter, it resulted in Ch. Inchidony Prince Charming. When Prince Charming was bred to a half granddaughter of Citation II, the great Ch. Salilyn's Aristocrat was born.

```
                        Ch. Salilyn's Sensation, C.D.      Ch. Frejax Royal Request
              Ch. Salilyn's Citation, II                   Queen Victoria of Salilyn
                        Salilyn's Princess Meg              Ch. King Peter of Salilyn
     Ch. Inchidony Prince Charming                          Ch. Salilyn's Animation, II
                        Ch. King Peter of Salilyn           Firebrand of Sandblown Acre, C.D.X
              Ch. Salilyn's Cinderalla, II                  Salutation of Salilyn
                        Ch. Walpride Gay Beauty             Ch. Chaltha's The Gainer
                                                            Walpride Sensation
PEDIGREE OF CH. SALILYN'S ARISTOCRAT
                        Ch. Salilyn's Citation, II          Ch. Salilyn's Sensation, C.D
              Salilyn's Royal Consort                       Salilyn's Princess Meg
                        Ch. Ascot's Estralita               Ch. Ascot's Ajax
     Ch. Salilyn's Lilly of the Valley                      Ascot's Diamond Lil
                        Ch. King William of Salilyn         Firebrand of Sandblown Acre, C.D.X
              Salilyn's Glenda                              Salutation of Salilyn
                        Ch. Salilyn's Good Omen             Ch. Cartref Bob Bobbin
                                                            Salilyn's Surprise
```

Ch. King Peter of Salilyn was an important aspect in the background of the legendary Ch. Salilyn's Aristocrat.

Tauskey

Potala Lhasa Apsos

Keke Blumberg, breeder of Group and BIS winning Lhasas, uses both careful inbreeding and strong linebreeding to a prepotent Best in Show winning sire, Ch. Tibet of Cornwallis. The mating of grandsire to granddaughter is illustrated in the pedigree of Ch. Potala Keke's Candy Bar. In this instance the sire of the dam was the grandsire of the sire on the sire's side.

```
                                    Ch. Karma Frosty Knight O' Everglo   Ch. Karma Kushog
                    Ch. Everglo Zijuh Tomba                              Ch. Hamilton Sha-Tru
                    Kambu of Everglo                                     Cubbi-Kyeri of Everglo
            Ch. Potala Keke's Tomba Tu                                   Ch. Kyima of Everglo
                    Ch. Zijuh Seng-Tru                                   Hamilton Toradga
            Ch. Potala Keke's Yum Yum                                    Ch. Hamilton Shim-Tru
                    Ch. Keke's Bamboo                                    Ch. Tibet of Cornwallis
    Potala Keke's Starsky                                               Ch. Keke's T'chin Ting T'chin
                    Hamilton Toradga                                     Ch. Hamilton Kalon
            Ch. Zijuh Seng-Tru                                           Ch. Hamilton Shim Tru
                    Ch. Hamilton Shim-Tru                                Ch. Hamilton Sandupa
            Ch. Potala Keke's Zin Zin                                    Hamilton Saung
                    Ch. Tibet of Cornwallis                              Karma Tharpa
            Ch. Keke's Bamboo                                            Ch. Licos Cheti-La
                    Ch. Keke's T'chin Ting T'chin                        Ch. Kham of Norbulinka
PEDIGREE OF CH. POTALA KEKE'S CANDY BAR                                  Ch. Keke's T'chin T'chin
                    Ch. Kham Te-Ran Rinpoche C.D.                        Ch. Shangrila Sho-George
            Merna's Rusti George                                         Ron-Si Rinpoche
                    Kinderland's Kimmi                                   Ch. Kham of Norbulingka
            Ch. Tabu's Pacesetter                                        Kinderland's Buddha
                    Ch. Tibet of Cornwallis                              Karma Tharpa
            Ch. Tabu's Golden Galaxy                                     Ch. Licos Cheti-La
                    Ch. Tabu's Kiss Me Kate                              Ch. Zijuh Seng-Tru
    Frakari's Vagrant                                                   Ch. Kinderland's Tonka
                    Cox's Royal Bow Bow of Yoshi                         Ch. Stoneyacres Bebe of Sikiang
            Ch. Pirk's Scaramouche                                       Tsing Tal of Yoshi
                    Helene's Fuji Yama                                   Ch. Stoneyacres Bebe of Sikiang
            Frakari's Kansas City Bomber                                 Glen Pines Sera
                    Intl. Ch. Ku Won of Yoshi                            Ch. Miradel's Won Boi
            Yoshi P-Nut Chu                                              Helene's Fuji Yama
                    Si-Kaing's Aj-Se                                     Ch. Stoneyacres Bebe of Sikiang
                                                                         Glen Pine's Sera
```

Hetherbull Bulldogs

Bob and Jean Hetherington are well known for their Hetherbull Bulldogs. The pedigree of Hetherbull Arrogant Harriet is an interesting one. The bottom line illustrates how the Hetheringtons went out and came back into their line every other generation. Ch. Hetherbull's Arrogance was also the sire of Ch. Hetherbull Westfield Imp in the fifth generation.

96

Ch. Potala Keke's Candy Bar was bred and is owned by Keke Blumberg. *Gilbert*

Jean said they always went out to a dog they admired which was bred by a breeder whose dogs they regard highly. Jean also said they attempted two inbreedings, both of which were complete disasters. More than half the pups had cleft palates and the survivors were much too small, almost dwarfs. By using the in-and-out system of breeding they have been able to avoid these deformities.

Harriet has been bred to the dam of Roberta's brother Ch. Hetherbull Arrogant Lazarus, UD.

PEDIGREE OF HETHERBULL ARROGANT HARRIET

Ch. Bayside Red Oak
Ch. Golden Carmel Coach*
Rosebud Brandy
Ch. Marinebull's All The Way*
Ch. Cherokee Morgan*
Ch. Marinebull's Here She Comes*
Ch. Tha-Mac's Windy Gal*
Ch. Dingman's Hunk of Hetherbull
Ch. Bayside Red Oak
Ch. Golden Carmel Coach*
Rosebud Brandy
Ch. Marinebull's Kaydee Too, C.D.*
Ch. Damar's El Domino
Ch. Tha-Mac's Windy Gal*
Ch. Logan's Frosty Snowflake

Ch. Hetherbull Arrogant Heir
Ch Hetherbull Arrogant Impulse
Brookhollow Dani Defiant*
Ch. Hetherbull Arrogant Robert
Ch. Bayside Mephisto
Ch. Rawburn Hetherbull Melissa
Naughty Rose Maburd of Muse
Hetherbull Arrogant Roberta
Ch. Taurus Tugboat
Ch. Taurustrail Houseboat
Wintersmoon Sissy Baby
Ch. Hetherbull Arrogant Dynamo*
Ch. Hetherbull Arrogance*
Ch. Hetherbull Arrogant Zsa Zsa
Ch. Hetherbull Arrogant Parlay

Cilgwyn Golden Prince
Ch. Bayside Ruby
Eng. & Am. Ch. Jackath Silver Rock
Pandora's Cotton Taffy
Ch. Snowman's Kenilworth Samson
Sandow's Seguel
Ch. Damar's El Domino
Ch. Logan's Frosty Snowflake
Cilgwyn Golden Prince
Ch. Bayside Ruby
Eng. & Am. Ch. Jackath Silver Rock
Pandora's Cotton Taffy
Ch. Marmac's Bold Charmer
Damar's Debbie's Sophia
Ch. Er-Leigh George
Mickey's Sweet Annie Logan
Ch. Hetherbull Arrogance*
Edelrich's Adorabull
Ch. Allin's High Hopes
Sherbord Princess Joangelyn
Ch. Bonnie Boy of Fearnought
Bayside Bikini
Rich Double Heritage
Naughty Susie of Jordon
Ch. Steamboat of Killarney
Aries Annie Oakley
Virgo Vixen
Wintersmoon Lisa
Ch. Plezol's Royal
Raefair's Pixie of Hetherbull
Ch. Bayside Doubloon
Ch. Hetherbull Westfield Imp.

*Bulldog Club of America
Top Producer's Hall of Fame   (Dogs: 10 champions
                             Bitches: 5 champions)

98

Hetherbull Arrogant Harriet at 15 months, being shown by Bob Hetherington.
Gilbert

"Harriet's sire, Ch. Dingman's Hunk of Hetherbull with Jean Hetherington handling.
Gilbert

99

St. Aubrey-Elsdon Pekingese

R. William Taylor, co-owner-breeder with Nigel Aubrey-Jones of St. Aubrey-Elsdon Pekingese, sent me the pedigrees of two outstanding specimens of his breed and several pages of his personal recollections on breeding as well. He illustrates how strains can be developed by using one dog as the basis.

Obviously when doing so, the ideal is to use the best dog or dogs available, one that has virtues in abundance and is free from any major defect or serious faults that are known to be hereditary. The dog need not be linebred himself, but that does not necessarily mean that his breeding should be haphazard. He should come from good, sound, healthy stock. Once achieved, the ideal dog can be introduced into a strain many times and its influence can be paramount.

Mr. Taylor began his recollections by stating that it is generally agreed there are two methods of breeding animals: line and inbreeding to develop type, and breeding individual to individual; animals that are complementary in characteristics, regardless of pedigree.

Line and to a great extent inbreeding will be the quickest way to establish a strain within a kennel and to develop certain characteristics of the breed. Its danger lies in accentuating the best point but at the same time accentuating faults, from which no animal is entirely free. The end results can be a family of many virtues, yet possessing certain faults to a marked degree.

It appears that constant use of one strain alone without addition of other blood from time to time will quickly lead to the best points becoming less obvious, while the serious faults become more dominant.

Line or inbreeding can be done to an already existing strain or it can be developed from an individual dog that need not be linebred itself. When contemplating line or inbreeding to a particular dog, the dog selected should be of very high merit and preferably lacking any major faults. To linebreed to anything less than outstanding is a waste of time.

One can also linebreed to an existing strain, a family already known for its consistency. Its introduction into a breeding program does not necessarily guarantee that the best points only will be introduced but there is less chance of disappointment if the individuals concerned are also complementary to one another. The presumption that breeding can be done by pedigree alone, without thought to the individual animals, can only lead to disaster.

Mr. Taylor continues with specific examples of Pekingese breedings and should be read with frequent references to the pedigrees of Am., Can. Ch. St. Aubrey Mario of Elson, and the lovely Am., Can. Ch. St. Aubrey Tinkabelle of Elsdon.

During the latter part of World War II, a dog by the name of Yusen Yu Chuo was bred in the Birmingham area of England. He was an absolute outcross with only one dog and one bitch appearing twice in the fifth generation. His sire, Yu Tuo of Pedmore, was a well-known wartime winner in the midlands and while he was full of various Alderbourne strains (this kennel usually carried on two or even three distinct lines), he was a product of an outcross mating. Yu Chuo's dam was one of the many beautiful matronly bitches for which the Yusen Kennel was noted. Yu Chuo died when quite young, but not before he sired the breed's first postwar champion, the nearly unbeatable Ch. Yusen Yu Toi, which was to die enroute to his American owner, Mrs. Quigley. Yu Toi's influence as a stud was cut short by his untimely death, yet he was to sire a famous bitch of the large matronly type in Ch. Mignonette of Rosterloy, and the well-known Eng. Ch. Bonraye Fo Yu, which followed his sire across the Atlantic and became one of Mrs. Quigley's noted winners.

Yusen Yu Chuo also sired another dog which was, perhaps, to become even more famous than his half brother, the outstanding stud dog Puff Ball of Chungking. Puff Ball's greatest achievement was to sire Ch. Ku Chi of Caversham, the celebrated winner and scion of the postwar Caversham kennel.

Puff Ball's pedigree is of great interest: although sired by an outcross, Yusen Yu Chuo, he was out of a bitch by Yu Tuo of Pedmore and consequently the result of a half-brother-sister mating. The double infusion of the best of the Alderbourne blood on the male line was obviously the reason for Puff Ball's great success at stud. It is a fine example of how a dog of individual merit, not line or inbred itself, when bred correctly produced an individual which became a celebrated sire. When Puff Ball was used as a basis in future breedings, the results were often outstanding.

In America, one of the best examples of half brother to sister breeding is Am., Can. Ch. St. Aubrey Laparata Dragon. In Dragon's case the doubling was on the maternal side. Laparata Miranda, Dragon's double granddam was a granddaughter of the famous Ch. Cherangani Chips, a linebred dog with three distinct crosses to that most famous of all Pekingese, Ch. Caversham Ku Ku of Yam. When bred to a great granddaughter of Ch. Chips, Dragon sired the litter brother and sister Chs. Dragonfly and Dragonora, and it is remarkable how the influence of their famous ancestor, Ch. Chips, shows in their wide, shallow headpieces with great detail in face and expressive eyes.

Am. and Can. Ch. St. Aubrey Mario of Elsdon, bred and owned by Nigel Aubrey-Jones and R. William Taylor.

Shafer

Ch. Caversham Ku Ku of Yam
Ch. Ku Jin of Caversham
Caversham Jin Jin
Am. & Can. Ch. Calartha Mandarin of Jehol
Tomi of Jehol
Anne of Jehol
Talgarth Vanessa of Jehol
Am. & Can. Ch. Rikki of Calartha
Ch. Caversham Ku Ku of Yam
Ch. Goofus Le Grisbie
Goofus Painted Lady
Adston Grizelda of Calartha
Rochard Wen Chu
Goofus Rochard Snowdrop
Rochard Wanda

Ch. Ku Chi of Caversham
Regina of Yam
Ku's Kin of Wethersfield
D'Juli of Wethersfield
Anton of Jehol
Miranda of Ambervale
Yusen Yu Fuh
Blondie of Chungking
Ch. Ku Chi of Caversham
Regina of Yam
Alderbourne Su Tuo of Elfann
Goofus Butterfly of Calartha
Rochard Young Foo of Lyall
Rochard Wanda
Wing's Owl of Alderbourne
Rochard Zinnia

PEDIGREE OF AM. & CAN. CH. ST. AUBREY MARIO OF ELSDON

Ch. Ku Chi of Caversham
Ch. Caversham Ku Ku of Yam
Regina of Yam
Am. Ch. St. Aubrey Ku Kuan of Jehol
Tomi of Jehol
Anne of Jehol
Talgarth Vanessa of Jehol
Can Ch. St. Aubrey Kumarie of Elsdon
Ku Chik of Caversham
Am. & Can. Ch. Chik T'sun of Caversham
Naxos Ku Chi Fille of Caversham
Chiquitta of Elsdon
Pagoda Prince Rupert of Tzumiao
Can. Ch. St. Aubrey Gay Whiki of Tzumiao
Wanga of Tzumiao

Puff Ball of Chungking
Marigold of Elfann
Ch. Tong Tuo of Alderbourne
Yu-Tu of Yam
Anton of Jehol
Miranda of Ambervale
Yusen Yu Fuh
Blondie of Chungking
Ch. Caversham KuKu of Yam
Ko Lee of Caversham
Ch. Ku Chi of Caversham
Caversham Psyche of Naxo's
Alderbourne Su Tuo of Elfann
Pagoda Piquette
The Giles of Tzumiao
Bryad Candid of Tzumiao

All champions in pedigree are English unless otherwise noted.

The most famous example in America of a complete outcross breeding that resulted in a prolific stud dog was Am., Can. Ch. Calartha Mandarin of Jehol. Mandarin became not only a top winner in his breed, but a truly exceptional sire. He produced not only champions, but great champions that are behind many of the American-bred Best in Show winners.

Mandarin was sired by Eng. Ch. Ku Jin of Caversham, and a good example of developing a strain using an outcross dog was when Mandarin was bred to a daughter of Ch. Goofus Le Grisbie and produced Am., Can. Ch. Rikki of Calartha. Both Ku Jin and Le Grisbie were sired by the famous Ch. Caversham Ku Ku of Yam, still the greatest Pekingese ever produced, in the minds of many.

Probably Rikki's best known offspring resulted from breeding him to a granddaughter of Ch. Caversham Ku Ku of Yam, producing the celebrated Canadian-bred stud dog, Am., Can. Ch. St. Aubrey Mario of Elsdon, who had still a fourth line to Ch. Ku Ku through Am., Can. Ch. Chik T'Sun of Caversham. Mario's four lines back to Ku Ku were through different dogs: Ku Jin, Le Grisbie, Ch. Ku Kuan and Chik T'Sun. Consequently Ku Ku was the great dominating factor in Mario's pedigree. He produced some twenty odd American champions despite the fact that he had the opportunity of breeding only within his home kennel and spent 18 non-productive months in California during what should have been the zenith of his stud career.

Ku Ku's most influential son was Ch. Ku Jin of Caversham. Although hardly the dog sire or grandsire Ku Chi was, he had a long and successful life as a stud and his influence was enormous. When used in a line where his sire was doubled, such as those of Rikki and Mario, the most typical results were attained. However, when breeders began to double on Ku Jin himself, thereby reducing the influence of his sire Ku Ku, there was a departure from the ideal Caversham type as exemplified by Ku Chi, Ku Ku, Ku Chik and Chik T'Sun. Faces became less broad and bodies, although short, were less slung between their legs.

It is evident how different strains can be altered and changed through the influence of an individual dog. I doubt if many kennels of any breed can keep a line going unchanged indefinitely.

In England today, the two most distinctive strains are the Jamestowns and the Changtes. The Jamestowns have been influenced to a great extent by Ch. Ku Jin of Caversham and are, in reality, an offshoot of the Caversham kennel. The Changtes are a highly individual strain. By breeding two descendants of Ch. Ku Chi, this kennel produced its first champion dog in Ch. Crown Prince of Changte. This dog has been the focal point on which the Changtes built a highly successful strain. Their famous Ch. Chuffy's Charm of Changte has at least five crosses to Crown Prince within the first four generations. A fascinating example of how one dog was able to shape an entire breeding program.

Am. and Can. Ch. St. Aubrey Tinkabelle of Elsdon, bred and owned by Nigel Aubrey-Jones and R. William Taylor.

Shafer

Ch. Ku Chi of Caversham
Ch. Caversham Ku Ku of Yam
Regina of Yam
Ch. Ku Jin of Caversham
Ku's Kin of Wethersfield
Caversham Jin Jin of Wethersfield
D'Juli of Wethersfield
Am. & Can. Ch. Calartha Mandarin of Jehol
Anton of Jehol
Tomi of Jehol
Miranda of Ambervale
Anne of Jehol
Yusen Yu Fuh
Talgarth Vanessa of Jehol
Blondie of Chungking

Puff Ball of Chungking
Marigold of Elfann
Ch. Tong Tuo of Alderbourne
Yu-Tu of Yam
Wei-Ku of Caversham
Tan Toi of Wethersfield
Ch. Don Juan of the Dell
Toy Me of Hinckford
Ch. Yu Tong of Alderbourne
Joanna of Jehol
Piers of Perryacre
Peat of Perryacre
Yu Tuo of Pedmore
Lady Jane of Pai-Choo
Puff Ball of Chungking
Chanti Angier of Malaya

PEDIGREE OF AM. & CAN. CH. ST. AUBREY TINKABELLE OF ELSDON

Ch. Caversham KuKu of Yam
Ku Chik of Caversham
Ko Lee of Caversham
Am. & Can. Ch. Chik T'Sun of Caversham
Ch. Ku Chi of Caversham
Naxos Ku Chi Fille of Caversham
Caversham Psyche of Naxos
Can. Ch. St. Aubrey Ku Tinka of Elsdon
Mingshang Ku Sun of Shynang
Sun Glow of Shynang
Tawney of Shynang
St. Aubrey Salome of Calartha
Alderbourne Sum Boi of Loofoo
Pamela of Calartha
Pandora of Kilbirnie

Ch. Ku Chi of Caversham
Regina of Yam
Ch. Caversham Ko Ko of Shanruss
Mo-Lee of Caversham
Puff Ball of Chungking
Marigold of Elfann
Wingco of Sherringham
Rena of Ifield
Ch. Ku Chi of Caversham
Sunshine of Caversham
Ki Chu of Caversham
Bessa of Caversham
Alderbourne Su Tuo of Elfann
Mignonette of Loofoo
Dragonfly of Calartha
Lady Amber of Kilbirnie

All champions in pedigree are English unless otherwise noted.

104

Vin-Melca Norwegian Elkhounds

There are no more important pedigrees for the novice to study than the two which follow. These are typical Vin-Melca pedigrees of young dogs, not shown much, but they illustrate the almost fautless linebreeding system used by Pat Craige in her Norwegian Elkhounds. A real craftsman in the art of breeding, Mrs. Craige is also well versed in the background of her breed.

In the fifth generation of Mrs. Craige's breeding stock is Norwegian Ch. Moa, one of the most influential bitches of all time in Elkhounds. Moa was not only an outstanding show bitch, but the pride of all Norway for her exceptional hunting abilities. Moa was bred several times to Norwegian Ch. Bamse, and once to his full brother Buster. The results of the Bamse-Moa breeding were nothing short of sensational, producing dogs that influenced the breed in Norway, England and the United States.

The greatest dog of this mating was Ch. Tortasen's Bjonn II, imported to this country in the 1950s by Catherine and Wells Peck. Bjonn was a multiple all-breed Best in Show winner both in Norway and in this country. He was the first Norwegian Elkhound to win the Group at Westminster. The five subsequent Group wins at Westminster by three different Vin-Melca Elkhounds all went to Bjonn descendants.

Ch. Vin-Melca's Rebel Rouser had one litter by Bjonn II which produced a trio of sisters that had tremendous influence on the breed. Since the late 1950s, the Vin-Melca breeding program has skillfully preserved and concentrated the genes of Bjonn II through the bitches, Rabble Rouser, Astridina, and Vikina, the dam of both Howdy Rowdy and Vagabond. Mrs. Craige also brought in outcrosses when they were needed.

Two very important dogs in the Vin-Melca breeding plan were the brothers Ch. Windy Cove's Silver Son and Ch. Windy Cove's Rowdy Ringo, grandsons of Bjonn II. They introduced strong heads and bone and each played a part in producing a Best in Show winner—Ch. Vin-Melca's Vickssen and Ch. Vin-Melca's Howdy Rowdy.

Mrs. Craige's breeding program now entered a new phase with home based studs whose progeny could be bred to each other in much the same way as one cross-ruffs at bridge. Vickssen, a grandson of Silver Son, was the produce of Rebel Rouser bred to her own grandson. Howdy Rowdy was the result of an outcross breeding of Ch. Vin-Melca's Vikina bred to Rowdy Ringo. In effect, Mrs. Craige

Ch. Vin-Melca's Howdy Rowdy, top Norwegian Elkhound sire, *Kennel Review* Hall of Fame, top Western
hound, 1968, three time top sire all breeds, sire of 165
champions. Bred and owned by Pat Craige.

Langdon

Ch. Vin-Melca's Vagabond, top dog all breeds, 1970 and Quaker Oats winner, 1970. Vagabond
is an integral factor in Vin-Melca pedigrees through his daughters. This great winner and
producer was bred and is owned by Pat Craige.   *Smolley*

had two separate lines from which to work but, when put together, continued to increase the prepotency of Bjonn II.

Howdy Rowdy's contributions as a sire are well known. He was several times Top Sire, all-breeds, and was voted into the Kennel Review Hall of Fame. He is the sire of 165 champions including a score or more of Specialty winners, Group winners, and all-breed Best in Show winners. Most Norwegian Elkhounds of importance today have one or more crosses to Howdy Rowdy, and for several years his progeny dominated the "Top Ten" for the breed.

However, it is Vickssen who is the "unsung" hero, siring three Best in Show sons—Ch. Vin-Melca's Vagabond, Ch. Vin-Melca's Valley Forge and Ch. Vin-Melca's Viscount. Vickssen continued to express his qualities through his daughters, and Vagabond is known as a "brood bitch" sire. Both Ch. Vin-Melca's Nimbus and his sire Ch. Vin-Melca's Nordic Storm were out of Vagabond daughters.

PEDIGREE OF CH. VIN-MELCA'S HEIR APPARENT

```
                    Ch. Trond's Son of Greenwood          Ch. Trond
          Ch. Windy's Tusko of Greenwood                  Ch. Karen of Highwood Range
                    Ch. Lady Kazana of Greenwood          Napoleon of North Gate
    Ch. Windy Cove's Rowdy Ringo                          Lady Tina
          Ch. Tortasen's Bjonn II                         Ch. Bamse
    Ch. Baadkarl's Tona of Windy Cove*                    Ch. Moa
          Ch. Kirsten of Bofe                             Ch. Trond
Ch. Vin-Melca's Howdy Rowdy                               Ch. Karen of Highwood Range
          Dal Gaard Viking, CD                            Ch. Rodin of Holfred
    Ch. Trygvie Vikingsson                                Inga of Holfred
          Ch. Marta Haakonsdotter                         Ch. Tari's Haakon, CDX
    Ch. Vin-Melca's Vikina                                Karen of Narvikwood, CD
          Vin-Melca's Carro Again                         Ch. Carro of Ardmere
    Ch. Vin-Melca's Astridina                             Ch. Ulf's Madam Helga, CD
          Vin-Melca's Rebel Rouser                        Ch. Koltorpet's Paff
                                                          Loha
                    Ch. Windy Cove's Silver Son           Ch. Windy's Tusko of Greenwood
          Ch. Vin-Melca's Hi Ho Silver                   Ch. Baadkarl's Tona of Windy Cove*
                    Ch. Vin-Melca's Rabble Rouser         Ch. Tortasen's Bjonn II
    Ch. Vin-Melca's Vickssen                              Ch. Vin-Mecla's Rebel Rouser
          Ch. Koltorpet's Paff                            Loveland Odd
    Ch. Vin-Melca's Rebel Rouser                          Skall Mucki
          Loka                                            Ch. Carro of Ardmere
Ch. Vin-Melca's Victoria                                  Kirsten of Nordkyn
          Ch. Windy Cove's Rowdy Ringo                    Ch. Windy's Tusko of Greenwood
    Ch. Vin-Melca's Howdy Rowdy                           Ch. Baadkarl's Tona of Windy Cove*
          Ch. Vin-Melca's Vikina                          Ch. Trygvie Vikingsson
    Ch. Vin-Melca's Hedda Gabler                          Ch. Vin-Melca's Astridina
          Ch. Roy of Pitch Road                           Tortasen's Los
    Ch. Wandec's Sylva av Vin-Melca                       Tortasen's Remi
          Ch. Vin-Melca's Silver Tyga                     Ch. Windy Cove's Silver Son
                                                          Ch. Vin-Melca's Rabble Rouser
```

*Sired by Ch. Tortasen's Bjonn II

Ch. Windy Cove's Silver Son
Ch. Vin-Melca's Hi Ho Silver
Ch. Vin-Melca's Rabble Rouser
Ch. Vin-Melca's Vickssen
Ch. Koltorpet's Paff
Ch. Vin-Melca's Rebel Rouser
Loka
Ch. Vin-Melca's Vagabond
Dal Gaard Viking, CD
Ch. Trygvie Vikingsson
Ch. Marta Haakonsdotter
Ch. Vin-Melca's Vikina
Vin-Melca's Carro Again
Ch. Vin-Melca's Astridina
Ch. Vin-Melca's Rebel Rouser

PEDIGREE OF CH. VIN-MELCA'S MANDATE

Ch. Windy's Tusko of Greenwood
Ch. Windy Cove's Rowdy Ringo
Ch. Baadkarl's Tona of Windy Cove
Ch. Vin-Melca's Howdy Rowdy
Ch. Trygvie Vikingsson
Ch. Vin-Melca's Vikina
Ch. Vin-Melca's Astridina
Ch. Vin-Melca's Hedda Gabbler
Tortasen's Los
Ch. Roy of Pitch Road
Tortasen's Remi
Ch. Wandec's Sylva av Vin-Melca
Ch. Windy Cove's Silver Son
Ch. Vin-Melca's Silver Tyga
Ch. Vin-Melca's Rabble Rouser

Ch. Windy's Tusko of Greenwood
Ch. Baadkarl's Tona of Windy Cove*
Ch. Tortasen's Bjonn II
Ch. Vin-Melca's Rebel Rouser
Loveland Odd
Skall Mucki
Ch. Carro of Ardmere
Kirsten of Nordkyn
Ch. Rodin of Halfred
Inga of Halfred
Ch. Tari's Haakon, CDX
Karen of Narvikwood, CD
Ch. Carro of Ardmere
Ch. Ulf's Madam Helga, CD
Ch. Koltorpet's Paff
Loka
Ch. Trond's Son of Greenwood
Ch. Lady Kazana of Greenwood
Ch. Tortasen's Bjonn II
Ch. Kirsten of Bofe
Dal Gaard Viking, CD
Ch. Marta Haakonsdotter
Vin-Melca's Carro Again
Ch. Vin-Melca's Rebel Rouser
Buster
Ch. Moa
Ch. Bamse
Ch. Moa
Ch. Windy's Tusko of Greenwood
Ch. Baardkarl's Tona of Windy Cove*
Ch. Tortasen's Bjonn II
Ch. Vin-Melca's Rebel Rouser

*Sired by Ch. Tortasen's Bjonn II

Matings that worked best for Vin-Melca Norwegian Elkhounds are grandsire to granddaughter and granddam to grandson; half-brother to half-sister; uncle to niece and aunt to nephew. Mrs. Craige is well aware of the fact that extended linebreeding in truth is a form of inbreeding, and she outcrosses from time to time to keep refreshing her lines.

Mandate's pedigree is a good example of what is known as "pattern" breeding, in which the same dogs are in similar positions in the pedigree of both the sire and the dam. Here littermates Hi Ho Silver and Silver Tyga are in a similar pattern with other family members in relative patterns.

5

The Mating Game

W HETHER this will be your first or 21st litter, take a good look at the bitch you are planning to breed and ask yourself some questions. What are her qualities, what are her faults? What does she have to offer to a breeding program? What was the quality of her siblings? What have her sire and dam produced in the way of quality? If she has already produced a litter, what virtues or faults did she pass along to her puppies?

Evaluating a Brood Bitch

Remember, there is only one reason to breed and that is to improve. And there are no short cuts to success, only hard work and perseverance. So take off those rose-colored spectacles and face reality. Read and reread the standard. Watch your bitch in motion, watch her standing free. Set her in a show pose with her front feet directly under the center point of her shoulder blades, and feel the outline of the bones that form the horizontal and axial structures, the muscles that hold them in place. Forget what others have told you. You and you alone must be responsible for deciding objectively whether or not the bitch is worth the time, effort and money you will be putting into your next litter.

Too often breeders allow what is currently winning in the show ring to influence their judgment and set breed type in their minds. What a judge likes or what he has been told by another breeder is correct, is not necessarily what the standard specifies. Breeders must constantly turn back to the standard and let that be the only deciding factor in judging their breeding stock.

109

Should the bitch you are evaluating be of overall excellence but with one major fault, it is a fairly simple matter to breed out that fault in a couple of generations and still maintain quality by selectivity. But if you find many niggling faults in a mediocre specimen, with no great virtues and no glaring faults, or if you find more faults than virtues, it would take you the rest of your life to get rid of each of the faults, one by one, and at the same time never come up with anything spectacular. Spay her and place her in a good pet home.

It's tough enough at best to upgrade the overall quality of one's breeding stock, but it is the constant striving for perfection—for that perfect animal, yet to be born, the one that is going to be in the next litter—that makes breeding fascinating.

Always keep one better than the one you have, and keep striving for still a better one. The true breeder is never completely satisfied with his own breeding because he is a perfectionist.

Getting a Foot in the Door

If you are about to become involved in the purebred dog world, start with superior animals only. If you can't afford them, wait until you can. Beginning with anything less with the idea they will produce better than themselves is foolish indeed. Chances are they will break not only your heart, but your bank account and, in a few years, you will be anxious to get "out of dogs" and into a gentler sport such as wrestling, sky diving or politics!

So start with the best. It's easy to say but not as easy to do. Breeders with select stock are reluctant to let a quality bitch get into inexperienced hands. What have you really got to offer? No amount of money in the world could repay the breeder for his time, energy, love, money and emotion already expended in developing an outstanding dog. Try to understand this and be patient. There is no way you are going to get your hands on that perfect bitch today or tomorrow. So take your time and spend it researching the history and background of your breed, the great dogs that have contributed to the present high quality dogs in the show ring. Look at as many dogs as possible, and don't take any one person's opinion. You'll get many; some honest, others colored by jealousy or greed.

Don't be overly impressed with the number of champions in a pedigree. There are champions and there are champions. Some finish only by the hair on their hackles or because of lack of quality competition. Others go on to win Groups and Bests in Show. None of these wins, however, are as important as the quality of the sire and dam that produced the show winner and the type and soundness that the dog passes along to his progeny.

Don't be pressured into buying a dog. Remember, if the dog is as good as the breeder says it is, chances are he will want to keep it himself, or will be most reluctant to sell it at any price. You may have to promise to employ a professional handler if you cannot gain a championship for the dog yourself. If a bitch, you may have to sign an agreement that will permit the breeder to select the dog to which it will be bred and, in addition, give the breeder "first option" to buy, at a fair price, any puppies you do not wish to keep for yourself out of the mating.

note

There are valid reasons for this last request. Breeders, who have spent many years developing a type and a strain which will breed fairly true, do not want their stock to get into puppy-makers' hands. They do not want the males bred to every bitch that comes along just because it has their kennel prefix before its name, nor do they want the females bred to that "cute little doggie down the street" that doesn't demand a stud fee. There go their years of work, washed down the genetic drainpipe in one misguided breeding.

One more caution: Beware the breeder who offers you a "brood bitch." As far as I am concerned there is no such thing *per se* as a "brood bitch." Any dog that free whelps and raises a litter of puppies is a brood. It is not born a brood bitch nor necessarily destined to become one. Just because it happens to be the largest in the litter or the least likely to succeed in the show ring, doesn't make it a "brood." Any female worth breeding should also be worthy of earning a championship or at least endowed with the virtues that would qualify it for such a title before fulfilling its destiny in the whelping box.

The best way to "get your foot in the door" of the dog fancy is to visit all the shows in your area, talk to professional handlers, talk to judges if they happen to have a free moment, talk to breeders, both the winners and the losers, visit their kennels and be flexible in considering any suggestion they might have as to how you can go about acquiring breeding stock.

While waiting to set your sights on an available bitch, you would be smart to buy a promising male puppy right out of the show ring. Learn how to handle it in and out of the show ring, get involved in a local kennel club and keep your ear close to the ground. You should be able to find a handling class in your area and might like to try the dog in obedience. Even though you are a novice, if you are a person of integrity and show you are anxious and willing to study and learn, if you can gain some knowledge of dogs in general and your breed in particular, you stand a much better chance of being able to coax a quality bitch out of a reluctant breeder on some kind of equitable terms.

Terms will vary from breeder to breeder, but a fair and honest breeder will not require you to devote the best breeding years of the bitch's life to "paying back" in puppies for what he has let you buy. Make sure every detail is in writing and the agreement is signed by both parties in front of a witness.

Never go back on your word or try to circumvent your agreement. And don't become an overnight expert! Keep the breeder as your friend and advisor. You have much to learn and your foot is barely in the door.

Organs of Reproduction

The reproductive organs of the bitch are composed of the ovaries, Fallopian tubes or oviducts, the uterus, cervix, vagina and vulva. The vulva is the external genitalia. The reproductive organs of the dog are equally few and even more simple, consisting of the penis and two testicles contained in a scrotum, or sac.

Both dogs and bitches have glands for reproduction known as gonads. The two gonads of the bitch are located in the ovaries and in them are her eggs or ova, the female germ cells. The two gonads of the male are located in the testicles and in them are the sperm or spermatozoa, the male germ cells.

When a bitch puppy is born she possesses in her ovaries all the unripened eggs she will ever have. Each time she comes into "season" or estrus, some of these eggs ripen and are flushed into the Fallopian tubes. The tubes extend from the ovaries to the two horns of the uterus. The number of eggs "dropped" by the bitch during one heat period is usually the number of puppies that results from a successful mating.

When the bitch is mated, the dog ejaculates millions of sperm into the vagina during one copulation. These male germ cells, with their propelling tails, then wiggle their way up through the horns of the uterus into the Fallopian tubes where the female germ cells or ova are waiting to be fertilized. The first sperm to reach an egg penetrates it and a zygote or fertilized egg is formed.

When all the waiting eggs are fertilized, the tiny one-celled zygotes descend from the Fallopian tubes into the uterus where they attach themselves to the walls and the uterus provides the necessary heat, food and protection for their development.

Reproductive Organs of the Bitch

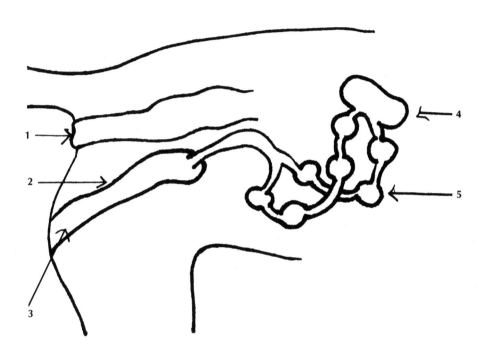

1. The large intestine
2. The vagina
3. The vulva
4. The kidney
5. The whelp in the uterus

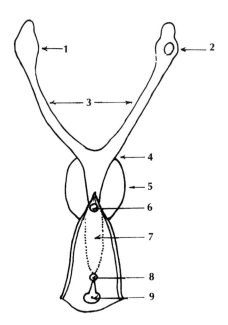

FEMALE SEX ORGANS: 1. Ovarian Bursa; 2. Ovary in sac; 3.
Horns of uterus; 4. Body of uterus; 5. Bladder; 6. Mouth of
uterus or cervix; 7. Vagina; 8. Urethral orifice (where urine
emerges); 9. Clitoris;

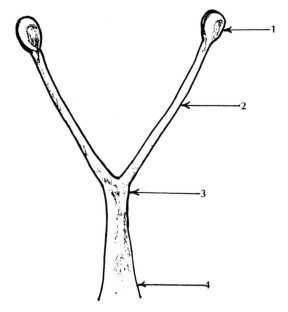

UTERUS OF THE BITCH BEFORE BREEDING: 1. Ovary; 2. Horn
of the uterus or Fallopian tube; 3. Body of the uterus; 4. Vagina.

The Bitch

Genetically the bitch contributes half the hereditary factors to the puppies; the dog the other half. Because the bitch will be the incubator for the zygotes that will develop into her whelps, her physical condition prior to mating, during the nine weeks of gestation and throughout lactation, are of utmost importance. So too are disposition and temperament. The bitch's attitude has an important environmental influence on the puppies.

The bitch should be bred from superior stock, as free as possible from defects, and the pedigree should be strong, sound and honestly representative of the dogs in her background. This is all a breeder has to fall back on when selecting dogs for a breeding program.

A bitch puppy will probably come into her first season anywhere from six to nine months of age. This is often an incomplete heat and, by no means should the bitch be bred at this time, even though some "experts" will tell you that it is okay, providing the bitch will be one year of age at the time the babes are born. I "bought" this once and the result was total disaster! Until the second full season, which should be six months later, the bitch is still growing and to breed her would be to rob her of the nutrients needed to build her own body. By the time the second full season rolls around she will be sufficiently mature, physically and mentally, to perform the rigorous duties connected with whelping and motherhood.

From the time a puppy has its first heat, the normal interval between the estrus cycles will be six months, but some bitches will be found in every breed that have a shorter or longer interval between cycles. This does not mean that Nature intends a bitch to be bred each time she comes into season. To do so would be a tremendous drain on her resources. An exceptionally strong bitch that whelps easily may be mated on two consecutive seasons but, if so, should be rested for at least a year. Generally breeders who do this get no further ahead than if they had skipped a season between litters to allow the dam to regain full strength and vigor.

The average bitch can be safely bred <u>every other season</u> until seven or eight years of age, providing she doesn't run into any whelping problems prior to this time. And a bitch should not be bred for the first time after three years of age. By then the elasticity of the uterine muscles will be diminished and the bitch is apt to run into trouble.

Each season will normally last for 21 days or three weeks. Periods that are prolonged much beyond the norm generally indicate some degeneration of the reproductive organs.

115

The Normal Heat or Estrus Cycle

Prior to the estrus cycle, you may be aware of temperament changes in your bitch. She may become more affectionate, demanding more attention, and at times will act unusually coy and playful. Her appetite may increase, she will urinate more frequently and will take a particular interest in cleaning her vulva or external genitalia. If you have another dog in the house, she will attempt to mount or "ride" it, regardless of sex.

These are the preliminary physical signs that her season is approaching, and shortly her heat will become apparent. Her vulva will become puffed and swollen to several times its normal size and will feel hard to the touch. The swelling of the vulva is shortly followed by a discharge, watery at first, then tinged with blood in varying degrees beginning with pale pink and gradually deepening to dark red. Some bitches bleed profusely while others have a discharge that is hardly noticeable. Some females show color before they begin to swell, others keep themselves so clean that a breeder is apt to miss the season completely. A safe procedure is to wipe the bitch with a tissue each day around the time she is due in season.

The estrus cycle may be divided into four phases, and specific changes occur in the external genitalia and vagina during each phase of the cycle.

The preheat season, or the gradual awakening of the sexual organs is called proestrum and lasts from four to 12 days, with the average being nine. It is during proestrum that hormones are secreted by the anterior pituitary gland, increasing the supply of blood to the uterus to prepare it to receive and nourish the fertilized eggs. At the same time the walls of the vagina thicken and the cells which line it become *cornified* or converted into horny tissue.

The bleeding and swelling of the vulva reach a peak in approximately nine days, and the true heat, or estrus follows. This is the time the bitch will begin to ovulate, or pass eggs from her ovaries into the oviducts or Fallopian tubes which lead to the uterus. There they rest waiting fertilization. This is the period of sexual receptivity. The bitch becomes aggressive toward males and encourages sexual intercourse.

This phase of the cycle is signalled by a lessening of the vaginal discharge, the color changing from red to straw, and the lips of the vulva, although still enlarged, become soft. The phase lasts from four to 12 days, with considerable variation existing among different breeds.

Ovulation

Ova or eggs are released into the Fallopian tubes on the third or fourth day of estrus. The exact time of ovulation can be determined by a series of vaginal smears taken throughout the proestrus and estrus cycles. You or your veterinarian must be experienced, however, in reading and understanding the smears.

When the bitch is not in season, a period known as anestrum, a vaginal smear will show flattened *epithelial* or skin cells and a few leukocytes, or white blood cells. As the heat progresses, and the discharge becomes more copious, the white blood cells decrease and red blood cells, or *erythrocytes,* and large cornified skin cells begin to appear.

During the course of the heat the epithelial cells of the uterus are entirely replaced by cornified cells. This is Nature's way of cleansing the walls of the uterus. So vaginal smears taken during early estrus show a majority of cornified epithelial cells and a few erythrocytes (red blood cells). As the time of ovulation approaches both the red and white blood cells disappear completely. When white blood cells reappear in small numbers, it signals that ovulation occurred about 24 hours previously, and the bitch is ready to breed.

When cornified epithelial cells decrease and *leukocytes* (white blood cells) again become abundant they herald the end of sexual receptivity and the bitch will no longer stand for the male.

The phase immediately following estrus or metestrus lasts for 60 to 90 days. It is the period when the bitch, if pregnant, will whelp and nurse her progeny.

Vaginal Smears

With the correct equipment anyone can learn to take and read vaginal smears. The first requirement is a high-power microscope, an expensive piece of equipment, which may be used for other simple tests such as stool inspections and, in large kennels, can pay for itself in a few years.

A sample of the vaginal fluid is obtained by means of a cotton swab inserted into the vagina, then placed on a glass slide. The slide is air dried and stained.

Each stage of the reproductive cycle of the bitch can be determined by knowing and correctly interpreting the cells characteristic for each stage of the heat cycle.

Stage	Reproductive Time Cycle	Cells Seen on Vaginal Smear
Proestrus	4 to 12 days (average 9)	Epithelial cells (skin cells) become cornified, many erythrocytes (red blood cells) appear, leukocytes (white blood cells) disappear
Estrus	4 to 12 days	Erythrocytes decrease
Ovulation	3rd or 4th day of estrus	Leukocytes reappear
Eggs enter uterus	5 to 6 days past coitus	
Eggs implant in uterus	15 days past coitus	
Pregnancy	60 to 65 days	
Metestrus	60 to 90 days	Leukocytes, non-cornified epithelial cells Erythrocytes disappear
Anestrus	70 to 105 days	Leukocytes, flattened or non-cornified epithelial cells from walls of uterus

Other Indicators of Ovulation

Some breeders utilize a glucose fertility test. At the time of ovulation, glucose is secreted into the vagina and can be detected by inserting a strip of glucose enzymatic test-tape into the vagina. If the edges of the tape or the entire tape turn green, the bitch will be ready to be mated in 24 hours.

Other breeders feel that the actions of the bitch are the best indicator of the time she is beginning to ovulate. She will make it quite obvious that her sexual instincts are aroused. This is usually at the same time that the vaginal discharge has lightened in color and the vulva has become soft and flabby. When tapped on one side with the finger, the bitch will move her tail to one side and clamp it to her thigh. When conditions are right an experienced male will seldom fail to breed her.

Best Time to Mate

Don't be in any tearing hurry. When the eggs are first shed they are immature and mating somewhere around the fourth day after the bitch indicates she is ready and willing may be more effective than an earlier breeding because the eggs will be at the right stage for fertilizing. Ideally, a fresh ejaculation of sperm at the time the eggs are ready to be fertilized is most desirable.

It has been demonstrated that if a bitch is mated on the first day of estrus, live sperm may still be found at the end of the estrus cycle, but whether they are capable of fertilizing an egg after the first 48 hours after ejaculation is doubtful. Some deterioration of the sperm may take place before 48 hours, so it is highly recommended that the bitch be bred a second time, no more than 36 hours after the first mating. This supplies the bitch with fresh, active sperm and eliminates the possibility of one of her eggs being fertilized by a disintegrating sperm, believed to cause a defective puppy.

The bitch can be bred a third time if it is desired, but if the first two matings were successful, if both the bitch and the dog were anxious, and a good tie was effected, a third mating is an unnecessary drain on the male.

More bitches miss from being bred too early than from being bred too late. Keep in mind that the most virile stud and the most anxious bitch will not have puppies if the eggs are not present to be fertilized. Only ovulation permits the presence of eggs, and they can be present for as long as four days.

Some breeders believe that too many matings can abort any ova already fertilized; others believe that it might be responsible for the resorption of the whelp by the dam.

After the matings great care should be taken to assure that the bitch does not come in contact with any other male for at least ten days, or until she indicates she is no longer interested.

Induced Abortion

Should a bitch have a misalliance with a stray or a dog of another breed after a planned mating, any resulting puppies should not be registered and should be placed in pet homes. Because it is usually impossible to tell which puppies were conceived by which male, it would be much wiser to have your veterinarian abort the fertilized eggs rather than let a valuable bitch deplete her energies in whelping and feeding a litter which can be of no future value to a breeder. Such abortion is effected by an injection of an estrogen hormone which prolongs the estrus cycle, creates a hostile environment, and prevents the zygotes from implantation in the walls of the uterus. The injection is effective if carried out in the early stages of pregnancy. No harm has been done to the bitch, and the owner of the stud dog will give a return service on the bitch's next season, providing such a clause is included in the stud contract.

Before Breeding Your Bitch

The right stud dog for your bitch should have been determined several months prior to her season. Photographs, if neither has seen the other's dog, and pedigrees should have been exchanged and the stud arrangements agreed upon.

At the first indication of the onset of estrus, have the bitch checked by a qualified veterinarian to be sure she is in condition, neither too fat nor too lean, and she is sound, healthy and free of external and internal parasites. It is also a good idea to have him check her pelvic area to see if she is correctly structured and large enough in this department to free whelp her puppies.

Problem whelpings are created by breeders who breed bitches that are too narrow in the pelvic area to free whelp a litter. When time comes to whelp they find these bitches unable to pass the head of a whelp between the pelvic bones and must resort to Caesarean sections.

Bitch puppies resulting from sections are then bred or sold for breeding with little or no regard for structural problems of the dam. There is every good chance they inherited the same defects and generation after generation of puppies will be born that are unable to whelp without surgery.

If breeders would check the pelvic area of their bitches before breeding, and would sell for pets, those that are structurally faulty, the present trend to more and more C-sections would soon be reversed.

If a breeder knows the approximate size of the head of a newborn pup, he should be able to estimate correct dimensions for his breed.

Place the bitch on a table and lift the tail. Measure the distance between the anus and the entrance to the vagina or the vulva. Then find the ends of the pelvic bones. The distance between the bones and the distance from the anus to the vulva is the area through which the head of the whelp must be able to pass. By measuring all bitches and keeping track of those able to free whelp and those that cannot, a breeder can, in a few generations, have a line of free whelpers. The fault is eliminated in the same way as any other fault—by not breeding any bitch having the fault and through selectivity.

In my breed, the Yorkshire Terrier, the distance from the anus to the vulva should measure three man's fingers, or approximately two and one-half inches. Space between the pelvic bones should measure two man's fingers, or about one and one-half inches. These measurements are ample to permit the free passage of the head of a Yorkie puppy to pass into the birth canal.

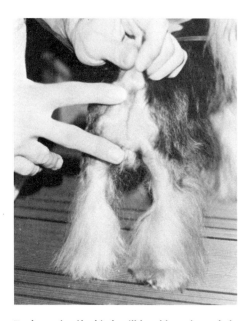

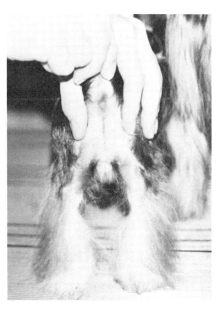

To determine if a bitch will be able to free-whelp a litter, first measure the distance from the anus to the vulva.

Then find the ends of the pelvic bones. The distance between these bones and the distance from anus to vulva is the area or circumference through which the head of the whelp must be able to pass.

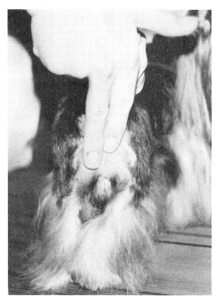

In Yorkies, the distance from the anus to vulva should measure a width of three man's fingers or about 2½ inches.

Distance between the pelvic bones should measure two man's fingers, or about 1½ inches wide.

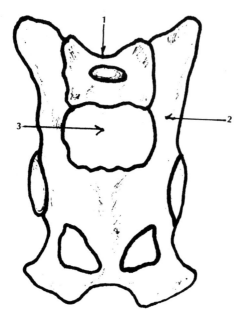

Narrow Pelvis: 1. The sacrum; 2. Bones of pelvis showing too narrow an aperture for a whelp to pass through without difficulties; 3. Aperture.

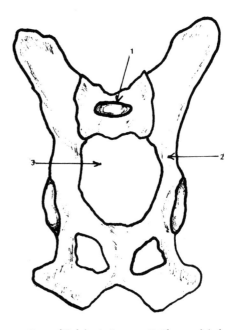

Normal Pelvis: 1. Sacrum; 2. These pelvic bones show an adequate aperture through which head of whelp can pass without obstruction; 3. Aperture.

In borderline instances, the bitch can usually free whelp if there are three or more puppies, because the number of puppies usually determines the size of each whelp at birth. The number of puppies can only be accurately determined by an X-ray, and the best time for this is on the 56th day of gestation.

Have the bitch checked for any possible internal parasites and, if necessary, have her wormed. It is most important that she be free of any worms before she is bred. She should also be given an immunization booster of DHL (distemper, hepatitis and leptospirosis) if more than six months will have elapsed since her last one and the time she will be due to whelp. This raises her titer and enables her to pass more immunity to infectious diseases on to her puppies. If you plan to ship her across state lines, the airline will require a health certificate from your veterinarian and a certificate of rabies given within a certain length of time, determined by the state and differing from one state to another.

Testing for Canine Brucellosis

The prebreeding examination should include a test for brucellosis, a highly infectious disease that attacks cattle, goats, hogs, some wild animals and dogs. It causes abortion, resorption, stillbirths and sterility.

Once the organism enters a breeder's kennel it rapidly attacks both dogs and bitches and renders the entire population impotent.

More and more stud owners are wisely insisting that they receive veterinarian certification that a bitch is examined a week or two before breeding, and is shown to be free from brucellosis infection.

Owners of bitches should also receive certification that the stud dog has been monitored at regular six-month intervals. Males can remain infectious, shedding the organisms in their urine or ejaculate for much longer periods than bitches. Bitches are infectious only while in season or following abortion.

Dogs may be infected by inhaling, ingesting brucella organisms or in mating. Those infected orally may develop enlarged lymph nodes in their throat area, while those infected vaginally may develop the enlarged nodes in the groin. As the disease progresses, the testicles in the male may become atrophied and edema of the scrotum results. The dog, because of painful testicles will, at best, be reluctant to breed, and will eventually become sterile. Some bitches fail to conceive or early fetal death follows conception. These are usually undetected except for a bloody or greenish discharge which may or may not be due to the presence of brucella organisms in the uterus. It is generally assumed that the bitch "missed" or the dog failed to impregnate the bitch. Other bitches may abort at the end of approximately 50 days gestation, or give birth to stillborn or weak puppies.

To date there is no cure for brucellosis. It is a self-limiting disease and can "burn itself out" in a kennel over a period of two or three years. The population is usually attacked during its most productive years and while it runs its course the dogs must still be fed and cared for. All breeding ceases.

Transmission of the brucella can probably be interrupted by castrating all infected dogs and spaying all infected bitches, but most breeders remove infected animals from their kennels by euthanasia.

Shipping

If you own your own stud dog, you and the dog can decide when the time has come to breed the bitch. If you are using an outside stud, check with the owner the moment your bitch starts to show color to be sure the dog is still available to service your bitch, and when the owner feels would be the right time to attempt the first mating.

If the mating necessitates shipping, decide on the day she should be shipped and make reservations with an airline during the week days when air traffic is not as heavy as on weekends. Some airlines refuse to accept dogs in transit on Saturday, Sunday, and holidays.

The bitch should be shipped at least three days before she is expected to ovulate. The entire experience away from home—travel to and from the airport, the flight, meeting strange people—may be traumatic for some bitches, especially those that are house pets. Kennel dogs are more likely to take it all in stride. But large, or small, kennel or pet, apprehensive or phlegmatic, they should be shipped far enough in advance of estrus to give them time to adjust and settle into their new situation and surroundings before being bred.

The owner of the stud dog should be willing to keep the bitch for a few days after a second mating to avoid early abortion due to trauma. Ideally the owner of the stud dog would keep the bitch for about three weeks from the time of the last breeding. By this time the fertilized eggs or zygotes will be firmly implanted in the walls of the uterus and chance of abortion or resorption is lessened. Most stud dog owners are reluctant to do this even for an additional fee, preferring to ship the bitch home as soon as possible at his convenience. As a result 50% of bitches shipped for breeding fail to conceive. Did the dog fail to impregnate the bitch or were the zygotes "shocked" out of the uterus before they had a chance to become implanted?

Care of the Bitch After Breeding

The gestation period in the dog is 60 to 65 days, with an average of 62. During this time the bitch should be fed a well-balanced diet containing all the nutrients, minerals, and calcium (in the form of bone meal) that she is normally used to eating. Neither the quantity nor the quality of the food should be changed during the first four to five weeks.

The bitch should not be allowed to become too thin or too fat. Either a fat bitch or fat puppies can complicate whelpings. Normally a bitch in whelp will instinctively reduce during the first few weeks, and many experience a few days of "morning sickness."

During the sixth and seventh week in whelp, ten percent additional protein should be added to her food in the form of raw beef, tripe, hard-cooked eggs or cottage cheese. During the last two weeks of pregnancy, the protein content of the diet can be increased by 25 percent, and the day's ration should be divided into several small meals a day instead of one or two. The enlarged uterus exerts pressure on the stomach and it is unable to hold the quantity of food needed at this time to maintain the health of the bitch and the whelps.

Do give hard cooked egg yolks to the in-whelp bitch. They contain everything to support life, including selenium, a nonmetallic element of the sulphur group, a lack of which is thought to cause crib-death in infants. Cooked beef liver is also important in the diet, but in modest quantities. Too much can cause diarrhea. And kelp is a valuable addition to any dog's diet, whether in whelp or not. This is a natural source of iodine from the sea and should be included in a dog's basic diet from young puppyhood through old age. It is an aid in reducing false pregnancies, helps conception, and is excellent for promoting a healthy coat.

Do not increase vitamins or minerals without the advice of your veterinarian and even then, not unless your veterinarian has had practical breeding experience. Many vets know little about diet and nutrition and even less about genetics and breeding systems.

Many years ago we used to give our in-whelp bitches one minicap vitamin capsule and three dicalcium phosphate capsules daily. The results were fat large-boned puppies that made whelping painful and difficult, and frequent attacks of eclampsia both before and after parturition. Since eliminating the oral calcium and vitamin supplement, we have never had a case of eclampsia in more than one hundred litters and our whelps are smaller, slimmer and more vigorous. Our basic diet is nutritionally well-balanced and additional vitamins and minerals throw it out of balance, upsetting the normal metabolism of the bitch.

The bitch in whelp should be given regular exercise to maintain muscle tone and prevent a build-up of fat, and plenty of sunshine. She should be allowed to romp and play and run and do all the things she did prior to the mating until the last couple of weeks, when vigorous exercise and excessive jumping should be curtailed. During the last ten days she should be given a clean, comfortable bed in a quiet place away from other dogs.

If the bitch is a house pet, she should not be allowed to run up and down stairs and care should be taken that she does not fall off a couch or bed. A fall of any kind could injure one or more of the whelps or rupture her uterus.

The Stud Dog

There is a great deal of difference between a dog that breeds a bitch and a stud dog. A stud dog is an experienced, willing worker. He is good natured and eager. He should be sound and typical of the breed, bred from sound, healthy and vigorous stock.

Responsibilities of the Owner

The owner of a stud dog owes it to the purebred dog world and to his breed, to offer that dog at public stud only after he has determined that the dog is endowed with good qualities which it is able to pass along to its progeny. It should be mated only to selected bitches of good quality owned by reputable breeders.

Far too many dogs are being bred, far too many breeders are unable to resist the lure of "fast money," and allow their stud dogs to be indiscriminately mated to any bitch regardless of quality. Remember that every puppy has a dam and that the dam and the sire each contribute equally to the puppy. Usually we get out of a breeding exactly what we put into it, and if the bitch is mediocre and faulty she should never be bred, especially to your dog. He may be God spelled backwards, but he can't perform miracles, and chances are it will be the stud dog that is blamed for any faults which crop up in the litter.

Before allowing your dog to be used at stud, evaluate the bitch, study her pedigree, assure yourself of the integrity of the breeder who owns her. A good question to ask yourself is, would you like to have a pup from this mating to use in your breeding program? If the answer is "no," then you should refuse to allow your dog to mate with the bitch.

126

Selecting a Stud Dog

The novice breeder would be wise to look to established kennels for a suitable dog for his bitch. Until he has had considerable breeding experience, it is best to follow this plan rather than to invest in his own stud dog. When he feels he is ready for his own stud dog, either one he buys or one he has bred, it should be of unquestioned excellence. And, generally speaking, a dog that is not of sufficient merit to warrant a championship is a risky stud.

Until the breeder maintains his own stud dog, he will have to go "out" to breed. The selection of a suitable stud will depend to a great extent on the breeding system the breeder has decided is the right one for him. But whether he plans to linebreed, inbreed or outcross, the stud selected should be correct in size, color, length of leg, quality of coat and every other breed particular. It should be a dog that is balanced, well-proportioned, typey, eye-pleasing and as free of faults as possible.

If you decide on a stud within a reasonable distance of your home, visit the kennel well in advance of the bitch's season. If the owner of the stud was also the breeder, ask him to let you see the dog's sire and dam and any other relatives that might also be in the kennel. Ask to see any puppies or young progeny it has sired. Keep in mind that there is more to a dog than visible virtues. It is capable of transmitting many qualities that it does not outwardly possess. Its total transmittable potential is contained in its genotype, and can only be judged by the quality of its get and often its grandchildren.

Although the laws of heredity tend to transmit the physical characteristics of one or both parents to the offspring, those characteristics may not be apparent until the second generation, when Mendelian segregation shuffles the genes and the hidden qualities surface. Because of this law, the second generation puppies may more closely resemble the grandparents or another prepotent ancestor than their own sire and dam.

Often the dog that is currently winning in the show ring may not necessarily be the most desirable partner for your bitch. It's entirely possible that the sire of the winning dog, especially if it has other quality puppies, would be better for your bitch than the attractive show star. These are questions that can only be answered by a visit to the home of the stud dog you are considering breeding to.

Managing a Stud Dog

When raising a future stud, give him plenty of love and freedom. Let him romp and play. Let him socialize with other dogs and other people. Play ball with him. Teach him to retrieve. Take him on long walks on lead. Take him to handling classes, enter him in puppy matches to accustom him to different situations and keep him extroverted and every inch a dog.

You will, of course, enter him in point shows when he is ready because you will want him to be a champion. At the same time, the demands made on a show dog are helpful in keeping him friendly and good-natured.

A stud dog should never be allowed to become too fat or too thin. His diet should be well-balanced, high in protein foods in the form of lean beef, liver, eggs and cottage cheese, mixed with wheat germ and kibble. He should have sufficient daily exercise to maintain good muscle tone and he should be kept well groomed at all times.

A good stud will be aggressive and will never refuse to breed a bitch when she is ready to be mated.

During his adolescence do not reprimand him for expressing himself sexually. It is instinctive for him to try to mount another dog, either a dog or bitch, and if you scold him he may be unwilling to mount a bitch when you want him to. Should he attempt to ride your leg, push him gently aside and distract him. A good game of ball is usually effective in directing his sexual energies into other channels.

With breeds that are known to be reluctant studs, simulated matings have proved an effective teaching aid. When the puppy is six months or older, encourage him to mount a bitch in season. Hold the bitch with one hand between her legs covering the vagina with your fingers. Cup your other hand in front of the fingers of the protecting hand and let the dog ejaculate. You will need another person to gently hold dog and bitch together in a simulated tie. When the dog draws his penis back into the sheath, allow him to dismount, praise him lavishly and give him a special treat.

When the stud dog is about ten months old, try to give him his first real experience, and make every effort to see that it is a happy experience. An experienced matron can do much to make a young stud's first service pleasant and easy. Attempting to mate a maiden bitch to an inexperienced dog is difficult and frustrating not only for the owner of the stud, but for the stud itself. In case of a painful first experience, a young stud can not only be ruined for future service, but can be seriously damaged. At an early age, with a cooperative bitch, a stud dog can be easily trained to do what you expect him to do in this and in future matings. He will accept the fact that you may have to handle him in case of a difficult mating. Through a happy first experience, you will have gained the dog's confidence, and he will look to you to hold the bitch if necessary.

Reproductive Organs of the Male

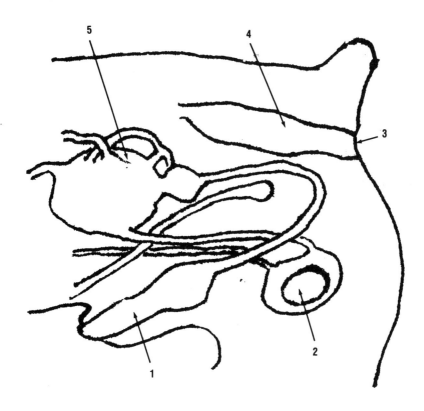

1. Penis in Sheath
2. Testicle in scrotum
3. Anus
4. Rectum
5. Bladder

A stud dog's second experience should not take place for several months. He was not fully mature at the time of his first service, and care should be taken not to overtax his virility when he is too young.

Should a dog fail to perform at his first opportunity, don't force him or scold him. Continue to try every couple of months or until he indicates by his behavior that he is ready. Meanwhile, keep him in good condition, happy and outgoing. If your stud is a house dog, don't make him into a lap dog!

After maturity, a stud dog can be used without strain at least once a week and, in the case of a very aggressive stud, twice a week. It would be wise, though, to curtail the services of a dog being shown. He is apt to lose not only weight but coat with too frequent breedings. He can continue to sire litters for many years. After the age of eight, his sperm may begin to lessen in fertility but successful matings have taken place between young bitches and dogs as old as 15 years.

However, an affidavit of fertility, signed by a qualified veterinarian, must accompany the registration of a litter whose sire at the time of mating was 12 years or older.

Reproductive Organs of the Male

The male genitalia are less complex than those of the female. Two testicles, or testes, each contained in a pouch, produce the spermatozoa, or male germ cells, and a small quantity of seminal fluid. The majority of seminal fluid is secreted by the prostate gland. The testes also secrete a hormone which acts on the brain to stimulate sexual desire.

The rest of the organs are accessory, concerned with the protection, storage and nourishment of the spermatozoa rather than their production. The scrotum protects the testicles and suspends them outside the body cavity. A convoluted tube, or spermatic cord, connects the testicles to the prostate gland and contains the sperm-carrying duct along which the spermatozoa pass toward the penis. It is believed that it acts as a storehouse for the sperm, which remain there until they are mature. The tube also contains a long muscle that aids in regulating the distance the testes are carried from the body, so that in cold weather they can be pulled close to the body for warmth.

The urethra in the male carries not only urine from the bladder to the penis, but serves as a duct for the semen. The penis, covered by a sheath of skin,or the prepuce, consists essentially of the urethra and erectile tissue. It has a bulbous enlargement at the base, which contains a small bone. When this bulb becomes engorged with blood during sexual excitement, the sphincter muscle at the entrance to the

Cross-Section of Male Reproductive Organs

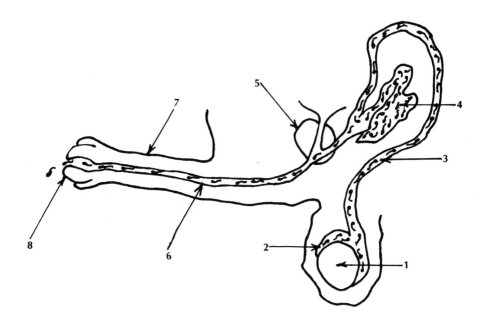

1. One of the two testicles shown in the sac
2. The Epididymis
3. The vas deferens, or spermatic cord
4. The seminal vesicle
5. The prostate gland
6. The urethra which conducts the semen into the penis
7. The Penis
8. Point of discharge of semen

female's vagina contracts and locks the dog and bitch together in what is known as a tie.

Cryptorchids

The testes normally descend into the scrotum just before birth. Here in the environmental temperature within the scrotum the testes are developed and when the dog reaches sexual maturity, it is said to be "entire."

Occasionally one or both testicles fail to descend and are retained within the abdomen. If only one testicle is retained, the dog is correctly described as a *unilateral cryptorchid,* rather than a monorchid. If both remain in the body cavity, the dog is described as a *bilateral cryptorchid.*

Due to the elevated temperature within the abdomen, sperm cannot develop in retained testicles, therefore bilateral cryptorchids are sterile even though their sexual drive may be unimpaired. The number of sperm produced in a single testicle of a unilateral cryptorchid are reduced by half, but the dog can still sire a litter.

A dog that is not "entire" is disqualified from the show ring and, since cryptorchidism is generally believed to be an inherited fault caused by a double recessive, it would be unwise to use such a dog at stud.

When a bitch is taken to the male, precoitus examination should assure the owner that the dog has both testicles and both are approximately of equal size.

The Actual Mating

Dogs and other animals in the wild mate without any human assistance. Most purebred dogs today, however, need some assistance from a capable handler. Experienced breeders never put a valuable stud dog and a willing bitch into close proximity and expect them to perform the sex act without help or, at least, close supervision. Either the dog or the bitch or both can be seriously injured. Should a bitch panic during a lengthy tie and attempt to pull away, it could be extremely painful for the dog and result in either his physiological or emotional damage.

The dogs should not be fed for several hours before mating and, before introducing them to each other, both should be given a chance to relieve themselves. It is also a good idea to sponge off the sexual organs of both dog and bitch with antiseptic soap such as Phisohex and water to avoid the possibility of infection.

Two people and often three are needed to breed large dogs. In this mating both dog and bitch are cooperative. Dog mounts bitch and breeder holds bitch's legs still.

Co-breeder assists the male in making an entry. Dog is accustomed to her touch and offers no objection.

Once tied, large dogs are usually allowed to stand rear to rear. One person supports the bitch to prevent her from sitting during the tie.

The stud thinks the bitch smells interesting. The bitch indicates she is receptive by flagging her tail to one side and holding it tightly against her thigh.

An assistant holds the bitch's head as the bitch elevates her rear to better position herself for the mating. The breeder makes sure the stud is at the right height.

A few strong thrusts and the stud enters the bitch. The expression on bitch's face shows that the dog has made an entry.

Trim any long hairs from around the vulva of the bitch and, if she is long coated, tie up the hair on the tail and on both sides of her hindquarters. A squirt of sterile lubricant into the bitch's vagina is often a help in case of difficult penetration.

The mating should take place in a restricted area as far away from kennel noises and other distractions as possible. Give them a firm footing to stand on, such as a rubber backed rug or rough matting. Never try to breed on a smooth surface. A carpeted ramp is often used for breeding and is particularly advantageous when the dog is smaller than the bitch, or when variations in the structure of the bitch pose a problem. Some bitches have a high set vulva that points up, others are low set and point down. In such deviations, adjusting the position of the dogs on the ramp can solve what might otherwise be an impossible mating.

Let the dogs become acquainted for a few minutes, holding both by their collars or on leads until you are sure the bitch is going to be friendly. If so, remove the leads and allow them a few moments of courtship. This helps make the stud more aggressive, and some breeders feel it encourages the bitch to ovulate.

It won't take long to determine if the bitch is ready to be bred or not. She will begin to flirt with the dog, flag her tail to the side and will present her rear to him in a seductive manner. The dog will attempt to attract her attentions by kissing her on the neck, playfully nipping her ear, and will smell and lick her vulva, all to the delight of the bitch.

If, on the other hand, the bitch tries to escape his advances, tucks her tail between her legs, snaps at his efforts or sits down as he approaches, she is not ready. Never force a mating. Try again in a few hours and, if still unsuccessful, put them into separate quarters overnight and try the next day. After three days, it may be necessary to restrain the bitch while the dog makes an entry. This can only be accomplished with an experienced stud. An experienced stud is also needed for a maiden bitch and usually, if the bitch is ready, the union is easily effected.

Two people should be present at a mating; one to hold the bitch and the other to help the stud. Some breeders place small dogs on a table, but most prefer the floor.

If the bitch is nervous or excitable, even though willing, she may swing around and snap at the dog at the moment of entry. This could frighten an inexperienced stud and he might refuse to mate for several hours, or until his confidence can be restored. Most breeders are cautious and will muzzle a strange bitch or tie a stocking or old necktie around her muzzle just tight enough to prevent her from biting.

The person helping the male should place a hand, palm upward and slightly cupped, under the bitch's vulva with the vulva between the first and middle fingers. If the dog is much smaller than the bitch and you are not using a ramp it may be necessary to place several layers of carpet or several sheets of newspaper wrapped in a rough towel under the dog to elevate him to the proper height.

Let the dog mount the bitch. If he does not yet know what is expected of him, help him to mount. With the hand in the described position, the person assisting the dog can maneuver the bitch's vulva into the right position to help the dog make a final thrust and effect an entry. If possible let the dog enter the bitch himself. Should he become too agitated or make repeated efforts to dismount, give him a few moments to "cool off," then try again.

At first the dog's thrusts will be long ones. When he begins fast, short motions and starts to tread, you know entry has been made. At this point, be careful not to let the bitch jerk or twist away from the dog. Hold the dog in position until he cannot slip out. The excitement of the sexual activity causes an involuntary swelling of the spongy erectile tissue in the penis as blood rushes into it, and the bitch and dog are physically attached to each other. This is the tie or coition. Hold the bitch firmly so she cannot sit down or pull away from the stud and damage the male organs.

As soon as a tie is secured, the dog will usually try to turn, and help should be given him if needed. The turn is not essential, but it is natural. It sets in motion muscular peristaltic contractions along the length of the female's genital tract, which serve to propel the sperm toward the eggs. Some breeders lift the forepart of the dog's body sideways off the bitch, and place both forefeet on the ground on one side of the bitch. The two are held comfortably in this position until the tie is over. It may be necessary to support the bitch's body from beneath to keep her in a standing position. Other breeders will help the male turn completely around. One hind leg is gently lifted over the bitch's back so the dog can stand on all four feet with his rear against the bitch's rear. The hind legs of both the bitch and dog should be held together so they cannot exert any strain on the other. At this point the bitch could be injured as well as the dog.

When the dogs tie, the seminal fluid ejaculated during the mating cannot escape and is forced into the horns of the uterus where, hopefully, the ova are waiting and ready to be fertilized.

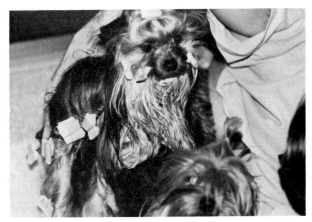

The stud is in the second stage of coitus or ejaculation.
The majority of the sperm is discharged at this point.

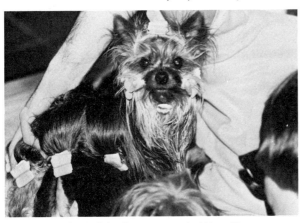

The stud dog is pretty proud of himself!

The stud attempts to turn, but the breeder keeps him and the
bitch side by side while the post-seminal fluid is ejaculated, and
the tie is finally broken.

In small breeds bitch's rear is elevated while a sterile
pad dipped in cold water is applied to her vulva.

The tie may last from five to fifty minutes and I have heard of some instances when it lasted for hours. The length of the tie is not important and has no effect on either the number of puppies or quality of the future litter.

As soon as the tie is broken and the dog eases away, hold a piece of sterile cotton dipped in cold water against the bitch's vulva for a few minutes. This will cause it to contract. She should be kept quiet for half an hour and not permitted to urinate.

Reward the dog with a special treat after a successful mating and let him know you are proud of him—he's a good boy. Make it something different from the bait used in the show ring. A lump of sugar, a chocolate chip cookie or other sweet will help restore the energy expended during the service. He worked hard and deserves a treat. Often it means that the stud will cooperate in a difficult mating, not only because he knows you want him to mate the bitch, but for the reward.

Give him a drink of cool water and allow him to urinate. Then put him in a quiet place to rest for a few hours, but not before inspecting his penis.

Occasionally and especially if a tie is abruptly broken, the sheath that normally rolls down to cover and protect the penis, rolls in a reverse direction. If not discovered it inhibits circulation of the blood and can cause the dog a great deal of discomfort. Usually the dog will indicate his distress by standing straddle-legged and refusing to walk or move. So before putting the dog away to rest, always check to be certain the sheath is back in its normal position. If not, insert the tip of a KY jelly tube under the edge of the sheath and squeeze out some of the lubricant. Gently uncurl the edges of the sheath and stroke it back over the penis.

What Happens During the Mating?

Many breeders feel that a full tie is necessary in order to impregnate the bitch. This is untrue and the purpose of the tie is not fully understood. It is doubtful if it has any special significance in modern dog breeding. In order to understand why it is not necessary, one should know what occurs when a dog and bitch are mated.

As soon as the stud makes entry, the penis begins to swell. Seemingly, he will become quite still except for some rapid panting. If, however, you place a finger at a spot just below the dog's anus you will feel a definite pulsation as the dog beings to pump out the ejaculate. Ejaculation is not involuntary as it is in humans. The dog accomplishes it by depressing the base of his tail.

Quite a large volume of fluid is secreted in the discharge, and it is produced in three separate portions. The first is ejaculated almost the moment the penis enters the vagina and the pulsations last about one minute, producing a clear, watery preseminal fluid from the prostate gland, which contains few if any spermatozoa. At the same time full erection takes place and the penis is held firmly by the contractor or sphincter muscles of the vagina until the ejaculation is complete.

After the preseminal fluid discharge the dog will be still for a moment, then begins again. It is this second porition of the ejaculate which comes from the testes that produces a milky fluid containing the majority of the sperm. This second fraction is the fertilizing portion of the emission and lasts from one to two minutes.

Again the dog will stop pulsating or pumping for a moment before going into the third and final stage that produces 80% of the total volume of fluid and may be ejaculated over a period of from ten to forty minutes. Again this comes from the prostate gland and is a clear watery fluid which serves to neutralize the slight acidity of the seminal fluid and helps the sperm achieve maximum motion. This has been determined to be in a slightly alkaline medium of from 7 to 8.5 pH.

If a dog and bitch do not tie but are held together for five to ten minutes, pregnancy will usually result. Millions of sperm, enough to fertilize thousands of ova, have been ejected in the first two to three minutes of entry, and a sufficient quantity of the alkalizing fluid has been introduced into the bitch in the next three to five minutes to serve its intended function.

Breeding Etiquette

The bitch is always taken to the male and the stud fee, agreed upon in advance, is payable at the time of service.

The owner of the stud dog should give a receipt and a certificate of service which records the registration number and name of the sire and dam of both the dog and bitch, the date or dates when the mating takes place, and the date when puppies would normally be expected. It should state the fee and any additional terms agreed upon by the owners of the stud and the bitch.

In the event that no puppies result from the mating, a return service is not obligatory unless specified in the stud service certificate and then it is to the same bitch at her next season and to the same stud.

Some stud owners specify that one puppy, dead or alive constitutes a litter; others will give a return service if at least one puppy from the mating does not survive.

If the bitch fails to whelp a litter, it is the obligation of her owner to notify the owner of the stud within seven days of the expected date of whelping.

Pick of Litter

Sometimes an arrangement is made between owner of the bitch and stud dog for a puppy out of the litter in lieu of a fee. The agreement might specify "pick of the litter," or second choice, allowing the owner of the bitch to make the first selection. In case of a one-puppy litter the agreement usually provides for payment of the stud service at this time, rather than the stud owner taking the only living puppy from the breeder and its dam.

The details of any such agreement, plus a specified age when any such selection of a puppy should be made, must be stated in the stud agreement at the time of the service.

The Importance of Integrity

The owner of a stud dog must be a person of complete honesty and integrity, who has the interest of the breed at heart.

Unfortunately there is an unbelievable amount of devious practices taking place in this mating game. Bitches are sent home as bred by unscrupulous people interested only in collecting a stud fee, when no mating occurred at all. The stud dog agreed upon doesn't happen to want to breed the bitch, so another, more aggressive stud is used without the consent or knowledge of the owner of the bitch.

American Kennel Club rules make it all too easy for this type of dishonesty to take place, and dog magazines, which have devised systems of recording top producers, aid and abet the ambitious breeder who must top all records at any cost. Too often the total champion progeny credited to one stud dog were sired by two or more different dogs.

Unless you can identify the dog to which your bitch is going to be bred and are able to witness the breeding, you have only the word of the stud owner.

Should the bitch turn out to be unbreedable because of a physical irregularity or some other reason, the stud owner should discuss the situation with the owner of the bitch. Some times a more forceful or more experienced stud can solve the problem, but this

```
┌─────────────────────────────────────────────────┐
│            CERTIFICATE OF STUD SERVICE           │
│                                                  │
│       This is to Certify                         │
│   That the bitch ......(Name)........ Breed ...................... │
│        Sire ...................... Dam ...................... │
│   Color: ...................... Reg. No: ...................... │
│   Owned by: ....................................... │
│   Address: ....................................... │
│   Was bred to: ...................... Reg. No. ................ │
│        Sire ...................... Dam ...................... │
│   On the ...... day of ......, 19...... and is due to whelp on │
│   or about the .............. day of ...................., 19 ...... │
│   FEE $ ...................... Terms: ...................... │
│   .........................     ......................... │
│      Owner of Bitch          Owner of Stud or Agent │
│                                                  │
│   If the above bitch does not prove in whelp, notice thereof │
│   must be given owner of stud within seven days from │
│   whelping date, in which case a return service will be giv- │
│   en to the same bitch at her next season, without addition- │
│   al fee, provided said stud is still in my possession. All │
│   transportation charges, if any, to be paid by owner of │
│   bitch.                                         │
└─────────────────────────────────────────────────┘
```

must be agreed upon by mutual consent. Other times the decision might be reached to resort to artificial insemination but in these cases the stud owner should not expect a stud fee until it is apparent that the bitch is in whelp. Should the services of a veterinarian be needed the cost of his service should be paid for by the owner of the bitch.

The stud owner is responsible for the well-being of the visiting bitch, and must take every precaution to protect her from the advances of any other male except the one selected by the owner of the bitch.

Artificial Insemination

This is the transfer of semen from the male to the female by means of instruments, and its success depends entirely on the skill and experience of the breeder or the veterinarian. The conception rate is still only about 50%. The semen should be collected two or three times over a 48-hour period and deposited into the cervix of the bitch with a syringe and long pipette.

The American Kennel Club accepts registration of a litter resulting from artificial insemination if both the sire and dam are present during the insemination, and if both the extraction and the depositing are done by the same veterinarian. A certificate of such a mating, signed by the owners of both the stud and the bitch must accompany the registration.

Infertility

The causes of infertility are many, but the most common are lack of exercise, improper diet, and mating either too early or too late in the bitch's season.

Lack of Exercise

Dogs that are constantly kenneled in close quarters and fail to get sufficient exercise, fresh air and sunshine are often temporarily infertile. If the condition persists, they can become permanently sterile. Not only do the muscles of the skeletal structure become atrophied, but so do the internal muscles of the heart and uterus, resulting in a general reduction of all bodily functions including reproduction.

We had this vividly demonstrated to us once when we bought a five-year-old dog that had spent the majority of his life in a small show crate. He was not only unable to breed a bitch, but incapable of an ejaculation. At the end of ten days of freedom and exercise, accompanied by a well-balanced, high protein diet, and affection, he successfully bred his first two bitches and continued to be a vigorous and fertile stud.

Proper Diet Is Important

Fertility depends on a diet complete in all necessary elements. Excessive carbohydrates and obesity can cause infertility.

Stud dogs and brood bitches need a diet high in protein from lean meats, internal organs and hard-cooked eggs. To this should be added Vitamin E in the form of wheat germ, tomato juice for Vitamin C, kelp for iodine, brewer's yeast (an excellent source of B-complex) and bone meal. Cod liver oil should also be added for the absorption and utilization in the body of the calcium and phosphorus present in the bone meal. The balance of these two important minerals, necessary for growth and bone development and for the prevention of eclampsia, is of prime importance.

To these nutrients should be added carbohydrates in the form of a high quality biscuit or kibble containing salt and some of the trace minerals.

Incorrect Timing

The most common cause of conception failure is due to mating a bitch too early in her season. Many breeders have a fixed idea that all bitches should be bred on their 9th and 11th days or their 10th and 12th days after the first show of color.

Conception depends on the time the ova are shed into the Fallopian tubes. There is no exact day of the heat on which this occurs in every bitch or every time a bitch is in season. The correct day is usually two to three days after the bitch indicates by her behavior that she is not only receptive but anxious to mate. The time of acceptance usually lasts for several days, although it is not uncommon for it to last for just a few hours.

We have bred a bitch as early as her sixth day, and have known other breeders to wait as long as 26 or 28 days. Both extremes resulted in live litters.

Some bitches come in and go out so fast that it is difficult to catch them at the exact time for mating without resorting to vaginal smears. Others may have silent heats with no external signs of a discharge. In such cases, the correct day for mating would be when the bitch will accept the dog.

Age Is a Factor

When a stud dog ages, his sperm becomes reduced in both number and motility. As the bitch gets older she sheds less ova and eventually will shed no ova at all.

For strong, vigorous puppies, breeding stock should be neither too young nor too old, but in their prime of life.

Mating a young dog too often before he is sexually mature can make him sterile.

Strictures

Some bitches have vaginal strictures which makes it difficult for a dog to penetrate. A strong stud can usually rupture the stricture, but in stubborn cases it is necessary for a veterinarian to dilate the bitch. Either way is a painful experience. In exceptional cases a stricture may require surgery. If so the bitch should be bred soon after surgery or adhesions will form preventing coition. Better still, remove her from your breeding program. Chances are the adhesions would prevent free whelping and the tendency to the formation of a similar stricture would be passed along to future generations.

Change of Environment

This affects the bitch in particular. If mating involves a long trip by plane or car, it is the bitch that must go to the dog. In addition to the need for time to adjust to her new surroundings, some stud owners are inconsiderate and do not allow sufficient time for natural courting to take place. As a result, a high incidence of misconception occurs.

Resorption

Often the mating is successful and fertilization of the ova takes place. Still the bitch does not whelp a litter due to some emotional problem or hormonal deficiency, which prevents the fetus from attaining full term. Resorption of the fetus normally takes place between 21 and 25 days of life. However, I have seen skeletal bones in the uterus of a bitch X-rayed on her 56th day, indicating that resorption can take place much later in pregnancy if anything interrupts the normal development of the whelp. The only outward sign of something amiss was a dark discharge from the vagina.

Psychological Impotence

The inability of a male to mate and the lack of desire on the part of the female is not uncommon in dogs. The general cause of such infertility is mismanagement during the adolescent months, and once a psychological barrier is formed it is usually irreversible.

Overaggression

Aggressive sexual behavior on the part of the stud dog is normal, but occasionally one comes across a dog which is not merely aggressive, but rather ferocious. He will attack the bitch when attempting to breed her. Even though muzzled, poor temperament is an inherited quality and any such dogs should be considered unsuitable for breeding purposes.

Hormonal Infertility

An imbalance of hormonal secretions can lead to infertility in either the dog or the bitch. At present there seems to be no hormonal supplementation that is highly effective in correcting this problem.

Infections

A high incidence of misconception is caused by several kinds of bacteria. Any disease such as canine distemper, hepatitis and brucellosis can cause infertility. Some good studs that have successfully sired many litters can suddenly become infertile as a result of a virus which involved a high temperature.

Orchitis, an inflammation of the testicles, can be a direct result of injury or infection, and nearly always affects the production of sperm in the male.

Epididymitis is another infection causing an obstruction between the urethra and the testes which prevents the flow of sperm down through the penis into the vagina of the bitch. Surgery is the only cure for this.

Streptococcus is another insidious infection which often can affect an entire kennel. It results in abnormal seasons and frequent abortions. It is necessary to take vaginal cultures of all the bitches in the kennel to determine those affected. Antibiotics are usually prescribed and are effective in arresting the infection but seldom bring about a cure.

Vaginitis may or may not cause fertility problems. Normally many different types of bacteria inhabit the uterus and vaginal cultures must be interpreted cautiously. It is only if there is a breakdown of immunity in the bitch that these different bacteria become pathogenic and produce disease. One of these bacterial infections could be metritis.

Overuse of Drugs

Generally tranquilizers do not seem to have much influence on the bitch's ability to conceive, but if given prior to mating can interfere with ovulation. Excessive use of steroids and antibiotics can render either a male or female sterile, and if administered to a puppy less than six months of age can seriously affect its fertility.

6

Pregnancy and Whelping

THE LENGTH OF TIME required for the complete development of the fertilized egg (zygote) into a newborn puppy is 63 days, give or take a couple. Gestation periods from 52 to 71 days have been recorded but whelps born earlier than 56 days are unlikely to survive. Bitches carrying large litters usually whelp a few days early, while those with only one or two puppies may go a day or two over full term.

If your bitch has not whelped by the 63rd day, keep an eye on her. As long as she remains bright and in good spirits and you can feel movement of the puppies in her abdomen, there is no reason for concern. Bear in mind that the actual number of calendar days may not coincide with the day the bitch ovulated and that fertilization may not have taken place for a day or two after the first or second mating. Should the bitch show signs of distress, however, have her checked by your veterinarian.

Signs of Pregnancy

A week or so after the mating, the bitch may experience a mild case of morning sickness and will vomit a bit of yellow foam. Because of a squeamish tummy she may go "off her food" for the first few weeks and lose weight. This may be Nature's way of slimming an overweight bitch; chances are she is pregnant. Otherwise there are no visual signs of pregnancy until about the fifth week. During the first five weeks the embryos are busy developing vital organs and do not increase much in size. After that time you will notice an increase in

147

your bitch's body weight and an enlargement of her abdomen. At the same time the nipples usually become enlarged and distended, and the pigment of the mammary glands becomes pink. The nipples will continue to enlarge until the bitch is full term and, a few days before parturition, a watery secretion can be expressed from them.

Vaginal Discharge

After the first five or six weeks, a clear, gelatinous substance will accumulate in the vulva of a bitch in whelp. For us, this is almost infallible indication of pregnancy and often, in cases of one or two puppies, tips us off before any enlargement of the abdomen is apparent. This discharge becomes more copious as pregnancy advances, finally becoming yellowish when the bitch is getting ready to whelp. Should the discharge at any time contain pus, it may be a signal of infection. Have the bitch checked immediately by your veterinarian.

Personality Changes

Often there will be a noticeable change in a bitch's personality after she is bred. A normally active bitch may become quiet and affectionate, a phlegmatic bitch may become extraordinarily active, and nearly all become more demanding. Such personality changes are a good indication that the bitch is in whelp, but are by no means infallible. Similar personality changes can take place in case of pseudo or false pregnancies, but usually not to the same degree.

Abdominal Movement

The most reliable sign of pregnancy is the movement of the whelps during the last week or ten days of pregnancy. It is usually easy to feel the restlessness of the unborn puppies by placing one hand gently on each side of the the bitch's abdomen. As the time of parturition approaches, the puppies become more active and often, when the bitch is lying on her side or back, can be seen twisting or kicking.

In cases of extremely large litters, the whelps may be so tightly packed they are unable to move. In such cases there will be little doubt in the breeder's mind that the bitch is in whelp.

Radiography

During the last ten days of gestation the spinal columns and crania (skulls) of the whelps may easily be seen in an X-ray. Radiography cannot be used to diagnose early pregnancy and is generally used only to confirm the presence of a single fetus, often carried so far forward under the ribs that it is difficult to know whether or not the bitch is in whelp.

Abdominal Palpation

Usually it is best to be patient and wait for the bitch to exhibit natural signs of pregnancy. Some breeders, however, are anxious to know if a mating was fruitful and will ask their veterinarian to diagnose pregnancy by palpation. This is an examination of the abdominal walls with the fingers. It is a fairly simple examination in a small bitch where only the fingers of one hand are required. The bitch must be totally relaxed. Nervous bitches tense their abdominal walls and make palpation extremely difficult. It is also difficult to palpate a bitch that is overweight. Some veterinarians feel that palpation can damage a fetus. Others with sensitive, trained hands can not only diagnose pregnancy with great accuracy, but can count the number of embryos in each horn of the uterus.

Between 25 and 30 days is the best time for palpation. By this time the embryos have developed from small, hollow, pear-shaped organisms to hard spherical lumps, ranging in size from a pea to a marble or golf ball, depending on the size of the breed. Beyond 30 days, palpation is almost impossible due to the development of protective amniotic fluids in which the embryos float in their sacs.

Resorption

Often a bitch will give all the physical signs she is in whelp. Her abdomen becomes distended and the mammary glands enlarge. But toward the end of the gestation period, all signs of pregnancy suddenly disappear. It is generally believed in such cases, that the embryos died in utero and were gradually resorbed by the uterine membranes.

Pseudo or False Pregnancies

Other bitches, mated or not, will display all the physical signs of pregnancy through actual time of parturition. The mammary glands become engorged with milk, the bitch will prepare her nest and may experience labor contractions. Yet there are no puppies. There are cases on record when such bitches with an abundance of milk have been able to play foster mother to an orphaned litter.

False pregnancies, depending on their severity, are generally believed to be an inherited factor caused by hormonal imbalance. It might be, however, that the eggs at that particular season were not fertile and, if the bitch is mated on a subsequent heat, she will whelp a litter of vigorous pups.

So don't "write off" your bitch after a false pregnancy. Plan to breed her again. Meanwhile give her a cuddly toy to "mother," and apply hot and cold packs alternately to her swollen breasts or pat on camphorated oil. Don't rub. That would just encourage the production of milk. Reduce her food and liquid intake and her problems will soon be over.

Nutritional Requirements and Exercise for the In-Whelp Bitch

Both these subjects were discussed in chapter 4. But to recap briefly, keep the bitch on her normal routine for the first five or six weeks. When her waistline begins to grow larger and there is little doubt she is in whelp, chances are she will become ravenous. Both the quality and quantity of her food should be increased and divided into three or four small meals a day. Her energy requirements will increase by 300% and her diet should be high in calories and protein. She needs raw and cooked meat, cod liver oil, vitamin D or plenty of sunshine, wheat germ, brewer's yeast, bone meal and kelp.

Giving excess vitamins or incorrect proportions of oral calcium and phosphorus can cause metabolic imbalance, anomalies in puppies and eclampsia in the dam.

If the bitch is very large with whelps she will become uncomfortable during the last weeks and may have to be tempted with special treats to keep her interested in food.

Normal exercise is necessary to maintain muscle tone and will help make whelping easier, providing there are no complications. After the seventh week, jumping or roughhousing with other puppies is verboten. Several walks each day should be continued right up to parturition. If the bitch is a house dog, don't let her jump off a couch or bed or run up and down stairs. When a bitch is heavy with whelps, it is easy for her to lose her balance and fall, causing injury to the whelps, abortion or a ruptured uterus.

Sporting dogs should not be used for hunting after the fourth week. Such strenuous activity could cause uterine torsion or abortion. This same rule applies to dogs involved in obedience competition or guard duty.

Normal Whelpings

The majority of our domesticated companion dogs, especially the small or large-headed breeds, need constant supervision if not help at the time of parturition.

The best assurance that a breeder can have that all will go well is a veterinarian who can be counted on to be available if you need him. Ideally he will be interested in your breeding program, perhaps a breeder himself of dogs or horses, and willing to work with you.

Normally the pregnant bitch will romp and play and eat well throughout the gestation period. The end of the eighth week is her "safe" period, and from here on there is a good chance that live puppies will result from the mating. Should puppies be born prior to this day, the lungs are not sufficiently developed to circulate the necessary oxygen through the body.

The Whelping Room

The place where the bitch will whelp her litter should have good light and be near a source of water. It should be a warm, quiet spot away from distracting noises of people or other dogs. Introduce the bitch to her whelping quarters at least ten days before she is due so she can become accustomed to her new surroundings. If the bitch normally lives outside, a corner of a garage or other outbuilding can be used in warm weather. In winter she should be brought into a heated garage or dry, warm cellar or playroom.

Whelping Boxes or Pens

As soon as the bitch is in her "safe" period, give her the whelping box. There are many different sizes, types, and styles that can be purchased or self-constructed. The box should be large enough to allow the bitch to stretch out to full length, but small enough to let her push against the sides when she has contractions. When parturition is complete, the dam needs a snug, compact area where she can keep her puppies near her for warmth and nourishment. Too large a box permits the puppies to stray in various directions.

The actual dimensions depend on the size of the bitch. The sides should be high enough to keep drafts out and puppies in. Within the box a railing should be fastened two or three inches above the floor to provide space for a puppy to crawl, thus avoiding the possibility of being pushed into a corner and smothered. This is known as a puppy guard rail.

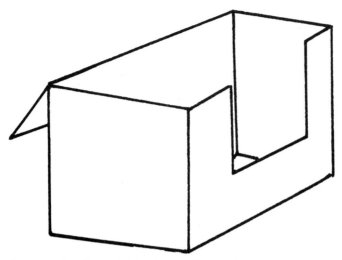

A warm and sanitary whelping box can be quickly constructed from a corrugated cardboard carton. Rough edges around top and door should be bound with masking tape.

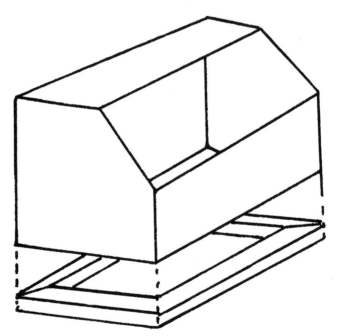

If cardboard carton is placed over a wooden frame of 2 × 2s, made the same dimensions as the box, the center of the box will sag, puppies will gravitate to it and the dam will curl around them. Such boxes closely simulate the nest a wild dog would make in the woods.

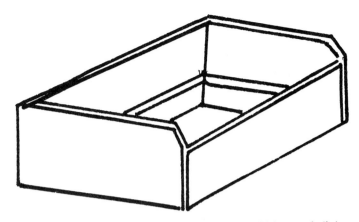

Reusable whelping pens constructed of plywood should have a built-in puppy guard rail. Three sides of this particular box are ten inches high, the fourth only 8 inches. Guard rail is made out of 1 × 2s and is attached two to three inches from base. Such size box is suitable for dogs from 10 to 20 pounds.

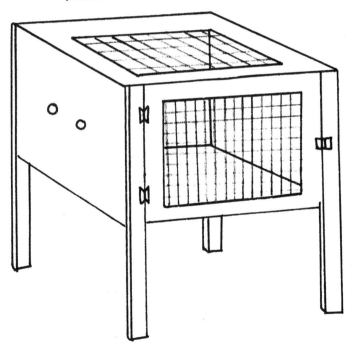

A ventilated cage makes a safe kennel for nursing dam and puppies. The high legs protect puppies from floor drafts.

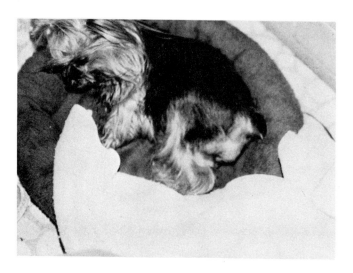

A washable cushion with raised sides makes a warm, comfortable whelping nest for small breeds or for those difficult to whelp. It permits close observation of proceedings and permits assistance as needed.

After the whelping dam, babes and pillow are transferred to a high-legged, wooden-framed pen with plexiglass sides. An electric cord leads to an infra-red fixture which is suspended above the new family.

One of the best whelping boxes is constructed from a heavy, corrugated cardboard carton. These cartons come in assorted sizes, are cheap, draft-free and can be burned after they are no longer needed. Such boxes are suitable for breeds ranging in size from the smallest Toy to a 50-pound dog.

A box about the same dimensions as a folded newspaper page (14 × 14 inches) and about 12 inches high is just right for Yorkies, Poms and Maltese. An empty paper towel carton is a good size for larger breeds.

Whelping pens made out of cardboard boxes do not have puppy guard rails. Setting one on a wooden frame made of 2 × 2s the same dimensions as the box, will allow the center of the box to sag. Puppies gravitate to the hollow in the center of the carton and the dam will curl around them. Such boxes simulate the nest a wild dog would make in the woods.

For a 20- to 30-pound dog a wooden whelping pen constructed of plywood should measure four feet square and 12 inches high. Divide it in half by means of a 12-inch wide removable partition. Attach a puppy guard rail around all sides except on the partition. The partition lets the dam escape from her puppies when she needs a rest and, when the puppies are four to five weeks old, it may be removed to give them more room to exercise and play.

Line the bottom of the whelping box with indoor-outdoor carpeting or rubber backed bathroom carpet. Protect the rug with sufficient layers of newspapers to absorb the fluids expelled during whelping. The top layer can be replaced as often as necessary with fresh layers.

Put a few soft towels or baby receiving blankets in one corner for small breeds. For larger breeds use an old matress cover or quilt or any warm, soft material that is machine washable. When the whelps are a few days old, the newspapers can be discarded so that the babes are raised on the carpet. Puppies raised on slippery surfaces such as newspaper, linoleum or plastic are slow getting on their feet. Once on their feet, a slippery surface is the cause of many a traumatic subluxation (dislocation) of shoulders or patellas.

Whelping Rings for Small Breeds

We used to use corrugated paper whelping boxes for our Yorkies but, not so long ago, switched to washable foam rubber circular cushions with high sides padded with polyester fibre. It's much easier to observe and to assist when help is needed. Soft towels and receiving blankets or disposable diapers are used to absorb the fetal

A satisfied Pembroke Welsh Corgi curls protectively around her litter of four. The thermometer on the guard rail of this wooden whelping box monitors temperature of the area.

156

fluids. After parturition and a post-whelping examination by the veterinarian, the ring is covered with a clean blanket and dam and puppies are allowed to rest for a few hours before being transferred to a high-legged, wooden-framed pen with plexiglass sides. Here mom and babes are kept under almost constant supervision until weaning time. The high sides of the cushion prevent babes from being crushed or smothered and the base of the cushion gives the pups warmth and a firm footing. The cushions are machine washable. Another advantage is they allow freedom for the bitch to run around the room to exercise during dilation and between puppies.

Preparing the Bitch for Motherhood

Around the 56th day of gestation, the bitch should be prepared for whelping. Hair around nipples and vulva should be trimmed, toenails cut, and teeth cleaned. Be careful in handling the bitch at this time. Any undue pressure exerted on her abdomen could cause premature whelping or a ruptured uterus. If she is not too heavy with whelp, she may be bathed and thoroughly dried. If she is bulging, forgo the bath and limit the ablutions to sponging off her teats and vulva with medicated shampoo.

Longhaired bitches should be trimmed or, in instances where it is important to preserve the coat, it should be heavily oiled, not tied up in paper packages or braided. Puppies are wigglers and can get their heads caught in the loose hair between the packets and the dam's body or between the braids. If not cut loose in time, puppies can be strangled.

Temperature Is the Tip-Off

On the 56th day start checking the bitch's temperature at the same time, morning and night, or at intervals of 12 hours.

Shake the thermometer down below 96 degrees, dip the end in Vaseline or KY jelly, and insert it gently into the rectum, where it must stay for three minutes. Meanwhile talk to the bitch reassuringly and rub her tummy gently. Moms are quick to respond to this unusual attention and will look forward to temperature time.

Normal temperature ranges from 101 to 102 degrees, and is always a little higher in the evening than in the morning. During the last week of gestation the temperature is usually slighly below normal, ranging from 100 to 100.8 degrees. When the birth of puppies is imminent, the temperature will drop one degree or more and will not go up in the evening.

No two bitches ever seem to go into whelp in the same way or have the same whelping temperature. The average whelping temperature is 99.2 degrees, but we have had bitches begin whelping with a temperature as high as 100 and as low as 98.2. It is that full degree drop without an increase on the next reading that means business. You can be fairly certain that pups will arrive before the end of 24 hours.

As the due date approaches, it's a good idea to take the temperature three times during the day (10 AM, 4 PM, and 10 PM) to pinpoint more accurately the time of day or evening the temperature took the downward plunge.

Should the temperature fall below 99 degrees and stay there for more than 48 hours without any signs of labor, get in touch with your vet. It could mean the beginning of eclampsia, which frequently occurs before any puppies are born. On the other hand, if the temperature rises to 102 or over, again call the vet. Any sustained temperature above normal may be a sign of infection.

Records Are Important

Keep a record of temperature and times taken and save for future reference. Although there will be variations in the same bitch from one litter to the next, these records provide a general temperature behavior pattern, and can often indicate if there is a distressed puppy among the whelps. A progressive whelping notebook is of great value to the breeder. Record name of dam, the stud, date mated, date puppies due, date of actual whelping. Jot down every detail whether you feel it important or not. In case of trouble it can be of inestimable help to your veterinarian. Did the bitch eat well up to whelping time or did she lack an interest in food? This is often an indication of approaching parturition. What other signals did the bitch give you that her time was near? What time did she give evidence of discomfort, did she pant heavily, vomit? When did she begin to have contractions?

Note the time each puppy is whelped, its sex, color or any distinguishing markings or abnormalities.

Temperature Patterns

Temperature Chart A
A normal temperature pattern gradually decreases as parturition approaches, but rises each evening. When it levels off, whelping time is imminent. Once it takes a full degree drop and does not rise at the

next reading, bitch will whelp within 24 hours. In this instance, bitch went into labor at 8:30 AM on the 62nd day. All puppies were normal and active.

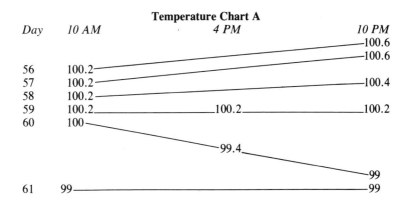

Temperature Chart A

Bitch went into whelp at 1:30 PM on the 63rd day from first mating. First puppy arrived buttocks first and upside down. Veterinarian assistance was required to release the puppy. Puppy was distressed, gums and tongue were pale and attempts to revive it failed.

The drastic temperature fall at 4 PM on the 60th day, with more than a degree rise in the evening is probably an indication that the puppy was breaking away from the walls of the uterus on the 60th day and was ready to be born.

Remaining two puppies were slow to take hold, but began to nurse at the end of 12 hours and were raised to maturity.

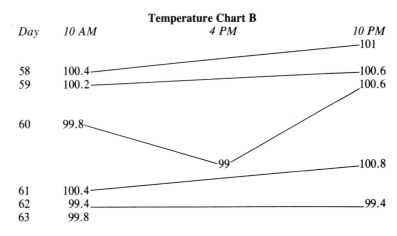

Temperature Chart B

WHELPING CALENDAR

Find the month and date on which your bitch was bred in one of the left-hand columns. Directly opposite that date, in the right-hand column, is her expected date of whelping, bearing in mind that 61 days is as common as 63.

Date bred	Date due to whelp	Date bred	Date due to whelp	Date bred	Date due to whelp	Date bred	Date due to whelp	Date bred	Date due to whelp	Date bred	Date due to whelp	Date bred	Date due to whelp	Date bred	Date due to whelp	Date bred	Date due to whelp	Date bred	Date due to whelp	Date bred	Date due to whelp	Date bred	Date due to whelp
January	March	February	April	March	May	April	June	May	July	June	August	July	September	August	October	September	November	October	December	November	January	December	February
1	5	1	5	1	3	1	3	1	3	1	3	1	2	1	3	1	3	1	3	1	3	1	2
2	6	2	6	2	4	2	4	2	4	2	4	2	3	2	4	2	4	2	4	2	4	2	3
3	7	3	7	3	5	3	5	3	5	3	5	3	4	3	5	3	5	3	5	3	5	3	4
4	8	4	8	4	6	4	6	4	6	4	6	4	5	4	6	4	6	4	6	4	6	4	5
5	9	5	9	5	7	5	7	5	7	5	7	5	6	5	7	5	7	5	7	5	7	5	6
6	10	6	10	6	8	6	8	6	8	6	8	6	7	6	8	6	8	6	8	6	8	6	7
7	11	7	11	7	9	7	9	7	9	7	9	7	8	7	9	7	9	7	9	7	9	7	8
8	12	8	12	8	10	8	10	8	10	8	10	8	9	8	10	8	10	8	10	8	10	8	9
9	13	9	13	9	11	9	11	9	11	9	11	9	10	9	11	9	11	9	11	9	11	9	10
10	14	10	14	10	12	10	12	10	12	10	12	10	11	10	12	10	12	10	12	10	12	10	11
11	15	11	15	11	13	11	13	11	13	11	13	11	12	11	13	11	13	11	13	11	13	11	12
12	16	12	16	12	14	12	14	12	14	12	14	12	13	12	14	12	14	12	14	12	14	12	13
13	17	13	17	13	15	13	15	13	15	13	15	13	14	13	15	13	15	13	15	13	15	13	14
14	18	14	18	14	16	14	16	14	16	14	16	14	15	14	16	14	16	14	16	14	16	14	15
15	19	15	19	15	17	15	17	15	17	15	17	15	16	15	17	15	17	15	17	15	17	15	16
16	20	16	20	16	18	16	18	16	18	16	18	16	17	16	18	16	18	16	18	16	18	16	17
17	21	17	21	17	19	17	19	17	19	17	19	17	18	17	19	17	19	17	19	17	19	17	18
18	22	18	22	18	20	18	20	18	20	18	20	18	19	18	20	18	20	18	20	18	20	18	19
19	23	19	23	19	21	19	21	19	21	19	21	19	20	19	21	19	21	19	21	19	21	19	20
20	24	20	24	20	22	20	22	20	22	20	22	20	21	20	22	20	22	20	22	20	22	20	21
21	25	21	25	21	23	21	23	21	23	21	23	21	22	21	23	21	23	21	23	21	23	21	22
22	26	22	26	22	24	22	24	22	24	22	24	22	23	22	24	22	24	22	24	22	24	22	23
23	27	23	27	23	25	23	25	23	25	23	25	23	24	23	25	23	25	23	25	23	25	23	24
24	28	24	28	24	26	24	26	24	26	24	26	24	25	24	26	24	26	24	26	24	26	24	25
25	29	25	29	25	27	25	27	25	27	25	27	25	26	25	27	25	27	25	27	25	27	25	26
26	30	26	30	26	28	26	28	26	28	26	28	26	27	26	28	26	28	26	28	26	28	26	27
27	31	27	1 (May)	27	29	27	29	27	29	27	29	27	28	27	29	27	29	27	29	27	29	27	28
28	1 (Apr.)	28	2	28	30	28	30 (July)	28	30	28	30	28	29	28	30	28	30	28	30	28	30	28	1 (Mar.)
29	2			29	31	29	1	29	31	29	31	29	30	29	31	29	1 (Dec.)	29	31	29	31	29	2
30	3			30	1 (June)	30	2	30	1 (Aug.)	30	1 (Sep.)	30	1 (Oct.)	30	1 (Nov.)	30	2	30	1 (Jan.)	30	1 (Feb.)	30	3
31	4			31	2			31	2			31	2	31	2			31	2			31	4

Temperature Chart C

This chart also shows a drastic drop in temperature on the 57th day with a two degree rise at the next reading. Trouble was anticipated.

Veterinarian was put on alert. Bitch went into whelp at 3:40 AM on the 59th day. Six hours later, veterinarian was called to help deliver a large puppy. Puppy was DOA. Veterinarian agreed that the puppy should have been born 24 hours earlier when 4 PM temperature dropped to 99 degrees.

As soon as the large puppy, which was blocking the birth canal, was removed, three more puppies arrived in the space of two hours.

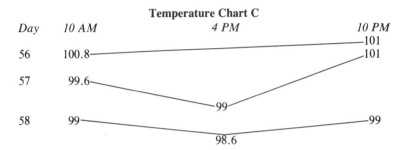

Temperature Chart C

Day	10 AM	4 PM	10 PM
56	100.8		101 / 101
57	99.6		
		99	
58	99		99
		98.6	

Whelping Equipment

Lay out basic equipment on a table covered with a clean towel. You are going to need: small rough towels, umbilical clamps known as hemostats, sterile gauze pads, a thermometer, alcohol or Roccal-D for sterilizing instruments, a chemical known as "monsel powder or salt" to stop bleeding of an umbilical cord, or iodine and cotton thread to tie the cord, a disinfectant soap and a couple of hot water bottles. A gram scale for weighing puppies and a small tank of oxygen are optional but useful.

You should have a heating pad or, preferably an infra-red brood lamp to keep puppies warm. The heat lamp quickly raises the body temperature of a cold, wet puppy and its rays can be adjusted. If a heating pad is used, keep it on low heat under the cardboard whelping box or under the carpet of a wooden one. An infra-red lamp should be suspended six to eight feet above the whelping box and the rays directed toward one corner. The whelp can crawl toward the rays when cold and away from them when too hot. If indoor-outdoor carpeting is used on the floor of the whelping box, it will absorb the heat of the lamp and diffuse it evenly across its surface.

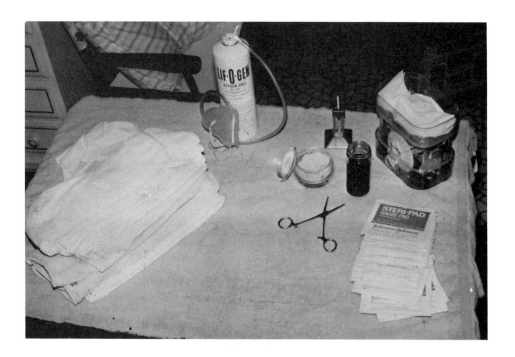

As soon as a bitch's temperature takes a one-degree drop, whelping equipment should be laid out on a table in a warm, draft-free room. Lots of clean towels, a thermometer, sterile pads, and a disinfectant such as alcohol or Roccal-D are essential, and a couple of hemostats or surgical clamps are helpful. A tank of oxygen is always a good precautionary measure if one must deal with a distressed puppy. For small breeds a gram scale should be available to record birth weights and daily weight gains.

Place a room thermometer beside the box to help adjust the heat. Room temperature at time of whelping should be 80 degrees; inside the whelping box a constant temperature of 85 degrees should be maintained for several weeks.

In addition to the whelping box you should have a small box or basket containing a hot water bottle wrapped in a blanket or towel into which can be put the first puppy and subsequent puppies when the dam is getting around to whelping another. If left with the dam when she gets restless and begins contractions, puppies could be injured. They can also get soaking wet from the parturition fluids. Most dams understand that you are helping, providing you leave the box within sight.

Stages of Parturition

Labor can be divided into three distinct stages. The first is the dilation of the passages, when the bitch is definitely uncomfortable and expresses her discomfort in many ways, usually by scratching and panting. Stage two is the expulsion of a whelp, which may take several hours from the first intermittent contractions until the bitch gets down to the strong, sustained pushes that finally expel the puppy. Stage three is the expulsion of the placental membrane or afterbirth which usually follows immediately after the birth of the whelp, but occasionally can be retained for five to ten minutes.

First Stage of Parturition

After the temperature drop, a distressed look in the eyes of the bitch may be your first sign that her time is drawing near. She may scratch at the bedding in the whelping box violently and begin to shake or pant. She may take a corner of the blanket in her teeth and try to tear it apart. She may run out of the whelping box frequently and squat as if to urinate or defecate. This means she is beginning to dilate to allow the passage of a whelp from the horns of the uterus into the uterus and thence into the birth canal.

As time for parturition comes close the vulva will relax and become soft.

During gestation the puppy has been floating on its back in a membranous sac containing amniotic fluid, which cushions the puppy as it comes through the birth canal. At the start of serious contractions, the puppy has to rotate. When the water sac appears at the vulva it means the blunt head of the puppy is just engaging the cervix. The cervix is a tight ring of muscle that has to dilate to allow the whelp to pass into the pelvic region and the birth canal where it awaits the last final strong, prolonged pushes that will expel it through the vulva into its new environment. The head must be presented accurately to the opening of the cervix if the birth process is going to proceed normally and without obstruction or complications.

Second and Third Stages of Parturition

Never let a bitch labor hard for more than one hour. You will have to be able to judge the difference between spasmodic or intermittent labor during the dilating period, and those really long, hard pushes that means business. Generally the bitch will have a few mild contractions, then will rest before her restlessness continues and the contractions increase in intensity until they are almost constant. Do not allow the bitch to become exhausted before calling for help. If you do, the puppies, which have started to break away from the walls of the uterus can die or at best will be what are known as distressed puppies by the time they arrive.

163

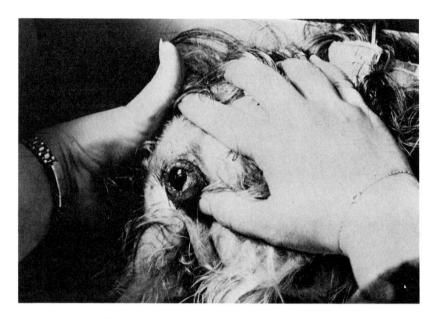

A water sac protrudes from the dam's vulva. It may be clear and gray in color or dark and tinged with blood. The sac is soft to the touch, meaning that the whelp has not yet come down the birth canal. *Duffy*

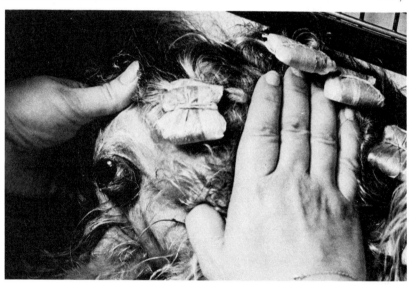

The sac may disappear and reappear with each contraction, but each time it should be a little further out. A few more good pushes and the water sac will break, or the dam may turn around and rupture it herself. The puppy is in no danger. This is Nature's way of lubricating the canal. The pup is protected in its own covering membrane and should make its appearance within an hour. *Duffy*

Once a puppy is ready to be born it must be delivered quickly if it is to survive. Any circumstance that delays its entry into this world calls for emergency action. In many cases an injection of post-pituitary hormone can help the dam eject a puppy. Such hormone should be administered only by a qualified veterinarian after a vaginal examination determines the degree of dilation, and that no obstruction is present. If given before the dam is sufficiently dilated it can rupture the uterus and you may lose not only the pups but your bitch. The drug causes involuntary contractions. In case of an obstruction it can act in the reverse and cause the cervix or neck of the uterus to tighten.

As stage two progresses labor pains will increase in intensity. The dam will often push her legs against the bottom or sides of the whelping pen and whimper. When the pushes become really strong and are almost continuous, a bubble or water sac will emerge from the vulva. The sac will appear dark, but the fluid inside is clear, sometimes tinged with blood. It frequently recedes but reappears with each contraction.

The pressure of the water sac on the cervix forces the bubble into the birth canal. Gradually the passage becomes more dilated until eventually the cervix, vagina and uterus all become one wide passage.

Scrub your hands with disinfectant soap and feel the bubble. If it is soft, relax and wait until a few more contractions propel the whelp into the birth canal.

At this stage the bag generally bursts from pressure within or from the bitch tearing it with her teeth. This is Nature's way of lubricating the birth canal. The bitch will rest for awhile to build her energies for those last final, powerful contractions that will expel the whelp.

Normal presentation is head first, but the whelp may arrive feet first or breech, which is a rear presentation. Neither usually cause any problem.

Once the head of the puppy can be seen, a few more good pushes should eject it. As long as the puppy protrudes a little more with each contraction, don't interfere. It is best to let the bitch do all she is able to do for her babes with the exception of some of the smaller breeds which usually require human assistance. But any time the bitch stops working you must help. Grasp the portion of the puppy that protrudes from the vulva with a clean cloth or rough towel and pull gently in a slightly downward angle each time the bitch has a contraction. Stop pulling when the contraction stops. Repeat the pressure until the puppy is extracted.

The afterbirth may or may not come along with the puppy but, in either case, unless the dam is experienced and in the past has taken complete charge of the whelps as each was born, you must help. The brachycephalic breeds such as the Bulldog and the Pekingese, with their foreshortened muzzles and undershot jaws, usually have difficulty severing the umbilical cord and tearing the membrane over the puppy's head. Other bitches whelp so easily they don't realize a puppy has arrived and it can drown or suffocate before they get around to doing something about it. So, the need for human assistance becomes obvious.

The puppy is generally born in a membrane which is attached to the placenta by means of an umbilical cord. If the membrane was not ruptured during delivery, which it frequently is, immediately tear it from the pup's head so the pup can breathe.

Open the pup's mouth and remove any mucous from its throat with a piece of sterile gauze. If the placenta is still in the dam, grasp the cord a good two inches from the belly of the babe with sterile gauze and, with a slight downward pull, gently withdraw it. Do not pull against the puppy. Should the cord rupture at the umbilicus (navel) the puppy could bleed to death. If you meet with any resistance, don't force it. The cord could be wrapped around the neck of an unborn whelp and forcing withdrawal of the placenta could strangle the puppy.

Usually it will withdraw quite easily. Leave it attached while you rub the puppy briskly but gently with a rough towel. Hold the newborn puppy between your hands, head downward to drain out any fluid from the lungs as you rub it. When the puppy lets out a good cry it is breathing on its own. Now it is time to cut the cord.

The placenta contains millions of tiny blood vessels which supply the whelp with a last surge of life-sustaining blood, fluids and nutrients from its dam. Before cutting the cord, raise the placenta above the puppy and gently squeeze the fluids in it toward the puppy. If mom takes care of the puppy herself, licking it with her tongue to dry and stimulate it, the placenta usually remains in her for several minutes following delivery of the whelp. The uterus contracts around the placenta and squeezes the blood through the cord into the puppy.

If you have a hemostat or umbilical clamp attach it across the cord one inch from the belly of the babe. With your fingernails, shred the cord on the far side of the clamp away from the whelp. Dab the end of the cord attached to the babe with monsel powder (a clotting agent) or iodine and press it firmly between thumb and finger until the cord dries and the blood clots. If you prefer, you may tie the umbilical

The pup was presented head first and the membrane covering its head and body has been removed. The umbilical cord, attached to the placenta, is still within the vagina of the dam.　　*Duffy*

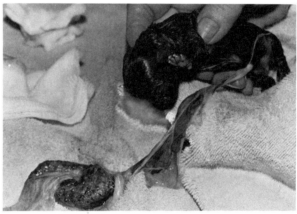

The membrane in which the newborn was contained may be seen lying between the puppy and the placenta (afterbirth). There is no rush to cut the cord. The placenta contains millions of tiny blood vessels which supply the whelp with a last surge of life-sustaining blood.

After the blood is milked from the placenta through the connecting cord into the babe's body, the cord is clamped with a hemostat prior to being severed.

Duffy

Cord should be tied at least one inch away from belly of babe. Note: Handle of hemostat rests on a towel so the weight of the hemostat cannot exert undue pressure on the puppy's navel of the puppy. *Duffy*

After second knot is tied, superfluous thread is cut away and end of cord is dabbed with iodine to prevent infection entering the pup's body through the cord. The dam's licking helps stimulate the whelp. *Duffy*

Breathing well on its own, warm and dry, the pup is encouraged to take the distended nipple in its mouth. This important first milk, or colostrum, contains antibodies against communicable diseases. It is important that the bitch's immunity be at its highest level during pregnancy and lactation.

cord with strong cotton thread. Tie it about one inch away from the belly of the whelp. Remember your boy scout's reef knot? Left over right, then right over left, making the second knot that secures the first. Cut or tear away the afterbirth and remaining cord and dab the end of the cut cord on the puppy with iodine. This prevents infection from entering the body via the cord. Shredding the cord with your fingernails more closely resembles the abrasive action of the dam's teeth if she were performing the same duty.

Occasionally there is a very short cord between puppy and placenta and the cord tears before the placenta has been expelled. To prevent it from slipping back into the dam, attach a hemostat on the end of the cord nearest the bitch.

Let the bitch eat the first placenta if she wants it. Many bitches do. Have faith in her instincts. In addition to being nourishing the placenta contains a high vitamin level and a hormone that helps the uterus contract, speeding the birth of the remaining puppies and inducing the milk supply into the teats. At the same time the placenta is highly laxative and care should be taken not to let the bitch consume more than two at the most, especially a bitch of a small breed.

Give the pup to its dam to nuzzle as soon as possible. A newborn must have contact heat as it cannot adjust its own body to the temperature of its new environment. Present it to the dam bottom up and encourage her to lick the anus to extract the meconium or first stool. This is a black tar-like substance that fills the puppy's intestinal tract prior to birth. Until it is expressed, proper digestion cannot take place and the pup can become constipated, develop colic or bloat.

The dam's first milk, the colostrum, is a mild purgative and the licking of the bitch also stimulates elimination. In the case of a weak puppy, it is frequently necessary to massage the anus gently with a fingertip until the meconium is extracted.

If a puppy does not immediately crawl to a nipple and take hold, it must be helped. Squeeze a nipple to make sure it contains fluid, distend it from the body of the dam with thumb and finger of one hand. Open the pup's mouth by pressing the jaws gently between thumb and finger of the other hand. Insert the nipple in the pup's mouth and hold it there until the puppy takes hold. You may have to do this several times until you are successful.

Every puppy must have some of the first milk. Colostrum contains antibodies that give the puppies immunity to disease until they can develop this on their own.

Let the first puppy nurse until the bitch indicates that another birth is imminent. At this point, place the first arrival on the towel-covered hot water bottle in the holding box, returning it to mom while you take care of the second born. Keep returning the puppies to the dam to nurse while waiting for the next. Be sure to keep track of the afterbirths.

The dam's milk is produced not so much by what she eats as by the hormonal activity caused by the nursing pups. If the milk is slow, the puppies will be hungry and will nurse almost constantly, creating more milk-stimulating hormones. Soon the supply and demand will be in perfect balance. Don't interfere by giving the puppies formula. They can survive very well without any food for 24 hours, and supplementing them at this time only causes them to demand less from the dam, fewer hormones are released, and a vicious circle is begun. The result of this can be a bitch that loses her milk and a litter which must be hand raised.

After the birth of the first puppy and each subsequent puppy, offer the dam a drink of warm evaporated milk or Esbilac, a puppy formula that simulates bitch's milk which can be purchased from your veterinarian. Make it according to directions on the can, but add one egg yolk to each cup of the prepared formula. Usually she will accept it gratefully.

When all the whelps have been born, the dam will settle down with her brood. However, it is always a good idea to have your veterinarian check the dam to make sure no more puppies remain in the uterus and administer post-pituitary hormone to clean out any bits of afterbirth which may remain in the uterus. This hormone also increases milk supply.

If your breed is susceptible to eclampsia, have your veterinarian give the dam a subcutaneous injection of calcium with vitamin D. Do not let him administer what is today a routine injection of antibiotic unless both you and he agree it is necessary. If the whelping was easy and sanitary precautions were taken, there is no reason for it. Many dogs are allergic to antibiotics, especially to penicillin, and there is ample evidence to support the theory that antibiotics may be the cause of many a ''fading'' puppy.

Have your veterinarian also check the puppies' mouths for cleft palates and other deformities. Deformed puppies should be given an overdose of a barbiturate.

Finally, all is in order. Cover the whelping box with a lid or blanket, stay close, but dim the lights and let the dam rest with her babes for a couple of hours. It is then time to take the mom out to relieve herself, clean her off with a warm wet cloth, and tidy the whelping box. Many moms are reluctant to leave their babes and must be carried or led out. Give her another warm drink, and move her to the place where she will remain for the first few weeks of raising her new family.

Normally the bitch will have a discharge for several weeks after whelping. This is Nature's way of cleansing the uterus. The discharge will range from light pink to dark blue-black. Fresh red blood, however, could mean an internal injury and the veterinarian should be consulted.

Various Ways Puppies Can Be Born

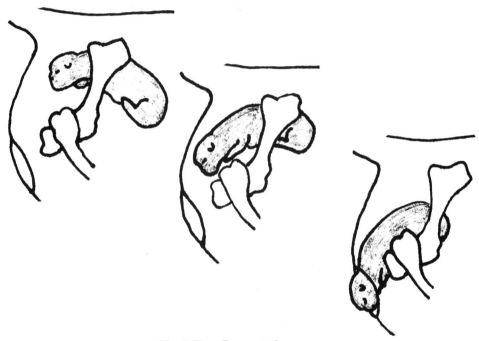

Head First Presentation

A. Puppy's head emerges first through the pelvis.
B. With each contraction puppy is expelled a little further toward the vulva.
C. Finally the head appears at the opening to the vulva. Shoulders should follow with the next few contractions, then come the final strong pushes that expel the puppy.

Various Ways Puppies Can Be Born

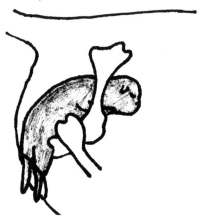

Posterior Presentation

Puppy is born feet first. Sometimes only one foot appears and the other gets "hung up" in the vagina. A sterile-gloved finger must be inserted to find the foot and bring it out beside the other before the whelp can make any further progress toward being born.

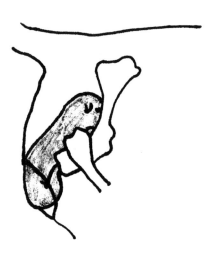

Breech Birth

Puppy presents its rear or buttocks first. If legs and feet remain tucked close to body, there should be no problem.

172

Various Ways Puppies Can Be Born

Posterior Presentation and Upside Down

This position causes the most problems. Sometimes a foot stretches out, preventing the birth of the whelp. Often it is necessary to completely turn the puppy in order to extract it. Usually veterinary help is needed.

Posterior Presentation

About forty percent of all puppies are born by posterior presentation, meaning tail or hind legs first or, in a true breech, buttocks first. Often such presentations cause no more difficulties to the dam than normal presentations but, sometimes, the dam is unable to expel the body of the puppy without assistance.

Should the umbilical cord be compressed by the body of the pup as it progresses down the birth canal, it will be cut off from the fetal blood supply. Breathing action may begin while the head is still encased in the membrane and fluid enters the lungs. Once in the birth canal, a puppy must be born within four minutes or it will suffer irreversible damage.

Place the dam on a work table or, if she is more relaxed remaining in her nest, lay her on her side. With one hand grasp the puppy's tail, feet or rear, whichever part has presented itself, with a sterile pad or warm wet towel and hold on firmly. Puppies are incredibly slippery! With the other hand push back the vulva from around the puppy and try to ease it out, pulling gently, slightly downward, each time the dam strains. Sometimes a gentle side to side motion will help align shoulders and front legs so they can pass through the vulva. Continue to pull with each contraction until the whelp is out of the birth canal. Then grasp the umbilical cord as close to the vulva as possible and gently withdraw the placenta.

Two people should be on hand at the time of whelping in case of trouble, one to hold the bitch and the other to extract the puppy and afterbirth. Sometimes the umbilical cord is so short that one person must hold the babe close to the vulva of the dam to avoid rupturing the cord and eviscerating the puppy. An assistant reaches slightly into the vulva, grasps the cord between layers of a sterile pad and tries to ease out the afterbirth, without putting any pressure on the thin fragile skin of the puppy's abdomen.

Should the umbilical cord tear away from the placenta, every attempt should be made to extract it. Usually a shred of the cord can be found protruding from the vulva. If not, again with fingers protected by a sterile pad, reach slightly into the vulva and try to find the end of the cord so the afterbirth can be withdrawn. If it does not come out easily do not force it. It will come along with the next puppy.

POSTERIOR PRESENTATION
The water sac in this breech birth (buttocks first) is still unbroken. Dam is having difficulties expelling the head. The puppy must come out once it is in the birth canal or it can either suffocate or drown in amniotic fluids.

Duffy

174

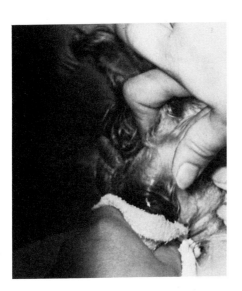

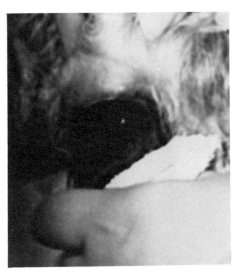

Puppy is still in its sac. Bitch has expelled enough of buttocks for a helper to get hold of pup. Puppies are unbelievably slippery, so a rough towel (preferably moistened in warm water) is needed for a firm grip. A second person present to hold the bitch is almost essential. *Duffy*

Still grasping the rear end of the puppy with one hand, push the vulva back from around the puppy with the other hand. Keep talking to the bitch, reassuring her that all is well, and ease puppy out with each contraction, pulling at a slight downward angle, and rocking the buttocks from side to side. The sac is now broken and there is no time to lose. Sometimes it is necessary to insert lubricating jelly into the vagina. *Duffy*

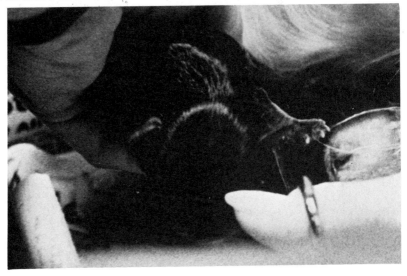

Puppy is finally out of the vagina, but cord was torn in the process. A hemostat or clamp is attached to the cord of the puppy until it can be tied.
Duffy

Keep track of the number of afterbirths. If one or more are allowed to remain within the bitch, complications or infection could result.

Length of Whelping Time

This varies greatly from one breed to another and from one breeding to the next. If the presentation of puppies is normal, some bitches will push out a whelp every 15 or 20 minutes; others will take as long as 12 hours to have half a dozen puppies or less. Difficult births extend the whelping period. If the interval between pups is greater than four hours or if the bitch passes large amounts of blood, she may be in trouble and a veterinarian should be consulted. The normal discharge is dark green to black.

Distressed Puppies

For a weak or distressed puppy, heat is as important as stimulation. Place the puppy directly on a hot water bottle that is hot enough

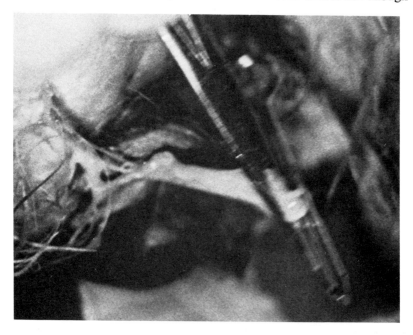

A second hemostat is attached to the end of the cord still dangling from the bitch's vulva to prevent the placenta from being withdrawn into the birth canal. Gentle pulling on the hemostat usually withdraws the placenta quite easily. *Duffy*

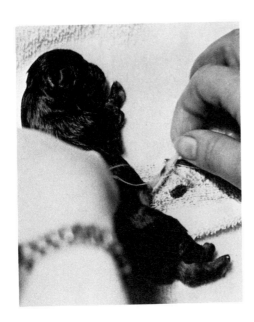

Umbilical cord is tied to prevent bleeding. A loop of cotton thread is tightened over the cord about one inch from belly of babe. *Duffy*

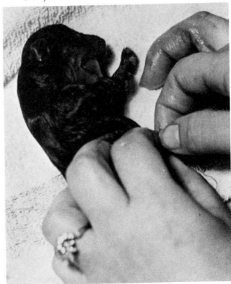

Thread is secured with second knot and excess is trimmed away. Puppy is gasping for breath and probably has fluid in its lungs due to the rear presentation. It needs to be "shaken down."
Duffy

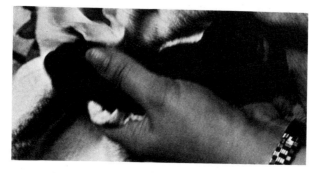

Briskly towel dry puppy first, then hold it firmly between palms of the hands, supporting the neck and head with the forefingers. Move arms above your head then down in an arc. The mucous will be expelled from lungs and nose of puppy by centrifugal force. The motion should be smooth and gentle. A fast snapping action could cause cerebral damage. *Duffy*

Hold puppy to your ear and listen to its breathing, or use a stethescope to hear if all the fluid has been removed from its lungs. *Duffy*

Before giving the puppy (obviously a bitch) to its dam, put a little vaseline on the end of your finger and gently massage the anus to extract the meconium. This is a black, tar-like substance which accumulates in the puppy's intestines prior to birth. If not removed it can cause constipation and colic in the pup. *Duffy*

to be uncomfortable to the hand. Massage the puppy's chest gently and turn the pup constantly from one side to the other until it grasps hold of life.

Auxiliary Oxygen

Sometimes the administration of oxygen can help in stubborn cases. Emergency oxygen tanks with regulator and mask are available at most drug stores. Read instructions carefully and do not administer oxygen near an open flame or a lit cigarette. Insert the entire puppy, head first, into the mask. Count two seconds each time you release the flow of oxygen. Repeat at intervals of one minute until, hopefully, the puppy gasps. Use in moderation. Overdoses of oxygen can cause brain damage.

Artificial Respiration

This must be correctly and gently performed. The lungs of a puppy are extremely delicate and if filled too quickly with too much air can easily be ruptured. Take a deep breath, cover the puppy's muzzle with your mouth and breathe gently into its mouth. Then press gently with thumb and forefinger on the puppy's chest to help it exhale. Repeat as needed.

Dystocia or Problem Whelping

Dystocia (dis-toe-she-ah) is the medical term for prolonged or difficult whelpings. It is generally divided into two categories— maternal and fetal.

We know that normal births depend on many things: the dam's physical condition, adequate pelvic structure, uterine muscles that contract rhythmically and vigorously to propel the whelp toward and through the birth canal, a cervix that is able to dilate at the right time. In addition, the whelp must be correctly positioned at the neck of the uterus, the cervix, to effect entry.

An abnormal pelvis, due either to trauma or inherited factors, will cause an obstruction to the passage of the whelp. Too large a whelp or those breeds with unusually large heads for the rest of their bodies, such as the Pug, Pekingese, and Bulldog, may be unable to progress through a normally structured pelvis. Sometimes two pups may be presented simultaneously, causing a "traffic jam," and making delivery impossible without veterinary assistance.

179

Uterine Inertia

The most common cause of maternal dystocia is uterine inertia, the inability of the uterine contractions to deliver a whelp. It may be sub-divided into primary or secondary, complete or partial inertia. Primary inertia means that the bitch is unable to expel even the first puppy, due to lack of exercise during pregnancy, overweight, or too many fetuses which stretch and distend the uterus to such a degree that contractions are ineffectual. Other causes may be a dysfunction of the pituitary gland or a hormonal deficiency.

Veterinary advice must be sought at once. If he finds the passages reasonably dilated, and part of the puppy can be felt in a normal position, he may give an injection of post-pituitary hormone to force the uterus to contract.

If little or no dilation has taken place, a hormone injection would be an unwise and dangerous procedure. The only alternative will be a Caesarean section, and the breeder has little or no choice but to agree.

Secondary inertia is due to exhaustion of the uterus after prolonged labor. It may be caused by an oversized fetus, too large to pass through the bony pelvis, a malpresentation, such as the head of a puppy doubled over onto its chest, or a puppy positioned transversely in the uterus, a deformed or a dead fetus.

Secondary inertia should not be allowed to occur. Veterinary assistance should be obtained before the bitch reaches the point of exhaustion.

Occasionally a veterinarian is able to work out an outsized or malpresented puppy by skillful manipulation and stroking of the vagina. Although painful for the bitch, after a short rest, she will resume contractions and free whelp the other puppies resting behind the troublesome one.

Episiotomy

An incision is made in the vulva in the direction of the anus. At this stage of parturition, the vulva is stretched to its maximum and is virtually paralyzed, so the surgery causes little discomfort to the bitch. Later, however, when parturition is complete, the incision must be stitched closed, and this is a painful procedure.

An episiotomy, while not pleasant, is much preferable to a Caesarean section, the only other alternative to a muscle-bound vulva. The C-section would save other whelps, but chances are the puppy already in the birth canal would be dead before it could be extracted by any other means than an episiotomy.

Sometimes the vulva does not dilate sufficiently to permit a whelp, already safely through the pelvis and in the birth canal, to be born. Quick action of the part of the veterinarian is necessary to prevent the bitch from useless straining, and certain death for the puppy.

Prolapse of the Uterus

Permitting a bitch to overstrain can cause a prolapse of the uterus, meaning the uterus literally turns inside out and protrudes from the vagina. It is very rare but should it occur, cover the protrusion with a moist sterile dressing and get her to the veterinarian immediately.

Caesarean Sections

Caesarean sections are frequently necessary to save the life of a bitch as well as the lives of the whelps and, if the bitch is in good condition and is not allowed to become exhausted, the prognosis for successful surgery is excellent.

The limit of two hours hard labor applies to either the birth of the first puppy or of subsequent puppies. Often a bitch will whelp several puppies normally, and then run into trouble.

In recent years the types of anesthetics used and the methods of administering them have improved so much that the risk of losing a bitch by Caesarean section has been greatly reduced, providing she has not been permitted to exhaust herself prior to the operation. It is more serious for Toy breeds than for larger ones, as is any other operation requiring anesthetic. Toys have a very low tolerance for stress and frequently go into shock just before the operation is completed or soon after.

From problem whelpings we have seen that there are many reasons why a Caesarean may be needed, and any one of these may occur in any breed and to any bitch regardless of size or past performance. Depending on the malfunction that caused the necessity for the section, having one litter by Caesarean does not necessarily mean that the next one cannot be born normally. If, however, a C-section is required because the pelvis of the bitch is too shallow to permit the head of a whelp to pass through, the bitch should not be bred again nor should any of her pups be used for breeding stock. The aim of every breeder should be to produce free whelping stock, and a narrow pelvis is an inherited fault.

In some breeds, bitches seldom free whelp due to the conformation required by the breed standard, a sad commentary on breed clubs that sacrifice normal parturition for abnormal structure.

Overanxious breeders and knife-happy veterinarians are the cause of many Caesareans. You, as a breeder, should turn to a section only as a last resort and, hopefully your veterinarian is a dog-caring person who will perform the operation only when all else fails.

Fortunately the majority of our bitches free whelp. Occasionally, however, a section is necessary because of some fluke. If the bitch has free whelped one or more puppies prior to the section, is young and in good health, we will breed her again at her next season before adhesions have had time to develop. But in no instance should a bitch ever be subjected to more than two sections.

Because our breed is a small one, we take the bitch to the veterinarian in her whelping box along with all the necessary equipment we might need should she suddenly whelp a puppy enroute, a not too infrequent and joyful occurrence. We take along clean blankets, lots of towels for rubbing puppies, and a couple of hot water bottles. We stay with the bitch at all times, talking to her as she goes under the anesthetic and when she is beginning to waken. We have found that the presence of someone she loves being with her goes a long way toward preventing any possibility of shock. Most bitches are licking their whelps as soon as the last suture is in place.

Puppies born by section have absorbed some of the anesthetic into their systems and are reluctant to begin breathing. Brisk rubbing, warmth, and artificial respiration are often required to induce the whelps to take their first big gasp. One of the loveliest sounds in the world is the cry of a whelp after it is born by Caesarean section.

You may have to take over stimulating the puppies to urinate and defecate until the dam is in full control of her powers and her instincts have returned. The puppies' intestines must be free of meconium as soon as possible.

The bitch is given a shot of cortisone to raise her stress level, a post-pituitary injection and an antibiotic. Although we have learned to distrust the general administration of antibiotics after a normal whelping, it is necessary evil in the prevention of infection after surgery.

The puppies are placed on a hot water bottle in one corner of the whelping box with the dam, and home we go. By the time we get there the dam is usually mothering the pups, and soon we are able to get them to take a teat. Milk is often reluctant to flow after a section, but the more the puppies suckle, the more milk will be produced, and the more quickly the uterus will contract.

When a Caesarean is required on a large breed, it is best to leave dam and pups with the veterinarian for at least one night, or until the veterinarian can assure you there are no complications.

The dam should be kept on a light semi-liquid diet for a few days, her temperature taken night and morning to assure that all is normal, and her incision inspected daily to make sure all sutures are intact and there is no inflammation. The incision should be kept clean and the dam's bedding changed frequently.

Usually the stitches are removed at the end of ten days or two weeks.

Care of the Dam After Whelping

For the first few days the dam will stay close to her babes, seldom leaving them except to eliminate. Gradually she will leave them more often for longer periods.

Most bitches are protective of their pups during the first week or two. Do not allow other dogs or strangers to come into the room. The dam and her puppies should be kept in a quiet place where they will not be disturbed.

Keep the dam on fluids for the first 24 hours. Her diet should be milk formula (Esbilac) to which may be added one egg yolk per cup of liquid and a few drops of baby vitamins (ABDEC), warm beef or chicken broth. Fresh, cool water should always be readily available. On the second day, solid foods can be introduced into her diet such as raw or cooked ground beef or poached chicken. Whatever it is, give her small amounts two or three times a day.

You may find this new mom extremely demanding. Often she will drink her milk or eat solid food only if hand-fed while she remains in the whelping box with her babes. Don't be afraid to spoil her if necessary. The bitch's need for food at this time is tremendous. She'll go back to her regular routine when she gets bored with her babes.

The National Academy Research Council recommends giving the dam 1½ times maintenance diet for the first week of lactation, two times maintenance during the second week and three times during her period of heaviest lactation which is her third week. The diet should be high in protein provided by cottage cheese, eggs, meat and some liver. It is only during the first week that it may be necessary to pamper her.

The dam's temperature may be slightly elevated for the first couple of days. If it registers over 102.5 or if an elevated temperature persists beyond 24 hours after parturition, consult your veterinarian.

Post-Parturition Complications

Eclampsia

Eclampsia is a convulsive condition that may occur during late pregnancy or lactation, probably due to a metabolic upset by which the calcium level of the blood becomes depleted. Some breeds are more prone to it than others, but nobody seems to know why.

Vitamin D enables the body to absorb calcium, yet some bitches, with adequate vitamin D intake, are unable to utilize calcium no matter how much is given orally. Giving oral calcium supplementation during pregnancy will not necessarily forestall eclampsia. On the contrary, we have proved fairly conclusively that over-calcification of the bitch in whelp interferes with the internal calcium-regulating mechanism, even when given along with the proper balance of phosphorus and vitamin D.

Eclampsia does not limit itself to small bitches or to large litters. A large bitch with a small litter may be equally susceptible.

The first signs are nervousness and excessive panting. The bitch may vomit or have trouble navigating. If you place your hands on her body you will be able to feel muscular twitches which will grow progressively stronger unless you act quickly. The dam's temperature will begin to rise. She may froth at the mouth and will eventually become convulsive. In extreme cases the temperature may rise to 106 degrees or higher.

At this point only a massive injection of calcium with vitamin D can save her.

Wrap her in a cold wet towel to keep her body temperature from elevating and get her to your veterinarian post haste. If she is able to swallow, administer six to 12 di-calcium phosphate capsules, depending on the size of the bitch. They may not help, but they cannot harm at this point.

Most veterinarians will insist on dripping calcium intravenously into her blood stream and, perhaps, in extreme cases or when a bitch has reached a state of unconsciousness, this is necessary, but we have found that a subcutaneous injection of sterile Cal-Dextro is equally successful. It is a little slower to act but much less dangerous. Having lost a valuable bitch from a massive heart attack 12 hours after the intravenous calcium, we refuse to permit the intravenous. We keep a bottle of Cal-Dextro on hand and, with veterinarian approval, administer it at the slightest suspicion of the onset of eclampsia. The correct dosage is most important as too much calcium is as dangerous as too little, so consult your veterinarian for the amount for your dog's size.

We have virtually eliminated eclampsia in our kennel with a breed that is prone to the condition, although we remain always on the alert. The maintenance diet of our dogs contains adequate amounts of bone meal and Pervinal (a dog vitamin). It also contains wheat germ and brewer's yeast. When a bitch is in whelp, the amounts of bone meal (calcium phosphorus) and vitamins remain unchanged; only the protein content is increased during the last few weeks of gestation.

When a bitch goes into whelp or directly after parturition, Cal-Dextro is administered subcutaneously. If the litter is three or more, or if the bitch is lactating heavily, a second injection is given when the whelps are ten days old. Years ago we used to give still a third injection to bitches who had a history of eclampsia, when the pups were three weeks old. Today we find that one injection is generally sufficient protection. When given prior to parturition it seems to stimulate labor.

Should your bitch develop eclampsia, the pups should be taken away from her during the acute stages and early weaning should be planned—the sooner the better.

If the puppies are too young to wean, supplement the largest puppies in the litter every four hours, eliminating an excessive drain on the dam's milk supply. Taking puppies away completely is traumatic for her and difficult for you. Often a bitch will become hysterical if separated from her babes. If you have begun to wean them and want to prevent them from nursing, wrap a towel around mom's body, fastening it across the back with large safety pins. For Toy breeds, cut the foot off a stocking, cut holes for the legs and slip it over the towel to hold it securely in place. The dam can then remain with her puppies and help them eliminate without danger of them nursing.

Metritis

A bitch that is lethargic and shows no interest in her puppies or in food is usually in trouble. These symptoms may be the first signs of acute metritis, an inflammation of the uterus. It is usually precipitated by a retained placenta or fetus, unsanitary bedding, or the introduction of bacteria into the genital tract by inept and unsanitary manual help.

If the condition is not attended to promptly, it will not be long before her temperature elevates to 103 or above, she will have an odoriferous vaginal discharge, the uterus will become swollen and the bitch will develop severe abdominal pain.

If caught in its early stage the infection can usually be cured by antibiotics and will run its full course in less than a week. When the infection is severe and the bitch fails to respond to antibiotics, spaying or death are the inevitable outcome.

Unless metritis is treated professionally at the onset of early symptoms, the bitch's milk will become toxic and the pups will become septicemic if allowed to nurse. Hand-raising the puppies may be the only way to not only save the litter but to relieve the bitch from stress.

Metritis can also be a chronic disease and a slight vaginal discharge after the bitch is bred may be the only symptom. The infection will exhibit itself in abortion, stillborn or weak puppies that fail to survive. Positive diagnosis must be determined by means of a vaginal smear, and the administration of antibiotics is usually an effective treatment.

Mastitis

This is an inflammation of the milk glands rather than the uterus, and occurs in bitches with an excess of milk. Milk accumulates in the gland, either because there are not enough puppies or because they are too weak to express the milk fully. The glands become congested and painful for the bitch. Usually the condition can be prevented if a teat which looks inflamed is gently milked or if puppies are rotated and encouraged to nurse from the congested nipple.

Mastitis may also be caused by a bacterial infection and, in such cases, must be treated with antibiotics.

Toxic Milk

If a puppy starts to bloat and cry any time from four days to two weeks after birth, has a greenish diarrhea and a red, swollen rectum, it may be affected by toxic milk syndrome which is symptomatic of an incompletely retracted uterus. The syndrome must be differentiated from bacterial uterine infection but, in either case, the pups should be taken away from the dam and fed formula by hand. The dam should be treated with antiflammatory drugs and antibiotics. Toxic milk should not be called acid milk, a term that should be eliminated from any discussion of canine disease. Whether the milk is acid or alkaline is not important. What is important is that infected milk can cause the early death of puppies.

Everything seems to be going along swimmingly with this litter of five Old English Sheepdog pups. Would you ever recognize the dam in her comfortable maternity trim?

Ladykirk Chamisa of Claford, a lovely Golden Retriever with her ten day-old pups. Without supplementary feedings only the strongest ones, able to fight their way to the faucets, will make it. At one week of age, there were eight.

188

7

The Critical First Three Weeks

PRIOR TO PARTURITION the rectal temperature of a bitch in whelp drops from its normal 101–101.5 degrees to 99 or 98 degrees. This is Nature's way of making the environmental change less drastic for a newborn puppy.

Even so the trauma of birth is great. The puppy is abruptly cut off from both the food and oxygen it has been receiving from the maternal blood through the placenta. At the same time it must establish its own circulatory system. This can be helped to some extent by insuring that as much blood and fluid as possible is squeezed from the placenta through the umbilical cord into the puppy before the cord is cut. The dam's rough licking also stimulates circulation.

Lungs are not fully expanded at birth and must expand for the puppy to breathe. A puppy slow to breathe can be stimulated by rubbing its coat against the grain with a warm towel and encouraging it to cry. Some that have a hard time coming into this world, born with a blue tongue, can grow into perfectly normal, healthy pups. Others born limp with a white tongue, having been cut off from any supply of oxygen for several minutes, are likely to have suffered brain damage and if revived will not grow into healthy dogs.

189

The Neonatal Period

The first 21 days of a puppy's life, or from birth to the start of weaning, is known as the neonatal period. It is a time when an average of 30% of all puppy deaths take place. There are some lucky "first-timers," but generally keeping a litter of newborns alive is a challenge. There are many obstacles to hurdle during the first few days before one can feel he may be "home free."

A healthy puppy is quiet, warm, round, firm and has a full belly. It is a beautiful sight in a breeder's life to see a litter of strong puppies lined up at the faucets kneading vigorously, their back legs stretched behind them, their tails almost at right angles to their backs, their skin pink and resilient, their muscle tone good, and their coats glossy.

For the first three weeks a puppy will nurse approximately 10% of the time and sleep the remaining 90%. Much of this sleep is "activated" or hyperkinetic. The muscle-twitching during sleep is essential to the development of muscles, which will enable the pup to stand at the age of 17 or 18 days and to walk without tremors by the 21st day.

A healthy newborn will curl in the palm of your hand. After 48 hours it will stretch and wiggle and lie with its head out. Its eyes remain sealed for 10 to 16 days. Its ears, too, are sealed and will open between 13 and 17 days. Its body temperature registers from 94 to 97 degrees for the first two weeks of life, and from 97 to 100 degrees for the third and fourth week. After that time the puppy will have a rectal temperature approximating that of an adult, or from 100 to 101.5 degrees.

The heart rate of a puppy varies from 120 to 140 beats per minute during the first 24 hours, and the respiratory rate varies from ten to 15 breaths per minute. After 24 hours through the first five weeks of life, both increase, the heart averaging 220 beats per minute and the respiratory rate averaging 15 to 35 breaths per minute. When adult, respiration slows to 10 to 30 breaths per minute and the average heart rate ranges from 80 to 140 beats per minute.

The suckling reflexes of a healthy puppy are generally strong at birth. Yet it is wise to check every few hours to make sure the puppies are nursing and their tummies are nicely rounded. Sometimes a puppy appears to be suckling, but is getting no milk. If the teat is completely in the mouth you will be able to see the pink tongue clasped around the base of the nipple. Watch and you will see it swallow about every half second. If a puppy seems to be mouthing a nipple and making soft sucking noises, it is not getting nourishment.

Put it on the nipple every couple of hours and hold it there until the suction becomes stronger. When it gets a good hold of the nipple it will knead the breast vigorously with its front paws. Sometimes it will brace itself against the dam and push out strongly, its legs distending the nipple with its head as it does so.

In a couple of days, if the puppies are nursing strongly, the dam's breasts will become engorged with milk and it will flow more easily. Check the breasts several times a day to make sure they are soft and not becoming hard or caked with milk.

If the litter is quiet, tummies well rounded, you have an easy-to-care-for litter. The puppies may complain if the dam sits accidentally on one or backs it into a corner. Otherwise all you should hear are happy noises like birds in the nest.

Continuous Crying

Crying is the first indication that something is wrong with a newborn. It may be hungry and needs to be helped onto a nipple and held there until its tummy is full. Often this happens with the smallest one in a large litter, which can easily be pushed aside by the stronger siblings. Keep a constant eye on this one to make sure it gets its share of milk.

If it is not hungry, maybe it needs to urinate. Frequently in large litters, the dam will neglect one in her maternal duties. Pick it up and stimulate the opening of the urinary tract with your finger, then hand it rear-end first to the dam to finish the job. If this was the trouble, it will stop crying immediately and will usually begin to nurse again. If it tucks its tail between its legs and tries to hide in the corner of the whelping box, it may have a tummyache or an attack of colic, brought on by a change in the dam's diet. Reach for the bottle of Castoria.

Colic

Castoria is an old-fashioned remedy that works wonders for colicky puppies. It is the herbal laxative that "babies cry for." Fill an eye dropper and press out a few drops onto the crying puppy's tongue, drop by drop. Make sure it swallows after each drop. Although totally deaf and blind at this age, the puppy most certainly has a keen sense of taste. It will wrinkle its nose and stick out its tongue in a most amusing manner as it recognizes the difference between this magic elixir and mother's milk! Give it from 8 to 20 drops depending on the size of the puppy. Then hold the puppy tummy down on a hot water bottle. If the combination of heat and Castoria doesn't work in about ten minutes, give it a second dose. It can do no harm, believe me. I've given it to puppies as young as four hours old when a novice dam failed to clean their intestines of meconium and the babes could not digest their food.

If the puppy is still in distress, you have a problem on your hands—a sick puppy.

The Sick Puppy

A sick puppy presents a drastically different picture from a healthy one. Its muscles don't twitch. Frequently it sleeps with its neck bent to one side. It does not nurse. If you put your finger in its mouth, the pup will reject it or roll it around in its mouth. It may crawl away from the warmth of its dam and siblings and cry pitifully.

The color of the stool changes in sick puppies. A yellow color is indicative of the onset of disease. Green coloration indicates liver secretions and hyperacidity of the intestines. Grey or white stools predict an advanced problem and usually death.

The sick puppy may have diarrhea which will become more copious as its condition deteriorates. It may regurgitate any food in its stomach. The puppy begins to lose body temperature and becomes dehydrated. Its heart and respiratory rates lessen and unless immediate help is given, death is sure to follow; often not as fast as one would wish. A prolonged death can be painful not only for the puppy but for you.

Warmth Is Important

Warmth is the first essential for the neonate. At birth its temperature will be that of the surrounding atmosphere. The area where the whelping box is kept must be draft free and maintained at a constant temperature of 85 to 90 degrees. Rather than heating an entire room, it is more practical to depend on an infra red light overhead, which can be raised or lowered to increase or reduce the temperature within the whelping box and can be directed to one side of the box so the dam or puppies can move into a cooler area if they become too hot.

A thermometer should be placed on the floor of the box on a level with the puppies and the dam and checked frequently. In this way the temperature of the room itself may be lowered while the interior of the whelping box remains a snug 85 degrees.

The dam will stay close to her babes for the first six days or so, and may have to be lifted out or led out to urinate or defecate. Bear in mind that the dam generates a great deal of radiant heat from her own body so, if the room temperature is lower than the interior of the whelping box, throw a light-weight cloth, baby blanket or diaper over the pups to protect them from drafts for the short time the dam is away.

After six days the dam will begin to leave her pups more frequently and for longer periods at a time. Nature is quite fantastic. The dam knows when her babes have begun to develop a shivering reflex which creates body heat and raises the body temperature to about 99 degrees. It follows, naturally, that the temperature of the whelping box should be reduced three to five degrees weekly after the puppys' first six days until it reaches a comfortable 70 degrees. By this time the puppies are four weeks old and will be able to sustain an adult body temperature without auxiliary heat.

Dam Culling

If you constantly find a puppy off by itself in the whelping box, it usually indicates the puppy has been rejected by its dam. She knows the puppy is sick or malformed in some way. Its temperature has dropped to between 78 and 83 degrees. She pushes it aside rather than waste her energies on it, thereby denying it further source of heat from her own body. To her the puppy is not only cold but does not have the vitality of a healthy pup.

The experienced breeder will trust the instincts of the dam and will not waste energies on it either. Most beginners feel they must save all pups even if it means no sleep for days on end, only to find that, after all the care, work and heartache, the puppy dies. We have never been able to raise to maturity any puppy that was rejected by its dam, and our advice to the novice is to leave it where the dam pushed it until it quietly dies. The dam will know when death comes and will have no objection to you removing it from the nest.

The survival of the fittest is the first rule of Nature. We are only asking for trouble when we take matters into our own hands and try to save the weakling. Would that rejected puppy have a chance of surviving in its own animal world? That is the question we should ask ourselves before we break our hearts and backs to save the weak.

The Cold Puppy

Should a puppy become accidentally chilled, it is imperative that it be warmed slowly with hot, moist towels, and an infra red lamp or a heating pad. If a heating pad is used as a source of heat, the pup must be turned frequently.

193

The drop in body temperature is accompanied by a drop in blood sugar, and this must be replenished by means of sugar, corn syrup or honey in a very dilute solution: two teaspoons sugar or one teaspoon corn syrup or honey per ounce of water (2 tablespoons). Administer 1 cc per 100 grams of body weight every 30 to 60 minutes, either orally or by intubation until puppy is warm and able to resume nursing.

If the pup becomes dehydrated, subcutaneous fluid injections should be given.

The First 48 Hours Are Critical

Every puppy should be weighed at birth on a gram scale, then every twelve hours for the first 48 hours of life. After that, once a day for the first two weeks. From then on periodic weight checks should be made and recorded.

Thanks to Dr. David Van Sickle's research project on neonatal puppy survival, conducted at the College of Veterinary Medicine, University of Pennsylvania, we now know that the weight gain of puppies after birth is in direct proportion to their rate of survival.

Some puppies gain steadily for the first seven days; others lose weight. Those that lose less than 10% of their birth weight within the first 48 hours of life, generally begin to gain after that time and soon catch up with the others. Those that lose more than 10% of their birth weight within the first 48 hours are extremely poor survival risks unless supplementary feedings are begun immediately. If supplemented correctly, a high percentage of these marginal pups can be saved, providing their condition is not complicated by disease or congenital abnormalities.

A newborn puppy's hold on life, especially in small breeds, is tenuous for the first week, and anything that upsets the delicate chemical balance of the puppy's system can cause illness and eventual death.

At birth, puppies have no subcutaneous fat and the small supply of reserve glycogen, the animal equivalent of starch, in the liver is not restored until after several days of nursing.

At the same time, lactation in a bitch directly after parturition is often borderline for the first couple of days and many puppies literally starve to death. They may have exhausted their limited supply of glycogen in their struggle to enter this world and do not have enough left for the necessary suction reflex needed to extract the reluctant milk from the dam's nipples.

It is important to understand that what a puppy needs most during its first 24 hours of life is ENERGY, not milk or formula. Giving the newborn puppy warm milk or formula is, perhaps, one of

194

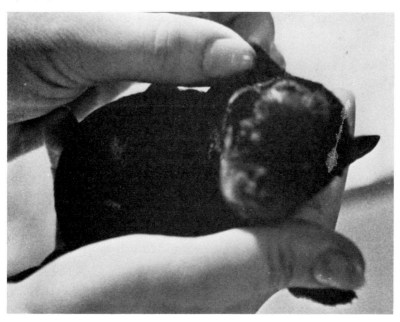

To check for dehydration, pinch and pull out the skin behind the head on the puppy's neck. If the puppy is not dehydrated, the skin will settle right back into place.

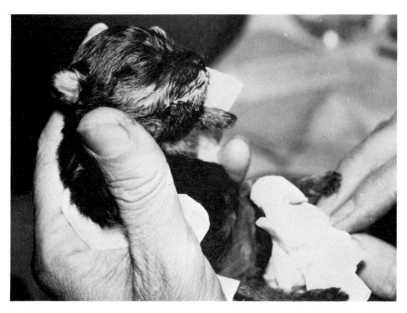

Stools and urine of an orphaned puppy must be constantly monitored to make sure they are normal.

195

the best ways to kill it. Giving it glucose (corn syrup) solution supplies the necessary energy to enable the puppy to nurse without interfering with its metabolism. When used correctly, glucose solution will not give the puppy diarrhea or colic or cause bloat, which milk or formula can do.

On the other hand, if glucose is not combined with water in the right proportion, it can create an imbalance in the blood sugar causing a stressful condition known as hypoglycemia, which unlike diabetes is not normally inherited but is the direct result of improper nutrition.

Hypo- and Hyperglycemia

To understand how glucose can save and glucose can kill, one must know a little about body chemistry.

Insulin, a hormone produced by a healthy pancreas, converts glucose into energy and, if this energy is not needed immediately, changes it into glycogen (body starch and fat) which is stored in the liver. Insulin not only enables the body to keep a reserve of glycogen on hand, but to release it for energy when needed. This means that both insulin and glycogen must be maintained in correct balance. If this balance is upset, stress occurs.

When too much glucose (corn syrup or honey) is given to a young puppy, the insulin production increases rapidly in its attempt to transform the excess into glycogen, causing a rapid drop in blood sugar to a point where the puppy can lose consciousness. This is known as hypoglycemia. Prior to unconsciousness the puppy urinates to a point of dehydration, and fat globules are discharged from the body into the feces. If the puppy is to be saved, a Ringer's solution containing potassium and sodium chlorides, injected by a veterinarian, replaces the loss of fluids, restores the level of blood sugar and urinary functions become normal.

If too much sugar and starch is included in the diet of an adult dog over an extended period of time, the pancreas becomes tired and its cells are no longer able to produce sufficient insulin to keep the blood sugar at a tolerable level. A rapid rise in blood sugar takes place and, again, stress or unconsciousness results. This is known as hyperglycemia or a form of diabetes. It explains why the diabetic must be supplied with insulin to lower the blood sugar level.

Hypoglycemia	*Hyperglycemia*
Blood Sugar ↓	Insulin ↑
↓ Insulin ↑	↓Blood Sugar↑

Using Glucose to Save Puppies

As soon as a bitch is approaching parturition, make a five percent glucose solution by mixing one teaspoon white corn syrup into four tablespoons boiled water. Add a few grains each of sodium chloride (ordinary table salt) and potassium chloride (salt substitute). This resembles a Ringer's Glucose-Saline fluid but, of course, cannot be used for subcutaneous or intravenous injection because it is not sterile.

Put the solution into a dropper bottle. As soon as a whelp is dry and breathing normally, weigh it on a gram scale and give it five or six drops of the solution for each 100 grams of body weight. It is best to administer the glucose drop by drop on its tongue and not introduce it directly into the stomach by tube. By giving it on the tongue the swallowing reflexes are being developed. Make sure the puppy has swallowed each drop before the next is given. Usually even the weakest whelp will accept it gratefully. Then put the puppy with its dam for stimulation and warmth.

Every four hours weigh the puppy, record the weight, and repeat the glucose, increasing the amount if the puppy wants it to as much as a full dropper or 1 cc for each 100 grams of body weight, until the puppy shows signs of gaining weight. Then offer it to the puppy every eight hours until it is 48 hours old. It should not be forced to drink it.

Usually even the smallest puppy will begin to take hold and nurse strongly with good suction at the end of 24 hours, and will reject the glucose, indicating it is getting sufficient energy and nutrition from its dam. You can tell when its suction is getting stronger for, suddenly, the puppy will close its mouth around the dropper and suck in all the solution from the tube.

If a puppy does not catch hold at the end of 24 hours, don't let anyone talk you into giving it milk or milk substitute. Do not introduce any supplementary food into the puppy's system for the first 48 hours. Energy and a reserve supply of glycogen is what it needs at this point in its tentative life.

After that, should a puppy need supplementation for any reason, a good formula is a standard mixture of Esbilac (one tablespoon Esbilac to three of boiled water), plus one teaspoon corn syrup and 3 drops of ABDEC to each eight tablespoons or ½ cup of the mixture.

Record the puppy's weight every 12 hours. After 72 hours, if a puppy is still not showing a consistent weight gain on the combination of dam's milk and Esbilac, try adding one egg yolk per cup of Esbilac-corn syrup mixture.

Dropper feeding must be done slowly and carefully. If a puppy inhales the fluid into its lungs it can develop inhalation pneumonia. Be sure to keep the pup's head up when dropper feeding.

This babe was the smallest of a litter of five Shih Tzu puppies. It lost an incredible 25% of its birth weight, and not only survived, but developed into a healthy adult. It was supplemented for 15 days and owes its life and normal development to the knowledge and understanding of the delicate insulin-glycogen balance in neonate puppies.

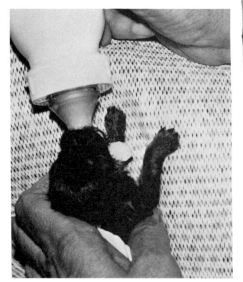

This puppy takes readily to a bottle after one week of tube feeding. Note correct position of puppy.

In general a puppy should gain 1 gram for each pound of its anticipated adult weight each day during the neonatal period. For example, a puppy which is expected to weigh ten pounds when adult should gain a minimum of 10 grams per day. It should double its birth weight in the first eight to ten days of life.

At this encouraging point in the neonate's life, discontinue the glucose or any other form of sugar in its formula and substitute protein in the form of two teaspoons scraped raw beef to 1 cup of the Esbilac egg mixture. The time has come when it is necessary for a puppy to manufacture its own glycogen without depending on corn syrup to stimulate the pancreatic production of insulin. If glucose is continued, the pancreas can become trigger-happy and whether the blood sugar rises sharply (hyperglycemia) or drops drastically (hypoglycemia) the results are the same—stress, possibly unconsciousness and, all too frequently, death.

Bottle Feeding

When a puppy is ready for formula supplementation, switch to bottle or tube feeding. Bottle feeding is much more satisfying to both puppy and breeder. The puppy's suckling instinct is preserved and encouraged, the dams readily accept the handling of their pups, and the babes themselves get the personal attention and fondling they need to help them become well adjusted adults. The extra handling or "gentling" as it is called by Ashley Montague in his fascinating book entitled *Touching*, pays off in healthier puppies, brighter, quicker to learn, better pets that are better developed systemically. In addition they are more resistant to disease.

In an experiment conducted with rats, the difference was impressive between a group that were fondled, petted and caressed daily for the first ten days of life and those, raised in the same environment, that were not petted.

The petted rats showed the following: 1) They learned faster and grew faster. 2) were livelier, more curious, and solved problems more quickly 3) skeletal growth was more advanced 4) food absorption and utilization was better 5) as adults they had better developed immunological systems 6) they had better emotional stability and were better able to handle stress 7) brain weight was greater, neural development more advanced and there was a greater development of both the cortex and subcortex of the brain.

The fondled rats made better mothers, produced healthier off-spring and had more surviving young. There were strong indications that fondling the female throughout pregnancy and during labor and delivery made the process easier. Males that were fondled were better producers.

Bottle feeding is less hazardous than dropper feeding as there is less chance of getting fluid into the puppy's lungs.

The puppy should be held in a normal nursing position, that is lying on its stomach with chest and head up. Make sure the puppy's tongue is in the right place and not held in the roof of its mouth. Guide the nipple into the mouth. Hold the bottle at a slight incline to keep the milk flowing toward the puppy. Give the pup a footing and, if you let it rest its front paws on a pillow or against your knee, it will knead as though it were the dam's breast.

Generally bottle fed puppies will fall off the nipple when they get tired, just as they would if they were nursing their dam.

Often air in the bottle gets into the stomach and the puppy should be "burped" after each feeding. Hold it on its stomach in one hand with head up and body at a slant and pat it gently on the back to encourage it to burp. If the bottle were just a supplementary feeding, give the pup back to its dam to stimulate and clean it. If it is an orphaned pup, it is important to gently massage its genitalia and anus with cotton dipped into warm water to be sure the pup is eliminating. If the stool is not normal or if the urine is not clear, consult your veterinarian immediately. Medication might be in order.

Intubation or Tube Feeding

All breeders should know how to tube feed and should have the necessary equipment on hand when expecting a litter. Often it is a means of saving the life of a sick puppy that is too weak to nurse.

In order to deliver formula into the stomach of a puppy you need a French catheter or feeding tube about fifteen inches long (size 8 for small breeds; 10 for large breeds) and a 10, 20 or 50 cc disposable plastic syringe.

The feeding equipment need not be sterile, but it should be scrupulously clean.

Refer to the feeding chart and use a commercial simulated dam's milk such as Esbilac. Mix it according to directions on the can. It's not a good idea to guess at quantities or improvise. The digestive

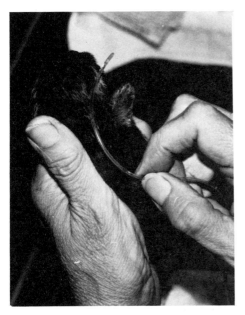
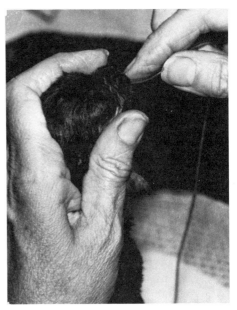

Using the catheter, measure from the puppy's nose to the bottom of its rib cage to determine how far the tube should be inserted.

Insert tube gently over the tongue, down the esophagus, and into the stomach to the pre-marked spot.

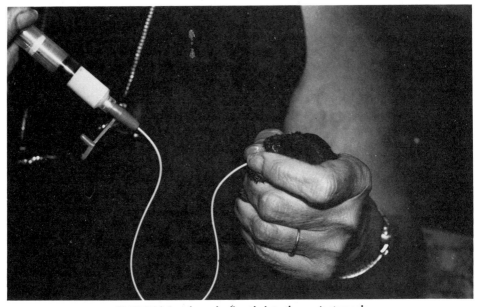

SLOWLY inject formula directly into the pup's stomach

201

system of the neonate is easily upset by overfeeding or using too rich a formula. Actually it is better to underfeed than overfeed. The amount can always be increased but, should you feed too much, the puppy may regurgitate and drown.

You may mix just enough formula for one feeding, using warm tap water, or make it in quantity in a blender and store in the refrigerator. In the latter case it should be warmed to body temperature or lukewarm before it is used.

Place the feeding tube along the puppy's side in a slight arc over the path of the esophagus, from the nose to the bottom of the rib cage. Mark the catheter at the point of the last rib by wrapping a piece of cellophane tape around it. This will be the depth of insertion of the tube into the puppy's stomach. If the puppies in a litter vary considerably in size you may wish to have more than one catheter; otherwise it will be necessary to adjust the depth of insertion according to the individual pup. It is a good idea to recheck the depth of insertion after every few days of feeding.

Attach the syringe to the tube and draw the amount of formula required into it. Filling the syringe after it is attached to the tube eliminates the air that would otherwise be in the tube.

Using the left hand, grasp the puppy's head and neck from the rear and open its mouth with thumb and finger of the left hand. Pressing on the side of the lips will cause the pup to open its mouth far enough to allow you to slip in the tube. Holding the feeding tube in the right hand, guide it gently over the tongue, which is often stuck to the roof of the mouth, and down the esophagus to the marked depth.

While the catheter is being inserted, the puppy's head should be held forward so the tube will be directed into the stomach. Should the pup's head be held back, the catheter could enter the lungs. If the formula is injected into the lungs instead of the stomach, the puppy would drown. If there is any kind of obstruction, the tube should be withdrawn and the process started again until it is certain the tube goes all the way down into the stomach. If the tube is inserted only partially and the end remains in the esophagus, the formula will overflow into the trachea, which leads to the lungs.

This must all sound pretty scary to the novice but, if we understand the anatomy of the puppy's throat and the relationship of the trachea to the esophagus, any anxiety about tube feeding should be dispelled.

For the tube to be inserted into the trachea or windpipe it must pass between the vocal cords, and if it does this the puppy is unable to cry. Pinch the puppy's foot or ear and if it cries you can be certain

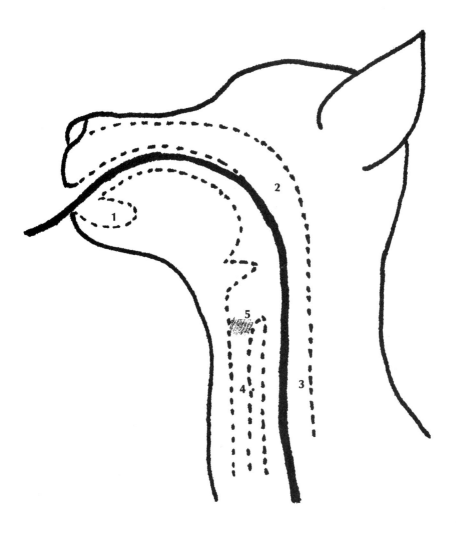

A DIAGRAMMATIC GUIDE FOR TUBE FEEDING

1. Tongue
2. Pharynx
3. Esophagus leading to stomach
4. Trachea leading to lungs
5. Vocal cords

the tube is not in the trachea. If it is inserted all the way to the cellophane marker, you can be certain it is in the stomach and not in the esophagus.

Hold the tube firmly in place so the puppy cannot spit it out and slowly administer the formula over a period of one and a half to two minutes. This gives the stomach ample time to dilate. Regurgitation rarely occurs with this precaution. Should it occur, remove the tube and do not feed again until the next scheduled feeding.

When removing the tube, do it with a quick, upward gesture. This prevents any formula remaining in the tube from entering the trachea.

After feeding, return the puppy to its dam or use moist cotton to stimulate it to urinate and defecate.

Should diarrhea develop, reduce the food intake by one half for one day. Should it continue, consult your veterinarian who might want to prescribe an antibiotic.

Wash equipment with hot soapy water and rinse thoroughly after each feeding. It is not necessary to wash it between puppies unless they are sick. They would all be trading nipples back and forth if they were with the dam. Nor is it necessary to sterilize it after use. There is nothing very sterile about the dam's nipples.

Plan to wean the puppies as soon as possible. They are perfectly capable of lapping from a saucer, with help, as young as ten days or two weeks of age.

How Much Formula to Feed

It is important to know that a newborn puppy stops nursing because of fatigue, not because its stomach is full. It is only after the fourth week that the control of food intake depends on the distention of the stomach.

Consequently in feeding orphan puppies or in supplementing the weakest pups in a large litter, the amount of formula must be determined on the basis of calories (energy) and water, and not on the apparent fullness of the stomach.

The water content required is two to three ounces per pound of body weight per day, while the caloric requirement is sixty to 100 calories per pound of weight per day. The caloric need increases each week until it reaches 100 calories per pound of body weight by the fourth week.

Commercial formulas contain approximately 1 calorie per cc when mixed with water according to manufacturer's directions.

Formula Chart

AMOUNT OF FORMULA (mixed according to directions) TO FEED AT EACH OF THREE FEEDINGS PER DAY*
1 ounce equals approximately 30 grams
1 cc or 1 ml of mixed formula equals approximately 1 calorie

Weight of Puppy	Amount of Formula at Each Feeding
60 grams (about 2 ounces)	4 cc
90 grams	6 cc
120 grams	8 cc
150 grams	10 cc
180 grams	12 cc
210 grams	14 cc
240 grams	16 cc
270 grams	18 cc
300 grams	20 cc
330 grams	22 cc
360 grams	24 cc
390 grams	26 cc
420 grams	28 cc
450 grams	30 cc (about 1 ounce)
480 grams (about 1 pound)	32 cc

*Published courtesy of Kenneth J. Davis, D.V.M.

Orphan Puppies

Sooner or later in a breeder's many experiences, he will be faced with the serious problem of orphan puppies. The dam may have died or is too ill to nurse her babes; she may reject them entirely, have a complete failure of milk supply or, in rare instances, have inverted nipples, making it impossible for the whelps to suckle. There are two options: either a foster mother or the full-time job of hand rearing the puppies.

Foster Mothers

By far the easier of these two alternatives is a foster mother. Care should be taken to settle only for a good-tempered, healthy bitch. The perfect one would be another of the breeder's dams with, perhaps, just one newborn puppy and sufficient milk supply to satisfy the orphans without depriving her own. Next would be another reputable breeder's dam that lost her babes and would welcome your

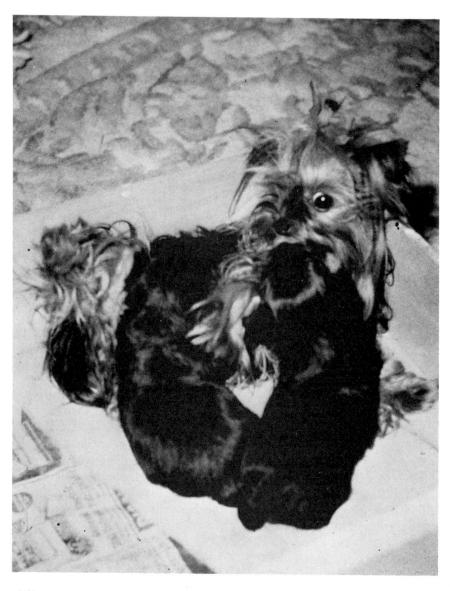

"Skiffles" a three-pound Yorkshire Terrier takes over the mothering of two orphan pups. They were hand-fed, but the petite foster mother kept them clean and warm. She seemed to enjoy her task, probably knowing that she was too small ever to have any of her own.

206

puppies. Kennel clubs and veterinarians are often helpful in finding such foster mothers. Sometimes a cat can be found that will readily adopt orphan puppies. Burmese and Siamese, especially, make excellent foster mothers. Hilary Harmar has a delightful picture of a Persian cat and her three Irish Setter orphan puppies in her book, *Dogs and How to Breed Them*. I have also heard of a rabbit successfully raising orphan puppies.

If you should be lucky enough to find a suitable foster mother, care should be taken in introducing the orphans to her. There are no two situations that are the same. In the majority of cases, maternal instinct takes over in short order, and there is little if any problem after the first few anxious moments of introduction. If the orphans are an addition to an already existing family, a good precaution is to rub the new puppies against the dam's own whelps and encourage them to urinate on the orphans before allowing the dam to approach them. In all cases, it is wise to keep an eye on the nest and the orphan babes for the first 24 hours.

Without such auxiliary aid, hand rearing is the other option.

Hand Rearing Orphan Pups

It's not going to be easy and, often, it is a thankless task. Orphan puppies, which lost their dam before having an opportunity to suckle are deprived of the dam's first protective milk or colostrum. They will be highly susceptible to all kinds of infections. Their environment must be kept scrupulously clean and anything that comes into contact with them, including the breeder's hands, must be well-scrubbed with disinfectant soap. Keep them as isolated as possible until they are old enough to receive their first immunizing injection, and do not permit strangers to handle them.

Warmth is, perhaps, the most essential requirement for orphan puppies if they are to survive. They have no thermal control and must depend entirely on their environment, which should be kept at a constant 85 to 90 degrees for the first week. They should be kept out of drafts in a small warm box or incubator on a soft towel or receiving blanket. A room thermometer should be placed beside them to monitor the temperature. The easiest and most economical way to maintain a constant environment is by placing the puppies directly under the rays of an infra-red lamp. It should be placed far enough above the puppies to create the desired temperature. The whelps will absorb the heat from the lamp, and should not be covered with a blanket.

Humidity should be kept high. Unless you have a thermostatically controlled incubator, spray the inside walls of the whelping box several times each day with warm water or tuck a warm, wet face cloth into one corner of the box. Refresh this several times each day.

The breeder must take the place of the bitch in keeping the environment clean and warm, in stimulating the puppies to urinate and defecate, first to remove the waxy meconium build up in the intestines, then after each feeding, in feeding and protecting them. They must be watched when not sleeping to make sure they do not chew on each other in their instinctive desire to suckle and in so doing harm each other. It may even be necessary to separate them by means of compartments within the box or incubator.

The breeder must decide if he is going to start them right out on tube feeding or can afford the time to bottle feed them. We go along, wholeheartedly, with bottle feeding, if a puppy is strong enough to suckle, in preference to intubation because of the personal attention involved with each puppy at six to eight hour intervals. Leave the tube feeding to the puppy mills. You might just have a winner among your babes! Go all the way and supply the attention, love and fondling they would otherwise be deprived of due to the loss of their dam.

Many more orphan puppies have been successfully hand reared on a commercial formula such as Esbilac than on homemade mixtures and few, if any, could survive on cow's milk unless scientifically fortified with fat and protein. Goat's milk has been successfully used.

Keep newborn orphan puppies on 5% glucose solution for the first 24 hours, then begin to introduce the commercial formula gradually. Make it according to manufacturer's directions, but dilute it 20% with boiled water. Once you know the puppies are going to tolerate the formula, the amount of liquid can be reduced until you are using the correct proportions as specified on the can.

Follow feeding instructions and amounts given under *Bottle and Tube Feeding*. When adding extra nutrients such as egg yolk or ABDEC do so gradually. Young puppies are very susceptible to digestive upsets. Avoid excessive use of honey or sugar.

Weigh and record the weight of the puppies at least once a day for the first week, then at regular intervals. A steady weight gain and a good firm stool are the best evidences that progress is satisfactory.

Nail Trimming

Puppies' nails grow fast and should be kept trimmed every few days throughout lactation so they will not scratch the dam's breasts.

Use small blunt-nosed nail scissors and remove just the white tips. They bleed easily at this tender age if cut too far back. Should bleeding occur cauterize it with a silver nitrate stick or hold a little monsel salt against it until the bleeding stops. Without either of these first aids, talcum powder works less quickly but well.

Removal of Dew Claws and Tail Docking

These minor surgical procedures should be done during the first week of life. We have found, with our breed, that puppies suffer less discomfort when the operation is performed at six days old, and their grip on life is stronger, than at four. So if you have had lengthy complaints from some of your litters, perhaps the puppies are suffering more from shock than from pain.

The dew claws are rudimentary thumbs set just above the other digits. They are generally present on the forelegs and sometimes on the hindlegs as well. If not removed, the nails grow long, curved and very sharp. They catch in fabrics and other materials and can become torn and painful. If not trimmed regularly, dew claw nails can also grow around in a complete circle until the tip penetrates the flesh of the leg. Soon the leg becomes sore and infected.

If you are breeding for show, it is important to check the standard of your breed. While many breed standards specify that dew claws may or should be removed, the standards for the Briard and the Great Pyrenees specify double dew claws on each hind foot.

If tails are docked in your breed, the standard may state the desired length of the docked tail on the adult dog. If your standard is not specific on this point, ask the breeder of your bitch to advise you. There is no practical reason why tails should be cut on the majority of breeds. It is done purely for cosmetic effect. For this reason many breeders prefer to perform the operations themselves. Only they know how important the correct length of tail is to the overall balance of a show dog.

If you depend on your veterinarian to remove dew claws and dock tails, it usually necessitates a trip to his office. The puppies must be kept warm at all times. Some bitches become upset if the babes are taken away from them at such a young age. This means taking the dam along too. Keep her at some distance from the puppies while the surgery is being performed.

When removing dew claws it is important to snip out the entire tiny joint. If the root is not removed the nail can grow again.

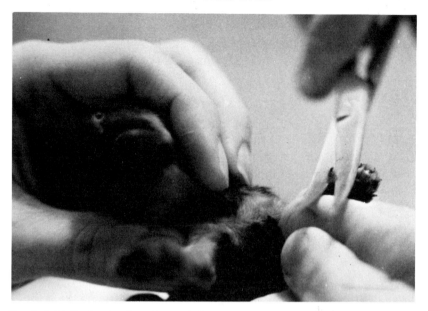

Paw is held firmly, the dew claw and the entire tiny joint is removed in one quick snip. If the root of the nail is not removed the dew claw will grow again.

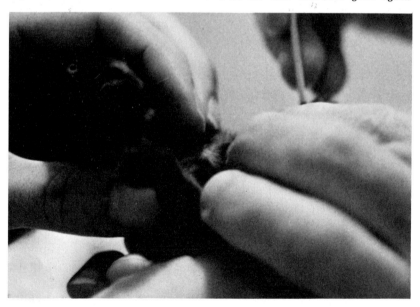

The spot is cauterized with a styptic stick. This seems to cause the pup more discomfort than the snipping out of the claw.

210

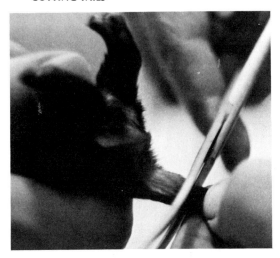

Tail cutting is far less traumatic for pups and causes less anxiety for the dam when they are five or six days old. Prior to this time, most puppies have not taken a firm hold on their fragile thread of life, and the dam is reluctant to let them out of her sight. A Yorkie puppy's tail is cut straight across at the point where the tan meets the black on the underside of the tail.

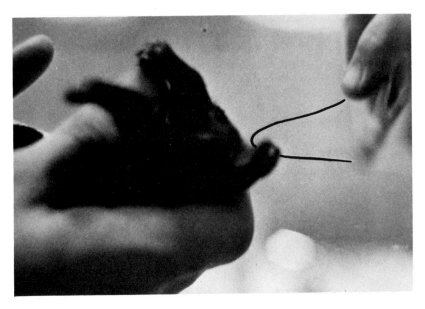

A stitch is taken to pull skin over the bone and prevent excessive bleeding.

211

There are various techniques used for tail cutting. We prefer a straight across cut and one stitch to pull the flesh together over the bone. Some types of stitches must be removed in a week, others are absorbed. Inspect each puppy's tail and the sites of the dew claw removal at least once a day to make sure they are healing properly and there is no infection.

Neonatal Mortality

One percent of neonatal deaths are due to abnormalities resulting from a failure of the embryo to develop properly in the uterus. The cause may be physiological or nutritional.

Many of the more common anomalies are thought to be inherited, caused by recessive genes. The majority of malformed whelps die in utero but should one be born alive it should be allowed to die or should be mercifully destroyed.

The more usual fetal anomalies are:

Chondrodystrophia fetalis

A malformation of the limbs, this disorder is often found in Poodles and some of the Terrier breeds.

Congenital hydrocephalus

Also known as water on the brain. It is a fairly common anomaly in the brachycephalic breeds and many of the Toys. Usually it can be diagnosed at birth by a malformed doming of the head, but becomes more apparent when the puppy is two or three weeks old. An abnormal accumulation of body fluids causes the soft bones of the skull to bulge. The puppy normally dies unless the breeder steps in and interferes for unscrupulous reasons or through ignorance. The puppy should be put down as soon as the abnormality is observed. Closing ones eyes to this lethal fault will not make it go away, and the puppy will eventually die of convulsions, after a great deal of suffering on the part of not only the puppy but the unfortunate person who buys it.

Cleft palate

This is the failure of the tissue of the palate to close at the midline and is a common hereditary cause of puppy death in a majority of breeds. It is generally lethal because the affected puppy is

212

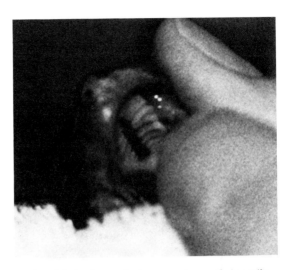

The cleft in the roof of a puppy's mouth is easily diagnosed at birth. Puppy should be "put down."

unable to nurse. Those that are able to suckle usually develop inhalation pneumonia. The roof of the mouth of all puppies should be examined at birth and any showing a cleft should be put down as soon as possible.

Harelip

This is a partial lack of fusion of the lips and is often associated with a cleft palate. In extreme cases the puppy is unable to suckle. If mild and with supplementary feedings by intubation, it is possible to force it to survive. It is much wiser to have the pup destroyed and not allow the dam to waste her resources on nourishing and caring for such a one, unless it is her only pup. In such a case it might be possible to find a home where it would be tolerated as a pet.

Diaphragmatic Hernias

Umbilical hernias occasionally occur while the whelps are still in the uterus, and a puppy can be born with its intestines floating in the amniotic fluid outside the abdominal wall. There is good reason to believe that such in utero hernias are inherited, and any puppies born with this anomaly should be allowed to die. Unfortunately, they are generally exceptionally strong puppies and often need help. A sleeping pill dissolved in a half teaspoon of warm water, administered orally, is a gentle, easy solution.

213

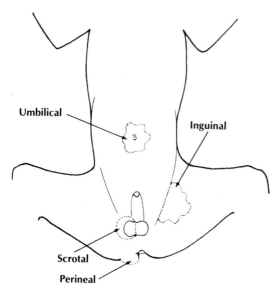

Common types and locations of hernias that can occur in the dog. Reprinted from The International Encyclopedia of Dogs, Copyright © 1974, 1971 by Rainbird Reference Books Limited, by Permission of the publishers Howell Book House Inc.

There are several types of hernias that are seldom fatal and can be repaired when the puppy matures. Inguinal and scrotal hernias are believed to be inherited and due to recessive genes. Umbilical hernias, on the other hand, can be traumatic or inherited. They can be caused by tearing the umbilical cord too close to the body or by overenthusiastic licking on the part of the dam. If there is any question as to the cause of a hernia in a puppy, the puppy should not be considered for future breeding stock.

Non-Inherited Physiological Neonatal Deaths

Alveolar Dysplasia

This is a failure of the lungs to inflate and is a common cause of death in premature puppies. The anomaly is not considered to be inherited.

Primary Atelactasis

Inhalation of fluids at birth is generally lethal depending on the quantity of fluids inhaled. It is generally caused by prolonged and difficult delivery.

Parasitical Neonatal Deaths

Hookworm

Hookworm can cause death in puppies as early as ten to twelve days due to severe anemia. These parasites attach themselves to the intestines by means of a hook at one end and feed on the puppy's blood.

Roundworm

Roundworm larvae, encrusted in the muscles of the dam, become activated during pregnancy and migrate to the uterus and into the digestive tract of the unborn puppies. Infested puppies become lethargic, their resistance to infectious diseases becomes lowered, and their gums become almost white. The best precaution a breeder can take against neonatal deaths from parasites is to make sure the bitch is free from all infestation prior to breeding.

Viral and Bacterial Neonatal Deaths

Fatal infections of newborns are caused by a rapidly increasing variety of viral and bacterial agents. Within the past two years several different types of viral enteritis in dogs have become of major concern to breeders and owners of show puppies. Because of the suddenness with which they strike, they are almost impossible to diagnose and treat and death is almost a certainty in the neonate. The older the puppy and the more quickly the disease is recognized, the more chance there is of recovery.

Herpesvirus

Seemingly healthy puppies that have been nursing vigorously, suddenly become limp, cease to suckle, cry continuously and die within 24 hours. This is generally symptomatic of herpesvirus, an insidious disease which may infect the fetus while still in the uterus, as it makes its way down the birth canal, or soon after birth through the saliva of an infected dam. Entire litters are usually attacked.

Herpesvirus multiply rapidly in a temperature of 95 degrees and the low rectal temperature of the neonate contributes to the development of the disease. It affects almost all organs, but especially the kidney and liver. Pathological changes which distinguish the herpesvirus from bacterial infections are the appearance of speckled kidneys and hemorrhages in various other organs.

The virus is destroyed at elevated temperatures, and treatment includes maintaining an environment of 100 degrees for short periods of time, plenty of fluids and antibiotics.

The preventive measure is in keeping the antibody titer of the bitch high by administering an immunizing booster prior to breeding. Although no vaccine for herpes has been isolated, there is evidence that a high percentage of commercial serum preparations contain the herpesvirus antibody. In adult dogs the virus may cause mild vaginitis in bitches or a nasal discharge in the dog. Only the young puppy suffers fatal infection.

Puppy Septicemia

There are many bacteria associated with the death of young pups. The most common of these are streptococci, E. coli, staphylococci and pseudomonas. If any of the microorganisms enter the bloodstream of a puppy, blood-poisoning or septicemia is the result.

Puppies are born healthy, suckle vigorously for the first 24 hours, then suddenly become weak, cry intermittently and soon die. Sometimes only one or two in a litter will succumb to the infection; other times the entire litter will be affected. Early symptoms are low blood sugar, low body temperature, abdominal bloat and rapid respiration. Usually such puppies are rejected by the dam, and little can be done to save them. Prevention is easier than a cure, and the best safeguards against such bacterial infections are strict sanitary precautions in the whelping area, use of sterilized instruments and surgically clean hands.

Umbilical Infections

The umbilical cord of a newborn is a means of easy access for microorganisms to enter the body. These most likely would be streptococcus or staphlococcus bacteria that are contaminating the whelping area at the time the puppy is born. Once the bacteria take hold in the bloodstream of the puppy, they can attack almost any organ of the body, including the brain, heart or lungs, and death can be early or delayed for as long as a couple of weeks. Precautionary measures should be taken to use sterile hemostats and scissors and to work with sterile hands. A dab of iodine on the cut cord is a good preventive

216

measure, especially if the dam is allowed to sever the cord. The prime source of infection is the dam's mouth. Teeth are an incubator for bacteria of every type and description.

Fading Puppy Syndrome

Most breeders have experienced the fading puppy syndrome. A litter of puppies appears to be completely normal at birth, fat, happy, nursing strongly for the first 24 hours. Shortly after that, one by one, they fall off the nipple, lose all interest in food and begin to fade. Their temperature drops, the dam pushes them into a corner where they cry weakly and incessantly until they die.

Many different theories have been suggested as to the cause of these dreaded symptoms in newborns, but nobody is really sure of the cause. Some feel it is the result of E. coli bacteria but the strongest evidence supports the presence of herpesvirus. Recently a new theory suggests that the administration of antibiotics to the bitch before or after she whelps is a contributing factor. It is believed that the antibiotic is transmitted through the dam's milk to the puppies.

All animals have normal intestinal bacteria; some are bad and some are good. As long as the good ones outnumber the bad, digestive disturbances do not occur. Antibiotics, however, are not discriminating. They kill off the good bacteria along with the harmful ones, leaving the intestines sterile and resulting in diarrhea and bloat.

Some breeders have had a good deal of success administering live *Lactobacillus acidophilus* bacteria to both dam and newborn puppies to restore the natural flora in the system. This is the same bacteria from which buttermilk is made and a similar one produces yogurt. It can do no harm, and perhaps it can help.

Lactobacillus acidophilus is available at drug stores under various trade names. It must be stored in the refrigerator and the expiration date should be observed. If in pill form, the pills should be crushed and added to a small quantity of five percent glucose solution. If in capsules, empty one into the glucose solution. No specific dosage has been determined but as close as I can estimate, from information passed along by a Collie breeder, about half a 300 milligram tablet to each puppy, per ten ounces of body weight, as soon as whelping is over, and the other half 12 hours later is a starting point. As in anything to do with a dog, let common sense be your guide.

This magnificent Standard Poodle is the result of intelligent breeding and thoughtful rearing and management—important factors for any well-adjusted pet or successful show dog.

Burwell

218

8

Puppy Rearing and Socialization

I<small>F A LITTER</small> has safely survived the first three weeks of life, a breeder can breathe a little more easily. The worst is probably over, yet there are many hurdles ahead. There are congenital abnormalities, which may begin to surface during the weaning and socialization periods. There are increasing numbers of deadly viruses and bacteria that attack puppies and may be carried into the kennel by visitors who have been around other dogs, by your veterinarian, or by yourself returning from a dog show.

From weaning time until the puppies receive their first immunization they face a high risk period. The antibodies received from their dam may have worn off and are no longer effective in protecting the puppies from disease. A breeder can do no more than protect puppies as best he can by keeping their environment clean, by keeping them isolated from other dogs and from exposure to visitors.

Weaning the Puppies

This is essentially the process of changing a puppy's diet from its dam's milk to the diet of a growing dog without disturbing its rate of growth or upsetting its digestive system. The transition must be made gradually from liquid to solid foods or diarrhea may result. Close attention should be paid to the puppy's elimination during weaning. If the stool becomes loose, mucousy, or discolored your veterinarian should be consulted. Diarrhea in a young pup can be serious.

In nature the dam regurgitates her own food, which has undergone partial breakdown, and the puppies readily accept this predigested mush. Our domestic dog will usually do the same if left to care for her pups beyond a period where she can cope with them without exhausting her own nutritional supply. But most breeders prefer to supplement them long before such a time beginning as early as three weeks with a milky formula.

When beginning to wean, don't try to feed a puppy when its tummy is full. Try to catch it after the bitch has been away from her babes for awhile or after they awaken from one of their frequent naps.

Put a little warm formula in a shallow saucer. Place each puppy, one at a time, tummy-down on your knee, hold its head steady because it is still pretty wobbly, and put the edge of the dish to the pup's mouth. Usually it will begin to lap immediately. If not, spoon a little of the warm milk into its mouth from a teaspoon much as you would feed a human baby. It's remarkable how fast the pups learn to lap. Repeat this two or three times a day, preferably morning, midday and late afternoon. Put the puppies back with the dam after each feeding, and leave them with her during the night.

If you prefer, you can place the saucer of formula beside the puppies and encourage them to lap by offering it to them from your finger or by wetting their muzzles with the formula. Although it takes longer, I prefer feeding each puppy individually so that I know which of them lap readily and which ones are reluctant. There always seems to be one exceptionally stubborn puppy in each litter but, in a few days, all puppies should be lapping hungrily without your help.

Keep the puppies' toenails cut during the weaning period so they cannot scratch the dam's belly.

From three to six weeks the consistency of the food should be gradually thickened to that of a thick soup or semi-solid with ground lean beef then, little by little, it can be made into a mush by the addition of some finely ground kibble, dog biscuit or cereal. By the time the pups are six weeks old they should be able to digest the same food as adult dogs, only in slightly softer consistency.

During this supplementation period the dam's food should be gradually decreased until she is back to her normal maintenance diet when the puppies are six weeks old.

From five to seven weeks weaning becomes serious and every effort is made to prevent the puppies from nursing although the dam should be allowed to play with them several times a day until they are seven weeks old. Then is the time for them to say good-by to her and hello to people.

At seven weeks the puppies are able to digest adult food. Because of variation in size of breeds and in individuals within a litter, it is difficult to give precise quantities of food which puppies should be eating. They need about 90 calories per pound of body weight per day, but the only way to insure that each puppy is getting its share during the weaning and post weaning periods is by weighing each puppy and recording the weight on a daily basis until they are ten weeks old; every other day from ten to sixteen weeks and finally once a week until they are eight months old or are close to their maximum growth and maintain a fairly constant weight.

Charts of the weight progress of various litters provide breeders with a valuable record of their breed's growth pattern, and can give an indication of the potential size of the adult dog.

During the weaning period, puppies should be fed four meals a day. A good basic formula is half meat (raw or cooked) and half cereal, biscuit, or kibble mixed to a consistency of soft mush with milk or formula plus vitamin and mineral supplements recommended by your veterinarian.

When weaning is complete, puppies need only two meat-cereal meals a day, usually fed morning and evening, with a bowl of milk or formula at noon and before bedtime. Fresh water should be available at all times.

As long as the diet is balanced in essential nutrients and the growing puppy is allowed to eat as much as it wishes twice a day, the exact formula of the food is not important. Meat, chicken, boned fish, cooked eggs, cottage cheese are all nutritious taste-treat additions to a basic diet. Liver is very laxative and should be used cautiously. Milk or formula should be continued until the puppy is six months of age or until it rejects it.

We have found the addition of a baby vitamin, known as ABDEC, available at your local drug store, aids growth, promotes a healthy coat, and helps build bone. It has also been scientifically proved a valuable deterrent to internal parasites. It does not cure a puppy infected with worms but, once the worms are treated by medication, they will not recur if ABDEC is included in the diet. We also include wheat germ, bone meal, brewers' yeast and Pervinal in our basic diet for adult dogs.

Teething

Dogs have two sets of teeth. The first, milk or deciduous, teeth begin to erupt at about three weeks. They have shallow roots and are generally shed at the age of four or five months without assistance from the breeder.

The milk teeth number 28. They are soft and penetrating with sharper points than on the permanent teeth. They are also more widely spaced and often it is difficult to tell if the bite will be correct or not when the dog is grown.

In all breeds except those which should have an undershot jaw, the teeth should meet, the upper incisors slightly overlapping the lower. This is known as a scissors bite. In an even bite, permitted in some breeds, the upper and lower incisors meet edge to edge. In an undershot jaw the lower incisors project beyond the upper. The reverse of this, the overshot, is when the upper incisors project beyond the lower incisors.

If a puppy is definitely undershot or overshot by the time its milk teeth are all in place, chances are it will not reverse, and if one or more incisors is missing between the canines, they will also be missing when the permanent teeth erupt.

There should be six incisors between the canines or "eye" teeth. If there are six baby incisors, there will almost always be six permanent ones. If there are only five there may be six permanents if you are lucky, but if there are only four, the chances for the normal six incisors when the puppy is mature are very slim. If the standard for your breed specifies that the dog must have six incisors between the canines, a lack of one or more can count against it in the show ring. When there are only five and there is no space between them, indicating that a tooth is missing, this minor fault is often overlooked by the judge. And a Toy with a missing tooth should not be penalized. When breeding, however, care should be taken not to breed a dog with five incisors to a bitch that also has a missing incisor. No matter how small a fault, the conscientious breeder will work toward eliminating it from his breeding stock.

Occasionally a borderline mouth that is slightly overshot will correct, and those that are particularly level may remain the same in adulthood or go either way—under or over. A slightly undershot mouth seldom corrects and usually gets progressively worse.

In most breeds the permanent teeth begin to break through from three to four months of age. Toy breeds take a little longer. The upper molars are the first to erupt, the upper incisors appearing a day or two later, followed by the lower molars or incisors. There are 42 or 44 teeth in all permanent dentition. The last ones to break through are usually the canines.

Often cutting permanent teeth can be painful for the puppy and it may refuse food. The mouth should be examined and any temporary teeth remaining in a mouth after the permanent teeth have erupted should be surgically removed. Generally it is the canines that are troublesome, especially in Toy breeds. Whereas other milk teeth are shallow-rooted, the roots of the canines are longer than the teeth themselves, sometimes so long they penetrate the antrum and cause nose bleeding. To avoid traumatizing the puppy, a short acting anesthetic that puts the puppy just beyond the pain level should be administered by your veterinarian.

Immunizations

From the moment a puppy is born it is constantly exposed to a number of common communicable diseases. Fortunately, highly effective immunizing agents or vaccines have been developed to protect dogs, and there is little reason for any to die or become crippled from such diseases as distemper, canine hepatitis, leptospirosis, parainfluenza and rabies.

When a pup is born, the only protection it has from disease is from the antibodies transferred to it through the placental membrane of its dam. Every bitch should be given a DHL booster prior to being bred to assure a high titer (quantitative measurement) of circulating antibodies in her blood serum that she can pass along to her whelps, and every effort should be made to be certain the pups receive the dam's first milk or colostrum within 24 hours of birth. If the dam's titer is high her antibodies will generally protect her puppies for the first six weeks.

After six weeks of age the pup is extremely vulnerable to viruses or airborne bacteria and must be given its first of a series of inoculations. Because of its age and size the puppy is unable to tolerate a full dose of the vaccine and a divided dose is injected. It is therefore necessary to repeat the injection a second and a third time. Each of these three divided injections provides adequate protection for a limited time.

After the first divided inoculation, there is a time lapse before antibodies appear in the blood serum and this time lapse decreases after each subsequent injection as the antibody-producing cells become activated.

After the first divided injection the antibody titer begins to decrease at the end of three to four weeks and the second injection must be given. This time the titer is maintained at a higher level for a longer period than after the first. The third and final inoculation, administered when the puppy is three months old will protect it from distemper, hepatitis, leptospirosis and parainfluenza (kennel cough) for nine months. At that time the puppy should receive its first "booster" inoculation and from then on yearly boosters should be given religiously.

Should a puppy be sold before its immunizations are finished, it is important to provide the buyer with a complete record of inoculations, the type of vaccine used, and the date that further inoculations are due. The buyer should be impressed with the importance of following through with these inoculations at the time they are due, and should be warned to keep the puppy away from other dogs until immunization is completed.

Puppies that receive no colostrum at birth can be protected as early as two weeks of age. Discuss this with your veterinarian.

Rabies

This virus is communicable only through the saliva of an infected animal, and these may be dogs, foxes, wolves, skunks, bats, woodchucks, rabbits and other wild animals. These infected animals are a reservoir of rabies for any warm-blooded animal, including man. City pets or kennel dogs are unlikely to become infected with rabies, since they are seldom, if ever, exposed to a rabid animal.

Puppies may safely be inoculated for rabies as early as three months, but most breeders prefer to wait until six months or a year. If given earlier than six months, the rabies inoculation must be repeated six months later. After that, every three years gives the average dog adequate protection.

Inoculations for rabies should not be given at the same time as a DHL. At least a week should lapse between other inoculations or a "booster" and a rabies shot.

Gastroenteritis

Within the past year many cases of gastroenteritis or inflammation of the stomach and intestines, have proved fatal in puppies.

Both coronavirus and parvovirus attack cells that line the intestinal walls, causing vomiting, bloody diarrhea, and fever. Parvovirus also attacks the bone marrow and lymph nodes and a drop in white blood cells usually accompanies the disease.

It is likely that coronavirus has been around for years, but was not recognized as a major cause of sickness in dogs until an extensive epidemic occurred among show dogs in 1978. Parvoviral enteritis seems to be something new and horrendous. No vaccines have yet been developed to counteract either of them.

The source of both viruses appears to be contact with the feces or saliva of an infected dog, and the show ring seems to be primarily the place where the disease flourishes and spreads rapidly from one dog to another. Exhibitors and spectators take it home on their hands and shoes.

Both parvo and corona are impervious to the majority of detergents and to alcohol. A 30 percent solution of regular household Clorox, however, is effective in destroying parvoviruses.

On returning from a show or after contact with other dogs, it is a good idea to keep a spray bottle of a one to thirty dilution of Clorox near the kennel or house door. Spray both hands and soles of shoes before entering. It is also highly recommended that if there are young puppies in the house, in addition to the spray, a complete change of clothing be made before touching the puppies.

Internal Parasites and Worming

Not all puppies are born with worms, and no puppy or grown dog, for that matter, should be indiscriminately wormed without good reason. Why give it poison? That's what you would be doing!

Dogs can become infested with five different types of worms, and no single drug is effective against all of them. A sample of each puppy's feces should be collected and taken to the veterinarian. After centrifuging the sample for a few minutes, the absence or presence of parasites can be determined by microscopic examination, and the type of parasite identified.

If the worms are allowed to live in a dog's intestinal tract, they rob it of nourishment and sap its vitality, lowering its resistance to disease.

Symptoms of worms may be vomiting or bloody diarrhea, a ravenous appetite without weight gain, stomach bloat or a dull brittle coat. Round worms can generally be seen in the feces.

Some breeds are more susceptible to worms than others. They contract them from the earth where infested dogs have been, from other dogs' feces, or from insect bites.

Scientific tests have proven that worms more readily infest dogs fed a diet deficient in protein and vitamin A. If the worms are destroyed by medication, they will not reoccur if the diet is made highly nutritious and vitamin A is included.

We have never had a worm in a Yorkie puppy. This may be because we give both the dams and the puppies a few drops of ABDEC daily. This is a human baby vitamin, high in vitamin A.

Heartworm

The mosquito is the carrier of the deadly heartworm in dogs, and all dogs, large or small, are potential victims, although those which sleep outdoors during the mosquito season are more apt to become infested.

Heartworms used to be found only in tropical climes, but in recent years it has become a threat to dogs in all parts of America, especially in areas heavily infested with mosquitos. If not destroyed they can completely fill the heart cavity and the heart is then unable to pump blood through the dog's body. Fatigue is the commonest symptom. Unfortunately the effects are so slow to develop that a dog owner may be unaware of any problem until it is already a serious one.

As each puppy matures, it is recommended that dog owners have them tested for heartworm as part of an annual physical examination. It's a simple test that shows the presence of heartworm microfilariae in the blood. If diagnosed at this stage of development it can be easily cured.

Ear Cropping

Cropping dogs' ears originated during the days when certain breeds were used for fighting. To protect them from becoming torn, part of the ear leather was cut away and the remainder encouraged to stand. Today, in America, it is nothing more or less than a style set forth in the standard of perfection for 14 breeds.

In almost all countries except America ear cropping is considered barbaric. It was abolished by the English Kennel Club and in Australia early in this century.

The operation is painful for the puppy, even though the actual cropping is performed under anesthetic. After cutting the ears to the desired size and shape, the edges must be stitched, then taped so they remain erect until healed.

The American Kennel Club is strict in policing the use of any artificial means of enhancing the appearance of a dog in the show ring. It seems incongruous to permit the alteration of the normal appearance of a breed by ear cropping.

If yours is one of the unfortunate breeds which requires its puppies to suffer this tortuous experience, your bitch's breeder is the one to advise you when the operation should be performed, and the name of a veterinarian qualified to cut a stylish ear. Show puppies can be easily ruined in inexperienced hands.

House Training

Even though one is breeding for the show ring, all puppies are not going to live up to exhibition quality. At least some of the pups will go to pet homes as good companions. It is therefore wise to establish good habits at an early age.

Defecating and urinating are automatic reflexes that take place usually after feeding or after a nap. If puppies are put outside first thing in the morning, last thing at night, and immediately after they have eaten, before they have had time to soil their living quarters, they will soon become accustomed to this routine and will be well on their way to being house trained by three months of age.

Congenital Abnormalities

Many abnormalities in dogs cannot be recognized in the neonatal period. The symptoms of affected puppies develop gradually as the puppy approaches maturity. Some may be corrected by surgery but, always, it must be kept in mind that the hereditary condition remains and the animal should not be used for breeding.

Elongated Soft Palate

This is a serious inherited defect affecting Bulldogs, Chow Chows, and other short-nosed breeds. An obstruction in the organs that control breathing causes breathing to be labored during and after exercise. It is particularly aggravated by stress and by hot weather. Due to cramped conditions in the back of the throat, the supply of oxygen to the brain is restricted and affected dogs may suffer brain damage in later life. In extreme cases the dog's tongue will turn blue and the dog will come close to death through suffocation.

Collapsed Trachea

In this congenital condition, found primarily in Toys, the windpipe becomes flat. Like the soft, elongated palate, breathing becomes labored especially in warm weather or if the dog becomes excited. In mild cases the affected dog can lead a nearly normal life but is a poor anesthetic risk.

Dilated Esophagus

A dilated esophagus is seldom diagnosed until weaning time. The affected puppy collects the food in a pouch in the gullet rather than swallowing it and later regurgitates. The condition is generally fatal.

Pyloric Stenosis

Pyloric stenosis is the scientific term for a faulty narrowing of the opening between the stomach and the duodenum which causes the projectile vomiting of food, in a completely undigested state, several hours after it is eaten. The condition cannot be corrected by surgery but can be tolerated by feeding the affected dog small meals several times a day, and avoiding any kind of stress. The animal should not be used for breeding.

Entropion

This condition is prevalent in breeds with small, deep-set eyes such as the Shih Tzu. One or both eyelids are inverted so that the eyelashes constantly brush the cornea causing an accute irritation of the tissue of the eye. Unless corrected by surgery, the irritation will lead to conjunctivitis and eventual blindness. Entropion may be caused by accident, but is generally considered to be an inherited condition.

Congenital Deafness

Deafness should be suspect in puppies when they are four weeks old. If a metal pan is struck by a metal spoon or a whistle is blown, every head in a litter will go up alertly except those of deaf puppies. Deafness is a seriously inhibiting condition caused by recessive genes and affected puppies should be destroyed. Deaf puppies may be anticipated in any litter from parents that have produced deafness in other puppies either when bred together or to another partner.

Progressive Retinal Atrophy (PRA)

This is another hereditary condition caused by recessive genes but, unlike congenital deafness which can be diagnosed when the pups are still young, congenital retinal atrophy is exactly what it says—progressive. Experts in PRA can recognize the condition when a puppy is about eight weeks old at which stage the vision is only slightly impaired. Gradually, however, the condition develops into total and permanent blindness.

Canine Hip Dysplasia (CHD)

Malformation of the hip joints was recognized in man as early as 370 B.C. About fifty years ago, when it was first diagnosed in dogs, the dog world came close to panic. Many dogs were declared dysplastic because of a laxity of the joints due to lack of tissue and muscle, and were discarded from breeding programs. But after a study conducted in Sweden on 11,000 German Shepherds proved that ten years of selective breeding failed to reduce the number of affected offspring or reduce the severity of the condition from extreme to moderate, hip dysplasia was put into its proper prospective.

Today the condition is known to be polygenetic in character. It encompasses not only faulty growth of the hip joint itself but of all the surrounding tissues. The dog may develop the condition in different degrees, and the rate of bone maturation plays a greater role in its development than inherited genes.

In extreme cases the round head of the femur (the large upper bone of the thigh) flattens and slips out of the deep rounded socket, the acetabulum, into which it normally fits closely and to which it is attached by a strong ligament.

Affected dogs can live long and near-normal lives with only minimum discomfort. Under no circumstances should surgery be used in an attempt to correct the situation. More often than not, surgery creates a dislocated hip rather than corrects the condition.

Breeders on the lookout for CHD should be able to recognize symptoms during the period of rapid growth or at about five months. Affected puppies will exhibit discomfort in the region of the hips in various ways. They may have difficulty navigating on slippery floors and may be disinclined to jump or roughhouse with other puppies.

Subluxed Patellas or Knee Caps

Subluxed patellas, more commonly referred to as slipped stifles, like all inherited factors will continue to cripple a breed as long as breeders continue to mate affected animals.

However, a breeder must be able to recognize the difference between a subluxed patella that is a congenital abnormality and those caused by an injury to the leg muscles and tendons which hold the patellas or knee caps securely in the grooves of the stifles.

229

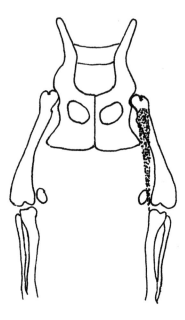

Figure 1. Thigh bones are bowed outward. Tibias bowed inward. Because of these bowed legs, the thigh muscles pull the kneecap or patella to the inside of the leg.

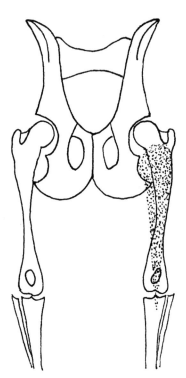

Figure 2. Normal legs with straight alignment of thigh muscles. They pull over the stifle joint, attach to the patella and then to the tibial crest. The patella is held firmly in place in the central groove over the center of the knee or stifle.

In normally developed legs (Fig. 2), the bones of the femur or upper leg bone, and the tibia, lower leg bone, are straight. The thigh muscles are aligned with the bones and run from the hip joints in a straight line, very much like the strings of a violin, over the knee joint, attach to the patella or knee cap, then attach to the tibial crest.

The only way that a dog with straight legs and good muscle can have a slipped stifle is from a trauma or injury in which the muscles and tissues holding the knee caps in place are accidentally torn or weakened. Many bad stifles are caused by allowing young dogs too much freedom to jump or play on slippery floors. Such stifles are not inherited.

To be inherited the thigh bones must bow outward (Fig. 1). There is no way that the taut muscles of the leg can follow the curve of a bone. Instead it pulls to the inside of the legs and the patellas are luxated or slipped to the inside of the legs from their correct position. It is the bowed legs that are inherited and cause subluxation of the patellas rather than the subluxed patella that is inherited.

When a dog with straight legs runs, the action of the muscles is free and they pull in a straight line over the center of the knee caps, but when the legs are bowed and the dog runs, the knee caps are pulled to the inside of the legs. In so doing, the supporting tissues around the patellas are weakened and become torn so that the patellas are free to slip in and out anytime there is the least amount of angular pull.

It is not necessary to exert an angular stress on a dog's back legs to determine if it has a slipped stifle. Every time a judge does this to a dog in the show ring he causes more extensive injury to the muscles and tendons and further cripples the dog. It makes no difference whether the subluxation was a direct result of inherited genes or caused by trauma. If the upper thigh bones are straight, the knee caps are logically in correct position. If the eyes of a judge cannot determine if the thigh bones are straight, his hands should be able to and if his hands can't, he shouldn't be allowed in the show ring.

Legg-Perthes

Legg-Perthes disease is another malformation of the leg bones which affects growing puppies and may be genetic, but more likely is caused by infection or trauma.

It is common in breeds weighing twenty pounds or less such as Manchester Terriers, Fox Terriers, Miniature and Toy Poodles, Pugs, Miniature Schnauzers, Yorkies, Silkies and Pekingese. It has also been reported in Cocker Spaniels and in Shetland Sheepdogs. The incidence is higher among puppies born by Caesarean section or by a traumatic birth than among those born freely.

At birth or shortly thereafter, the blood supply to the femoral head is cut off. The femoral head gradually undergoes necrosis or dies. When the puppy is six to seven months of age the diseased socket reaches a decalcification stage. It becomes abnormally soft and is easily crushed or flattened by the dog's body weight. The leg is pushed farther up into the socket and as a result appears to be abnormally short.

Legg-Perthes is characterized by the sudden onset of lameness without apparent cause, and some degree of lameness and resulting muscle atrophy usually persists for the remainder of the dog's life. In only about one-fourth of the cases do the dogs recover completely. In most of these the dog's movements are restricted and the animal confined for from three to six months to prevent pressure from being exerted on the affected joint.

During these months the bone recalcifies, although it will never again regain its original shape and is easily recognizable through X-rays.

The administration of anti-inflammatory drugs relieves the pain but encourages the use of the affected leg and increases the danger of the destruction and deformity of the femoral head which causes permanent lameness.

If the dog's hip joint could be completely immobilized as soon as it begins to favor the leg, it would regain complete use of it again.

Occasionally Legg-Perthes is bilateral and the dog may reach maturity without displaying any lameness at all. In such cases both legs become equally shortened during the decalcification stage. The only tip-off a breeder would have is a marked reduction in the range of motion of the back legs. Suspicion may be confirmed through X-ray.

Socialization

Breeding today is a science, not the hit-or-miss approach used by puppy mills, backyard breeders, and by the majority of well-meaning novice breeders, who become overnight authorities and prattle on about the excellence of their first litter with little or no experience or knowledge to back up their superlative evaluations.

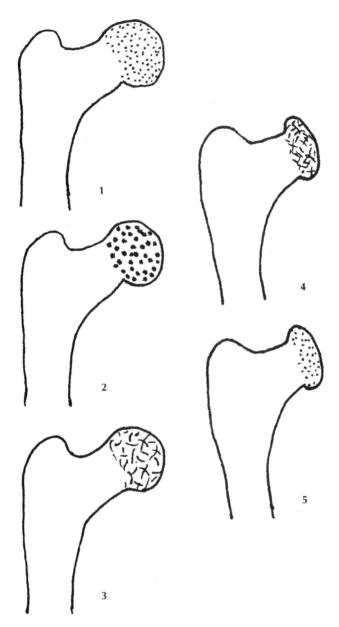

Legg-Perthes is a degenerative disease of the femoral head in certain small breeds (proportional miniatures). Diagram 1 shows a normal femoral head. Diagrams 2 and 3 show the gradual death (necrosis) of the femoral head due to an interruption in the blood supply. Diagram 4 shows the decalcification of the dead bone and Diagram 5 shows the flattening of the joint which causes lameness.

To hundreds of breeders in all parts of the world, producing high quality dogs is an all-engrossing, time-consuming, fascinating avocation. Seldom a day goes by that new information on rearing and socializing puppies, on structure and gait, on nutrition and genetics is not brought to their attention through articles in the *American Kennel Gazette, Gaines Progress, Kennel Review* and various other newsletters and bulletins. Every valuable bit of new information is carefully added to the overwhelming accumulation of facts and figures the veteran breeder has already absorbed and put into practice over the years.

These breeders know that a puppy is born with certain characteristics and traits. These are inherited but may never reach their full potential unless cultivated by environment and training during the early weeks of the pup's life. The goal of socialization is to see that each puppy matures with confidence and without fear.

The Critical Periods

Behavioral scientists such as Drs. Scott and Fuller, followed by Clarence Pfaffenberger and Dr. Michael Fox, and most recently by Joachim and Wendy Volhard determined critical periods in a puppy's life and proved that early environment and socialization make lasting impressions on the puppy. These critical periods begin at birth and extend to 16 weeks of age, with a peak between six and eight weeks.

Any trauma occurring during the second and/or fifth critical period(s) will have a permanent effect on the dog and, although the effect may be modified through training, the dog will never be as well-adjusted to people, new experiences, or to its characteristic work in life as it would have been if the traumatic experience had never occurred.

The First Stage (Birth to 3 weeks)

This is the neonatal period, discussed in chapter 7, when puppies need warmth, food, and lots of sleep in close proximity to their dam. Neurologically the puppies are not developed and are essentially unable to learn. They respond, however, to gentle stroking and caressing. The tactile stimulation is the beginning of a dog interacting with man. If quiet music is played in the room with dam and pups, it will provide auditory stimulation when they are ready to receive it. Their ears start to open about the tenth day and the breeder should talk softly to the pups so that voice stimulation becomes a part of the environment. When their eyes open, between ten and fourteen days, the pups will begin to receive additional sensory input by their interaction with different shapes, textures and other stimuli that encourages them to early environmental responses to variation.

The Second Stage (3 to 5 weeks)

At three weeks of age the puppies begin to take a few wobbly steps. In another couple of days they will start to play with their siblings and dam. By four weeks they should start to growl and bark. It is a period of very rapid sensory development. Suddenly the brain is receiving messages, and the puppies can see, hear, and have the ability to learn. At the same time they are vulnerable, and care should be taken to handle them gently and to avoid trauma of any kind.

Supplementation of the puppies to relieve the dam may begin, especially if the litter is large, BUT THEY SHOULD NOT BE WEANED. It is vitally important that they remain with their dam during this extremely critical stage.

As the puppies begin to play and become more active they need more space to move around than they had in the whelping box. The dam needs an avenue of escape more often than during the first three weeks of caring for her litter. However, they should remain in familiar surroundings and still be protected from extreme changes in temperature and from drafts.

A fine screened or fiberglass-sided play pen makes an ideal environment for growing, learning puppies. The bottom should be raised off the floor to protect them from floor drafts, and the sides should be high enough to prevent them from jumping out. A washable indoor-outdoor carpet should be placed at one end to give them firm footing with a snuggly blanket for a nest. Spread layers of newspapers at the other end. Puppies are instinctively clean animals and dislike soiling their bed. They learn quickly to wobble out to the newspaper to relieve themselves. This is the beginning of their house training.

During this period the puppies should be individually fondled and introduced to various auditory stimulation, such as bells, vacuum cleaners, unfamiliar voices and so on. The intensity levels should be kept low in the beginning and gradually increased.

The Third Stage (5 to 7 weeks)

This is the time to get serious about weaning, but the puppies should be returned to their dam after each feeding and they should all remain together as a family during the night. Puppies need their dam and littermates during these two weeks. The influence of the dam aids

At six weeks of age puppies respond readily to the visual stimulus of a new object such as a stuffed toy. By seven weeks they have the mental, but not the emotional capacity of an adult dog.

By living and playing together from seven to ten weeks, puppies develop a secure canine relationship. If taken away from playmates during this time a puppy will find it difficult to form attachments to other dogs later in life.

Puppies should have frequent but short play periods.

in the development of sibling behavior. This does not mean she is constantly confined with them. She sees them for short periods of time, allows them to try to nurse her breasts, almost depleted of milk, plays with them and disciplines them. It has been proved that puppies removed from dam and siblings during this period may be unable to socialize with other dogs, and are the ones most likely to become fighters later in life.

Short periods of individual training may be started, and contact with humans is important. This is the period when puppies are gradually encouraged to transfer their dependency and affection from their dam to people, while still in association with the dam and litter mates. It is the period when the "stage is set" for each pup to become an ideal companion dog later in life.

Hand contact with pups must be gentle, never rough or corrective. Should a pup be accidentally stepped on or carelessly dropped or hurt accidentally in any way, it should be picked up, reassured, told GOOD PUPPY and put down immediately. Every pup has to get some bumps growing up, just like children, but a breeder's calm approach to a minor accident, can reverse an unfortunate, harmful stimulation to one of trust and affection for humans. Puppies handled with love and care will not shy from people or from a judge as he approaches them for examination. They will trust man.

By six weeks of age puppies should run eagerly to children and strangers. If they don't, a problem may already exist and it will take time and lots of work on the part of the breeder to raise such puppies to be outgoing individuals.

The puppy's ability to move with agility should be encouraged at this time by teaching it to go up and down a step, chase a rolling toy or ball. Lead training may be started, but a puppy should never be pulled or jerked on lead.

Introduce them to the great outdoors as soon as practical. Here they will experience different tactile surfaces such as snow, grass, gravel, concrete. Let them smell the flowers, rub noses with a friendly cat, listen, perhaps, to children playing, cars roaring by and trucks back-firing. Such environmental changes should all be a part of puppyhood.

The Fourth Stage (7th week or from 49 to 56 days)

By this time the puppies should be fully weaned. Their brains are neurologically complete. Their bodies, obviously, are young and they cannot be expected to perform the same tasks or exercises at this point that older dogs can accomplish easily.

The puppies should live and play with their siblings or other puppies of comparable age but, at the same time, they should be introduced to an entirely different environment from where they were born and lived securely with their dam. The time has come for puppies to transfer their affections and dependence from their dam to people. They should be moved to another area of the house, among new sounds, smells, and new faces. Here the puppies face a multitude of new experiences as they play and romp and sleep.

A small room adjacent to the kitchen, a playroom or sun porch are ideal for a bunch of exuberant puppies to learn that life is more than a warm nest and a doting dam. Set up a play pen in one corner where they can be confined and let them out for short play periods when you have time to watch them. Puppies running free around a room can defy imagination! There is no end to the mischief they can get into.

Take stock of the playroom or area where the puppies will play and remove as many hazards as possible. Puppies are curious. Like children, anything that attracts their attention will go into their mouths. Such items as safety pins, straight pins, rubber bands, or buttons can cost a puppy a great deal of grief, if not its life. Puppies are also naturally destructive at this stage of growing up. So make sure that breakable dishes, ashtrays, cigarette packages and lighters are out of reach. Electric and telephone cords are equally intriguing. If punctured by a puppy's sharp teeth they can give it a nasty shock, often of sufficient intensity to traumatize it forever.

The floor of the play area should be covered with indoor-outdoor carpeting or should have a non-skid surface. Like the human child, whose clavicle is the first bone to ossify, the cartilage holding the bones together in a dog gradually hardens and forms connecting joints. Until about nine months of age, when bone formation is complete, avoid the pitfalls of slippery hardwood, linoleum or tile floors. Many a show puppy has been ruined by a torn leg muscle or tendon, dislocated hips, knees or shoulders.

Brief excursions into all parts of the home will accustom the puppies to novelty and will provide additional visual, auditory, tactile and olfactory stimulation. Work with each puppy individually. Carry it around the room in your arms. Let it look out the window at rain, snow or sunshine. Let it look at itself in the mirror, listen to the ticking of the clock, see and smell what's cooking on the stove, and inspect various objects on tables and mantlepiece, normally outside its line of vision.

Everything is a new experience for a young puppy.

Puppies are taught to heel by following their caretaker who clucks like a mother hen to coax them along a carpeted pathway. If an obstacle is put in its path it is interesting to observe the puppy's reaction to it.

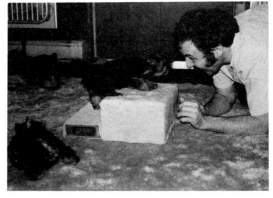

Giving the puppy a simple problem to solve encourages locomotive agility.

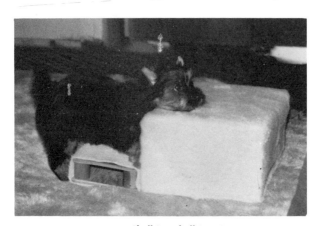

Shall I or shall I not?

Learning to retrieve is a real fun game.

Short, individual training periods should be given to each puppy to teach it to pose on table and to walk on lead.

240

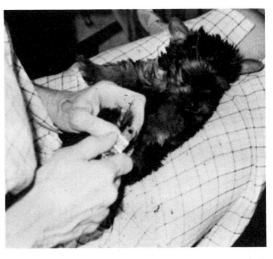

Before the eighth week (flight or fear imprinting period) each puppy should be introduced to its first bath routine and to the initial grooming and trimming characteristic of its breed. Toenail trimming is one aspect of grooming that every puppy must learn to tolerate.

Puppies should never be pulled or jerked on a lead.

Weather permitting, puppies should be introduced to the great outdoors as young as six weeks, and allowed to smell a rose, rub noses with a friendly cat, feel sidewalk grass or gravel under foot.

242

A screened or glassed in playpen makes an ideal environment for growing, learning puppies. The bottom should be raised off the floor to protect them from floor drafts, and the sides should be high enough to prevent them from jumping out. Casters on legs allow the playpen to be easily rolled from one location to another.

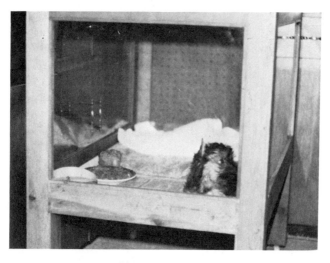

The period of segregation is a time of literally and figuratively "cutting teeth." Each puppy has its own blanket, toy, water, and food. It is not isolated because it is surrounded by other puppies and older dogs, and has visual contact with them. Generally, puppies enjoy this critical period and develop into well adjusted adults. It is the time they discover they are dogs.

The breeder must be able to devote a great deal of time to his puppies at this time, even if just for five minutes per puppy each day. Without daily contact with humans during this critical week, a pup's attitude to people can be drastically affected.

Each puppy needs individual play-training. Playing on lead, standing on a table and posing on the floor are all valuable experiences. Now is the time to begin to teach a puppy its name and simple commands such as NO, COME, STAND, STAY, FETCH, HEEL and GOOD. All this is done in the spirit of fun.

Teach the puppies to go in and out a door. Introduce them to the car and take them for a ride each day, short at first, then gradually increasing the distance. Take them to busy shopping centers, through traffic and encourage strangers to talk to them and touch them. When traveling in a car each puppy should be confined to its crate for security reasons.

Under supervision, allow a child to sit on the floor, hold a pup in his lap, and play with it.

Each pup should be introduced to its first bath routine and to the initial grooming and trimming characteristic of its breed. The trainer should handle the puppy around its muzzle, pretend to clean its teeth, fondle its ears, turn it over on its back on his knee and trim its toenails. Should the puppy struggle, it should be held down firmly by its chest and praised lavishly when it settles down.

The Fifth Stage (8 to 10 weeks)

This is the critical stage in a puppy's development known as the flight or fear imprinting period. Great care should be taken that nothing traumatic happens to the puppy during these critical weeks. No routine immunization injections should be given, no ears should be cropped, and no punishment or severe correction of any kind should be administered. If your puppies come through this period safely with love and affection from their human companions, they will respond with trust and affection.

Play training should continue to be a happy game until the pups are eleven or twelve weeks old. At that time they will be on the threshold of a satisfactory behavior level, without having been deprived of the joys of puppyhood.

The Sixth Stage (10 to 16 weeks)

Sometime during this period play-fighting among the puppies becomes a little too serious as one puppy in a litter will decide it is going to be "boss."

If puppies are left together, one will exercise its dominance at the expense of the personality of the others, and the firm relationship with humans that was beginning to take shape during the previous weeks will cease to develop. The puppies will begin to relate only to other dogs, taking their leadership from them rather than from their breeder or owner.

Each puppy should be separated or segregated in its own individual pen or run. It should be given its own blanket, toy, water and food. It is not isolated, because it is surrounded by other puppies and older dogs and has visual contact with them. It is a period for each puppy to develop its independence and self-confidence, and to form a strong association with man. It is literally and figuratively a time of cutting its teeth.

If not segregated and allowed to remain with its litter mates or other young puppies during these crucial weeks, it would be deprived of the dignity of becoming an individual dog. It could turn into either a bully or a cringer. It would seriously limit its ability to learn to adapt to various situations and changes in environment, and would make poor material for later training as either a well-adjusted house pet, an obedience dog or a show winner.

Peter Vollmer summed up puppy behavior development in an article in the Fall, 1978, issue of *Gaines' Progress* as follows:

> By providing your puppies with these early experiences you are, in a sense, challenging them to develop toward their genotypical potential. Cubs whelped and reared in the wild are customarily exposed to a demanding, challenging environment. Man, in domesticating canines, has inadvertently removed much of the stimulation that now appears vital for maximum psycho-physical development.

9

Evaluating Puppies and Young Adults

E VERY BREEDER is faced with the problem of selecting the best puppies in a litter to keep for future showing and breeding. For most breeders it is necessary to make this selection while the pups are still young and cuddly enough to be appealing to pet buyers.

To Sell or to Keep?

Usually space limitations and the daily mounting costs incurred by labor, food and care of the litter make it impossible for the average breeder to keep all puppies until they are six to nine months of age. At this age it is fairly easy to make the right decisions, but not as easy to find good homes for the ones that fall by the wayside.

But long before this, as soon as the puppies have their legs under them and are beginning to romp and play, the eyes and hands of the show-breeder are beginning to evaluate the puppies.

Many years ago a breeder-judge told me an amusing story. She had been waiting for a puppy from a particular kennel for some time. One evening her phone rang and the voice at the other end said, "We finally have your show dog for you!" "Great," replied the judge. "When can I come to get it? "Oh," replied the breeder, "it was just born."

Don't let anyone tell you he can pick the best puppy or even a good show prospect before it is at least ten to 12 weeks old. Even then it is a calculated guess at best. The smallest may turn out to be the largest, even outsize for its breed; that pretty head may develop too long a muzzle, the jaw may go either overshot or under, and that gorgeous male, so perfectly colored, so beautifully structured may fail to let down both testicles.

Culling a Litter

The first culling, of course, should have been made at birth. The responsible breeder will raise only those puppies that are correct in color and normal in conformation. Any malformed or mismarked puppies or weaklings should be put to sleep.

The second culling should be done at around twelve weeks. Many faults begin to appear during the weaning and socializing periods, so that by the time a puppy is three months of age, the experienced breeder will be able to say, "Let that one go to a pet home," or in the case of the manifestation of a crippling, congenital abnormality, "This one must be put down."

Twelve to 13 weeks is a perfect time for a puppy to go to a new environment, providing there are no young children. It is the critical period in a puppy's life when it should be separated from its litter mates so it can develop its own individual personality.

A breeder will generally want to hold on to borderline puppies in the hope that some small fault may correct and from three to seven months potential show puppies should be watched very closely. Heads go through several stages of development, shoulder placement and toplines can change, fronts can straighten, rears can tighten. The brisket will begin to develop, muscles will harden, so that by the time a puppy is six or seven months of age—depending on its breed—personality, conformation, temperament, soundness, teeth, testicles and movement are fairly well established. A breeder will then be safe in making the last culling or in selling that promised show puppy to someone who will do well by it, and not waste its potential through lack of experience or knowledge.

Kennel Blindness

The most serious fault that can creep into a kennel, and it does so insidiously, is something called myopia or "kennel blindness." The dictionary defines it as "lack of insight or discernment." It is a condition all too common among the breeders of purebred dogs, in which the breeder sees all dogs belonging to his competition as poor specimens and only those owned or bred by himself as exquisitely representing the standard of perfection.

Such a breeder is incapable of recognizing the shortcomings in his own dogs, refusing to admit to the slightest fault and belittling all others. He twists and distorts the standard to fit the type of dog which he happens to be breeding at the time, regardless of its quality.

Don't let this happen to you! Take a good hard look at your breeding stock and your puppies. Evaluate them objectively. Read and reread the standard. Many different types of the same breed can fit into its confines, but the overall quality, soundness and showmanship must be there. There is no such thing as the "perfect dog." You don't have it and neither do I, so every breeder should be striving constantly to improve and make his best even better.

The Importance of Keeping Records

There is a staggering amount of book work connected with breeding dogs. Accurate and detailed records of every whelping, of every puppy bred, sold, bought or shown are essential. The information must be kept up to date and in such a manner that it is readily available when needed.

You need a pedigree book in which five-generation pedigrees of each litter you have raised, of each of the dams and stud dogs responsible for producing these puppies, are kept. This is not only for your own use but for visitors, prospective buyers, and other interested people to use for reference. If possible a picture of each of the individuals should accompany each pedigree. If kept in a large ring binder, the pedigrees may be filed either alphabetically or by date.

You need a breeding book in which details of each whelping are recorded: names of dams and sires, date of mating, date due, actual whelping date, when whelping began and ended, any problems occurring throughout the whelping, and the final results—number of puppies and their sex, any defective puppies or those dead on arrival.

You need a card file or small drawer-type filing cabinet with a card for each individual puppy, filed alphabetically and cross indexed under the name of a new owner, if any. On each card should be the full name of the dog, its litter registration, names and registration

LITTER INFORMATION

Breeder's Litter No.   AKC Litter Registration No:

Name of Bitch: Dates bred:

Sire: Due:

Dam: Whelping date:

What type of breeding was it?

Age of Dam: Weight of Dam: Age of Sire: Weight of Sire:

What litter is this for the dam?   1st   2nd   3rd   4th   5th

How did she whelp: Free?   Assisted?   Caesarean?

No. of males?   No. of females?   No. & Sex of any DOA.

Neonatal deaths: Before 3 days?   Before 2 weeks?   Before Weaning?
(give sex)

Any abnormalities or defects in the puppies?
(give sex)

Any reproductive problems such as eclampsia, inertia, dystocia, retained placenta, metritis or other?

Details of whelping, time puppies born, etc.

Name of Puppy:	Sex:
	Date of birth:
	Litter Reg. No:
Sire:	AKC Individual Reg. No:
Dam:	
	Price:
Date sold:	
	Address:
To:	
Telephone No.	
Conditions of sale, if any:	

numbers of the dam and sire, date of birth, date sold, price paid, name, address and telephone number of the buyer, any conditions of the sale, color, any identifying marks and its "call" name. When someone phones to say she bought "Dolly" three years ago and wants you to know how much fun she is, you can quickly find the card under the name of the caller and carry on a little more intelligent conversation than if groping around for the registered name of the puppy.

Each breeder can develop his own particular system of recording important information for future reference and study.

Ideally puppies should be watched closely, both at ease and at play, every day as they grow, and a detailed record should be kept of their development. It is a wealth of material, so easily forgotten, which can be used as reference when the puppy is adult. By comparing the adult dog with the puppy record, litter after litter, the breeder will become more adept at selecting his show puppies at an early age.

Once a week works out for some people to trim each puppy's nails, weigh it, stack it, observe it critically and make some notes. You will want to include an overall impression of the puppy, its condition, balance, bone and substance. Check its bite, testicles, eye color, ear set, pigmentation, body color and measurements, size of markings, coat texture, tail set and carriage, length of neck, layback of shoulder, straightness of legs and angulation of hock and stifle. You will want to observe the puppy as it moves on lead. Some are

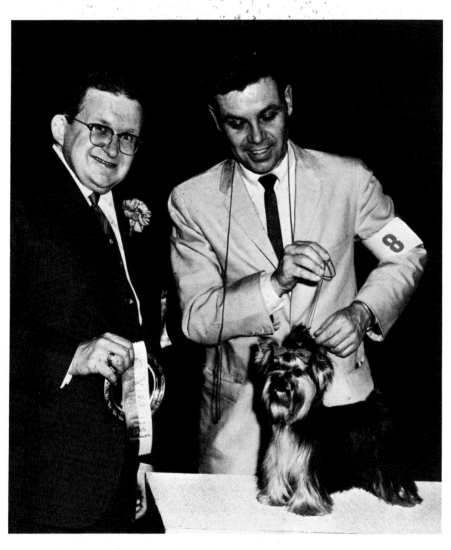

Dog enthusiasts speak with great admiration about the "natural show dog." Such a one was Ch. Danby's Belziehill Panque, shown here being awarded Best of Winners at the National Capitol KC under judge Anthony Brueneman, handler Wendell Sammet. Bred by Mildred Hornbrook and owned by the author and her partner, Barbara Wolferman, this talented Yorkshire Terrier completed her championship requirements at the tender age of nine months, with a commendable record of excellent wins. *Gilbert*

"naturals" and seem to have the essential show spirit built right in. They will start showing off, walking, head up, on lead from the first play-training session. Others will take patience and perseverance in order to develop this sparkle.

There are no shortcuts to time and patience to bring out and develop the maximum potential of each puppy. Unless a breeder is in the enviable position of affording a knowledgeable staff of skilled assistants, he should breed no more litters per year than he can give enough time to train, socialize and observe.

For large litters where the difference in size, sex, or color are not sufficient to enable a breeder to readily identify individual puppies, Peggy Adamson, one of our foremost breeders of Dobermans, recommended an excellent idea in an article she wrote for *Dog World* in 1974. With her permission I am quoting her:

> When picking a stud puppy, or helping someone else evaluate a litter, much time must be lost initially by having to study each puppy individually in order to tell which is which while watching the whole litter. This is especially true in well-bred litters where the appearance is quite uniform. The less good the litter, the easier it is to identify the individual puppies quickly.
>
> To take care of this identification problem, the ideal solution is ribbons. A litter of puppies, each with a fresh, different-colored ribbon around its neck, is a delight to the eye. The ribbon can be bought at the local variety store and costs very little. It should be quite narrow and in as many colors as there are puppies.
>
> Starting at four or five weeks, each puppy should have its own color and stay with it. For this reason, two or three yards of each shade should be bought, since it will have to be replaced about once a week as the puppy grows in size and the ribbons need refreshing. Each puppy's ribbon collar should fit loosely on its neck and should be tied in just a knot with the ends clipped short. If there are no bows or dangling ends, puppies will not show the same interest in chewing ribbon as they do with leather. In the period from four to ten weeks, during which puppies usually do not yet have names, such designations in one's records as "Red Collar," etc. will make it easy to note the weights and individual characteristics as they develop.
>
> Without the ribbon, in a uniform litter, one cannot be sure that it is the same puppy which constantly catches the eye or is always the one doing interesting things, unless the puppy is picked up and examined each time. The ribbons solve this problem, serving much the same function as the handlers' armbands in the judging ring.

Another record book which I find absolutely indispensable in planning future breedings is a four-ring looseleaf binder large enough to accommodate 8½ × 11 inch pages. These are cut in half horizontally. On the upper half is written the name of the stud dog, registration number, date of birth, and show record. If the dog is still being actively campaigned, the show record is noted in pencil so it can be erased as new wins accumulate. If the dog's show career is over, it is permanently recorded in ink. Below this is a four-generation pedigree. Usually I use just the call names of the ancestors, but put CH. in front of those that were champions. On the back of this half page are recorded the names of the puppies the dog sired, date born and dam of the litter.

On the lower half of the cut pages, the bitches are recorded in the same way. When planning the next breeding for a bitch, it is so simple to keep the bitch's page on the bottom, flip over the possible stud dogs, and see at a glance where future quality and prepotency lie.

Herein is one type of behavior report, CHART A, which different breeders can adapt, if desired, to suit their particular breed. It starts at weaning time and takes each puppy through its first four months of life.

At three weeks BEhavior is noted simply as normal or abnormal. As the puppy develops, its behavior is recorded according to the code at the bottom of the chart, that is A for aggressive and so on. INtelligence and SPirit are rated from one to ten. At four months puppies are sorted into show, brood, or pet categories, and are rated on SPirit on lead, movement, conformation, color and texture of coat from one to ten.

At three months, when the puppies usually have names, a quality evaluation is also made. Each puppy has its own chart as illustrated in CHART B and is rated on structure, personality, and show potential. It follows through to maturity those puppies kept for future show or breeding. If and when a puppy is sold to a pet home, the reason for disposing of it is noted at the bottom of the chart.

Following Chart B is a sample whelping record, which provides invaluable information when combined with Charts A and B.

A Breeder's Responsibilities

Every time a litter is born, the breeder has a responsibility to the small lives he caused to come into this world. Any puppy he decides to sell is entitled to a home where it will be cared for, loved and have the opportunity to live a long, rich life.

CHART A. BEHAVIOR REPORT

LITTER: _____ WHELPED: _____

SIRE: _____

DAM: _____

NAMES	Sex	Ears up at:	3 wks.		6 wks.				8 to 10 wks.				3 mos.			4 mos.				
			Wt.	BE	Wt.	INT. 1-10	SP. 1-10	BE.	Wt.	INT. 1-10	SP. 1-10	BE	INT.	SP.	BE	SP on lead	Conf.	Move.	Coat.	Show Brood Pet.

GENETIC PREPOTENCIES AND EXPECTATIONS

Aggressive   Fearless   Independent   Stubborn   OBedient   LOving   Eager to please

CHART B.

QUALITY EVALUATION RATING

NAME OF PUPPY: **SEX:**

	10. 12 wks or 3 mo.	4 mos.	5 mos.	6 mos.	8 to 10 mos.
COAT					
Texture					
Length					
Volume					
Head and/or body break					
HEAD					
Type					
Ears					
Eyes					
Muzzle					
Mouth					
AXIAL STRUCTURE					
Skull					
Neck					
Topline					
Back					
Tail Set					
APPENDICULAR STRUCTURE					
Forelegs					
Hindlegs					
PERSONALITY Score 1–10					
SHOW POTENTIAL Score 1–10					
Congenital or Inherited Faults (Explain)					

Adult Measurements

lbs.	wks. 8 10	3	4	mos. 5	6	8	10
7½							
7							
6½							
6							
5½							
5							
4½							
4							
3½							
3							
2½							
2							
1							

Screening the Buyer

If the puppy is sold as a show prospect, the breeder will want to know what experience the person has had in the show ring. Has he made other dogs into champions or is he a novice? No matter how good the intentions, some people are just plain klutzes and will never develop a knack for handling a dog. The breeder may insist that if the buyer is unable to finish the dog, he will bear the cost of a professional handler. If sold for breeding, the breeder has every right to make sure the buyer is not a puppy mill and will not breed the dog too often or indiscriminately.

Then there are those adorable pets! No matter how well a breeder plans a litter, regardless of the quality of the sire and dam, we all find ourselves with puppies that fall short of expectations. Perhaps the bite is off a little, the size is outside the limit set by the standard, a male may lack two testicles of equal size and so on—variations from the standard that rule the puppy out as a show dog. Each breeder must solve his own problem as to how he plans to handle the pet puppies he breeds. He cannot keep them, and each puppy deserves its own home and its own family.

We have a policy that all pet stock, regardless of price, must be altered before the buyer will receive AKC registration papers. We explain that if the puppy were good enough to be used for breeding, it would not be for sale, and that if it isn't good enough for us to use for breeding it isn't good enough for anybody else.

Most sincere buyers readily understand and agree. If they don't, you're better off not letting them have the puppy anyway.

We screen a potential owner carefully, and ask a great many questions—tactfully. The first is, generally, how many children do you have? Children are potential hazards to a puppy. They can be rough without realizing it. Even if supervised, children don't talk, they scream; they don't walk, they run, and these actions alone are enough to make a nervous wreck out of a puppy raised in a more serene adult environment. We advise such people to settle for a cuddly toy until the girl is at least seven years old, boys preferably older. The smaller the breed, the older the children should be.

We ask the potential buyer what other breeds of dogs he has owned and what happened to them? People whose dog died of old age are usually good prospects. Where do they live? Apartment or house? What facilities do they have for protecting the puppy from accidents? If they live in a house, do they have a fenced-in yard? If not, are they willing to construct an exercise run or do they plan to walk the dog several times each day, come rain or come shine? I would think that breeders of larger breeds would want to know if the puppy is destined to a chain attached to an outdoor dog house or will become a member of the family.

A Breeder's Responsibility to the Pet Buyer

The breeder is responsible for furnishing the buyer with a healthy puppy, free of external or internal parasites or disease.

If registration papers are being withheld until a veterinarian's proof of spaying a bitch or castrating a dog is made available, the breeder should be willing to send the new owner a neat copy of the puppy's pedigree, or family tree, consisting of the names of its ancestors for at least three generations, a certificate of the dates of the puppy's inoculations, type of serum used, manufacturer of same, and date when the next inoculation is due.

If your breed has special coat care requirements, you should be willing to show the buyer of a pet puppy the fine points of grooming. Time permitting we let the buyer watch a puppy being bathed and groomed, and show him the correct tools he will need to keep his puppy in good condition.

The breeder should give the buyer a diet sheet showing the foods and vitamins the puppy has been getting, and the number of meals per day. Some breeders will also give the new owner a small packet of prepared food to take home to see the puppy through the first couple of days. When the diet is to be changed this can prevent any possibility of diarrhea which can result from too drastic and sudden a change in what a puppy is fed.

The buyer should be shown the reason why the puppy is being sold as a pet, and be warned that, even if house trained, it will need further training to adjust to its new home and new routine.

The breeder should remind a buyer that a small puppy is still a baby and that, in between frequent play periods, needs its sleep. For the first few days the new owner should guard against confusion of all kinds until the puppy's self-confidence is reinforced.

Even though the puppy is an active, tough little animal and was raised to be a well-adjusted, outgoing individual, the buyer is taking it away from its home, its friends, the breeder whom it has learned to love and trust, into a totally strange atmosphere. Everything will be new. It does not understand what is happening. It's security blanket has been pulled out from under it. It's going to miss the familiar noises of its kennel and pals, so there is little wonder that a puppy is

When a breeder sells a puppy as a pet he is obliged to explain to the new owner what makes the puppy a pet-quality specimen. In most cases it is risky, at best, to proclaim a very young puppy pet or show quality since dramatic changes can take place as puppies grow. As an example, these five-week-old Miniature Schnauzers will undergo many physical changes as they mature.

apprehensive in a new home. It needs a few days to adjust, but with gentle handling and love will soon realize it is once again among friends and that these are its very own to love and protect.

A Visit to the Veterinarian

Most breeders will urge the buyer to have the puppy examined by a qualified veterinarian of his choice sometime during the first two or three days after the puppy is purchased. If anything is amiss, the breeder will want to take the puppy back and refund the money. This precaution is as much protection for the breeder as it is for the buyer. The breeder will also want to know that the puppy is happy in its new home, is lively and playful, eating well, and that the. buyer is completely satisfied with it. The welfare of the puppy is more important to a conscientious breeder than any amount of money paid for it.

Your First Show Puppy

When you, as a future breeder, buy a promising puppy with the hope of exhibiting it in conformation at championship shows, both its training and yours should begin immediately.

Some puppies are born showoffs and enjoy being in the spotlight. They seem to know instinctively how to set themselves up to their best advantage and how to gait with spirit and animation. Other fine puppies need encouragement and training.

Hopefully you were lucky enough to get one with that built-in spirit. However, you can lose it in less than a week if you spoil the puppy.

You Are Boss

You must establish right from the start that you are boss—a kind one, and your dog's best friend but, in spite of the fun and games you have together throughout the day, when time comes for training, it is serious business. This takes patience and persistence, but if you know how, even a reserved or shy puppy can be turned into an extrovert.

Until you have received some training yourself in basic show procedure, the best advice I can give you is to treat your puppy like a dog. You'll never make a show dog out of a lapdog. Why should it go out of its way to please you? It doesn't have to. It gets all the fondling and attention it wants and still has its own way.

These Golden Retriever puppies, bred by High Farms Kennels, mirror the robust good health that all serious breeders and thoughtful buyers diligently seek.

These Cocker Spaniel puppies seem to wonder what their futures will hold. A new home where the owner exercises kindness and authority will help these babies become happy, well-adjusted adults.

Jones

259

Play with your puppy. Throw a ball for it. Have fun but, at the same time, teach it good manners. The same principles on which obedience training is based go into making a show dog. When your puppy pleases you, let it know it with a pat on the head and words of extravagant praise. When it refuses to cooperate, scold it, and put it into its room or run for awhile. Pay no attention to it and, before long, it will be begging for some indication that you have not banished it completely from your affections.

Puppies, like children, look to their owners for guidance and discipline. If they don't get it, they become objectionable adult dogs just as unruly children become obnoxious adolescents. When they get it, they respond gratefully and lovingly.

We have a strict rule around our kennel-home, and that is "Show dogs on the floor." This does not mean you cannot pick up a puppy and give it a hug. Of course you can but, after a brief display of affection, put it down and say "Good Boy." Once it is old enough to jump on a chair, let it sit quietly and undemandingly by your side. Don't make a fuss over it or continually pat and stroke it.

Good Health Is Important

Good health is essential to a show dog. Feed it nutritious foods, give it plenty of exercise, and keep it clean and well groomed. Make sure its toenails are clipped short and hair is removed from between the pads of its feet.

While your puppy is growing and developing, take it for frequent car rides, every day if necessary, until it loses any fear of the car. Expose it to distracting noises, new startling objects, other dogs. Take it with you into shopping malls and encourage strangers to approach it gently and touch its head and body.

Attending Dog Shows

Go to as many dog shows as possible as a spectator and watch ring procedure. Watch the judges and the different ways they ask handlers to move their dogs. Be familiar with the catalogue, judging schedule, progression of the classes to Best of Breed and the mechanics of exhibiting before trying your own wings in the ring.

Many novices have a complete lack of knowledge of and regard for ring etiquette. Don't be one of these! It won't take you long to spot this particular novice. Watch how he lets his dog pull him into the ring, how awkwardly he moves, hauling his dog, nose to ground, up and down the ring, stopping to chat with other people in the ring or

Absorbing the dog show scene from ringside is a good starter exercise for the novice. Go to as many dog shows as you can just to watch. If you can train your eye to recognize quality in any dog, you will have gone a long way to insure your own success in the fancy.

waving to friends at ringside. He lets his dog play and cut up in the ring as it does at home, and he probably thinks it's cute. The audience may enjoy it, but the judge is not apt to look kindly on the antics. He has only a couple of minutes per dog to make his decisions, and there is every reason why he should have little patience with any kind of distraction. Take a firm vow that you will never follow that route.

You will soon find these same novices are the experts on everything. Keep your ears open and your mouth closed. Don't join in with one of the cliques you find around your breed ring until you know which ones have a professional approach to showing dogs. Often it is better to make friends around other breed rings than your own.

Watch the professional handler in the ring and study his technique not only with your particular breed but with other breeds in Group and Best in Show competition. Notice how he conveys to his dog, both manually and mentally, what he wants it to do. He doesn't let it flounder at the end of a loose lead. He guides and directs it with calm, deliberate hands. He moves the dog at the best gait for the dog, not for himself. He is completely at ease, yet he is working every moment. He has a way of letting his dog relax when the judge is examining another entry, yet in some magical way his dog is always in perfect show pose the moment the judge turns to look at him.

A natural dog handler is born, not made. But in addition to his God-given talents, the professional has added all the tricks of his trade—those "extras" that come only with years of experience.

It's thrilling to see the rapport between a good handler and a responsive, quality dog in top condition. They are a team—working together as one to win.

Doing It Yourself

If you are determined to present and show your dog yourself, make up your mind that you are going to do it like a professional or not at all. There have been many outstanding amateur owner-handlers, as good as the best professionals, who have done a great deal of consistent big winning. It isn't done overnight or with one dog. Learning to handle a dog in the show ring expertly takes work and lots of it. But if you have a sound dog that fits the breed standard, it can become a champion. It depends on you. It's 50 percent dog and 50 percent the way it is trained, presented and handled.

Unfortunately not every owner is physically or emotionally suited to handling a dog in the ring. This is especially true of the

The late Louis Murr scrutinizing four finalists for the 1969 Westminster Best in Show award. It requires an excellent dog, impeccable training and tremendous ring presence on the part of handler and dog to achieve this lofty level of competition.

Gilbert

263

one-dog owner, who has allowed his dog to become the boss or a nervous person who constantly has butterflies in his stomach. The mental attitude of a handler is transmitted right down the lead to the dog. What looked so easy when you were an observer at ringside suddenly becomes an impossible chore. You realize you are sadly prepared or suited to the task of handling. So if you want your dog to win, and it is worthy of earning its championship, learn to be a good, confident handler before you enter your first championship show or turn your dog over to a professional.

Too often an impatient novice exhibitor will enter his dog in a show before it is properly ring trained and, instead of being proud of his new puppy and placing in the ribbons as the puppy should do, it becomes an embarrassing experience not only for the owner but also for the person who bred the dog. The best way to avoid this situation is to thoroughly and carefully train the puppy before investing money and time on entering a show.

Training should consist of daily work-outs where the puppy is gaited on a show lead and taught to stand quietly for examination. Practice sessions should take place not only in your own home environment but in a variety of environments, inside and outside, in familiar places and in strange places. There is no substitute for training and hard work, but unless you know what you are supposed to do, you are incapable of teaching your dog. One thing you can be sure of—an untrained dog plus an untrained owner does not equal a blue ribbon.

Handling Classes

Within reasonable driving distance of most major cities and towns can be found handling classes in school gymnasiums and other sport centers, conducted by local kennel clubs. A course usually consists of ten hourly sessions held once a week, taught by a professional handler.

You will learn how to handle the show lead, to present your dog to the judge, and to respond quickly to his directions. You will learn how to give your dog ample room to turn without putting yourself between it and the judge, to set the dog up and hold its attention, to always keep one eye on your dog and one on the judge.

It takes many hours of homework, in addition to the handling classes, to learn to show your dog. As you gain confidence, you will learn to make the most of your dog's good points and minimize its bad, both in grooming and in showing. No dog is perfect, so don't expect your puppy to be. Evaluate it honestly, objectively, and learn to make the most of its virtues. Have someone other than you gait it while you watch to see if it moves better on a loose lead than on a tight one. Enlist the help of family and friends to act as judge, to approach your puppy and handle it when on the ground and on a table if table examination is applicable to your breed.

Bring out your movie camera. Photograph the professionals at work, then get a friend to take pictures of you during a training session. If your camera is equipped with slow motion, you can find out a great deal about your dog's movement, its best features, its faults, and your ability to pose and gait it to its best potential. A film can be devastatingly revealing and often discouraging but it will dispel any illusions you might have about yourself or your dog and will bring you up short to face reality.

Not until the day comes that you know you are transmitting to your dog at the end of the lead what you want it to do, and it responds gaily, are you ready to enter your first championship show.

Brushed, combed, and coiffed to the "nines," this lovely Alekai white Standard Poodle is patiently waiting his turn in the ring.

Match Shows

While attending handling classes, by all means enter your dog at kennel club fun events or sanctioned match shows in your vicinity. They are excellent training grounds for amateur handlers as well as for the puppies. To learn when and where one is being held, ask your veterinarian or call the secretary of a local kennel club.

Match shows are informal affairs at which purebred dogs may compete, but not for championship points. Ring procedures and the process of elimination are the same as at championship shows, except that there are no classes for Winners. Puppies that are not old enough to compete in championship shows may be entered and introduced as young as three months of age to the confusion, noises, and smells of a dog show.

At match shows, novice handlers have no reason to be embarrassed by their inexperience. Everyone is there to learn. The members of the sponsoring clubs are learning how to conduct their own shows, stewards are learning the art of stewarding, and judges are getting experience in evaluating dogs and developing their own efficient ring techniques.

Match shows are the best possible training grounds for you and your show puppy. Competition is not as rough as at point shows, and everyone gains something by way of experience and confidence in showing his dog.

Bibliography

"Advances in Knowledge and Recent Discoveries of Viral Diseases of Puppies," Leland E. Carmichael, D.V.M. & Roy V.H. Pollock, D.V.M. *Animal News*

Basic Guide to Canine Nutrition, Gaines Dog Research Center

Book of Dogs, The, National Geographic Society

Breeding and Genetics of the Dog, Anne Fitzgerald Paramoure

"Canine Pediatrics," *Gaines Progress*, Spring and Summer, 1979

Canine Pediatrics, James Dorney, D.V.M. & Susan Tobias, D.V.M.

Care and Training of Dogs, The, Arthur Frederick Jones

Causes of Cleft Palate, Dr. E. Fitch Daglish

Complete Dog Book, The, American Kennel Club

Complete Herbal Book for the Dog, The, Juliette de Bairacli Levy

"Diseases of Dogs," Cornell Research Laboratory for Diseases of Dogs, *Veterinary Virus Research Institute, Cornell University Laboratory Report*, Series 4, No. 2

Dog in Action, The, McDowell Lyon

Dog Behavior, John Paul Scott & John L. Fuller

Dog Breeding, Dr. S.A. Asdell

Dog Talk, Gaines Dog Research Center

Dogs, National Audubon Society

Dogs and How to Breed Them, Hilary Harmar

Dogsteps, Illustrated Gait at a Glance, Rachel Page Elliott

Ecology of the Surplus Dog & Cat Problem, May, 1974, American Kennel Club

Encyclopedia of Dog Breeds, Ernest H. Hart

"First 18 days—Do or Die, The," Erwin Small, D.V.M., *Gaines Progress,* Fall, 1977

Genetics as Applied to a Breeding Program, Rev. Dr. Braxton B. Sawyer

Inheritance of Coat Color in Dogs, Clarence C. Little

International Encyclopedia of Dogs, Stanley Dangerfield & Elsworth Howell

How to Breed Dogs, Leon F. Whitney

Natural History of Dogs, The, Richard & Alice Fiennes

"Neonatal Puppy Mortality," Cornell Research Laboratory for Diseases of Dogs, *Veterinary Virus Research Institute, Cornell University, Laboratory Report,* Series 4, No. 2

New Art of Breeding Better Dogs, The, Kyle Onstott

New Complete Poodle, The, Mackey J. Irick, Jr.

"New Determinant for Puppy Survival," Dr. David C. Van Sickle, *Gaines Progress,* Summer, 1974

New English Springer Spaniel, The, Charles S. Goodall & Julia Gasow

New Knowledge of Dog Behavior, The, Clarence Pfaffenberger

Patellas Are Also Important, Wayne Riser, D.V.M.

Pedigree Utilization in Breeding, Dr. Roy C. Fanguy

Pet Genetics, Robert L. Gering

Planned Breeding, Lloyd D. Brackett

Practical Dog Breeding & Genetics, Eleanor Frankling

"Present Status & Outlook on Canine Hip Dysplasia," *Gaines Progress,* Spring 1973

Principles of Dog Breeding, Will Judy

"Problem of Fading Puppies," C.C. Lloyd, *Dog World,* September, 1967

"Puppy Behavioral Development, The Breeder's Challenge," Peter J. Vollmer, *Gaines Progress,* Fall, 1978

Seaward Kennels, Lois Meistrell, *Gaines Progress*

This Is the Silky Terrier, Betty Young

Touching, Ashley Leslie Montague

Tube Feeding, Catherine A. Marley, M.D.

Understanding Your Dog, Michael W. Fox, Dr.

"Veterinary Clinics of North America," *The Orthopedic Surgery in Small Animals, Vol. 1. No. 3*

Index

269